T0151365

Hipsters in Distress

Are You Lookin'?
and Other Plays
by Murray Mednick

Produced by Sideshow Media LLC, New York, NY

Editorial director and project manager: Dan Tucker
Cover and interior design: CoDe. New York Inc., Jenny 8 del Corte Hirschfeld and
Mischa Leiner
Supervising Padua editor: Guy Zimmerman

Guy Zimmerman
Padua Playwrghts Productions
964 Tularosa Drive
Los Angeles, CA 90026

Printed in the United States of America

Distributed in the United States and Canada by Theatre Communications Group,
520 Eighth Avenue, 24th Floor, New York, NY 10018-4156.
ISBN: 0-9630126-5-7

Contents

Hipsters in Distress

Preface by Guy Zimmerman

Shortly before his own death, the poet Czeslaw Milosz wrote a eulogy for Allen Ginsburg. Milosz praised Ginsburg's courage, his willingness to live out extremities. "Great poet of the murderous century," he writes, "who persisting in folly attained wisdom." These plays by Murray Mednick speak to a similar persistence. They depict characters who lean fully into their own confusion, in search of transformation, and they embrace the seemingly foolish idea that theatre, like poetry or music, is first and foremost an art form, able to elevate those it engages. Playwrights coming of age in this new era of threat and dread will find these plays highly relevant, and this bodes well for their fate in the long term; what artists of the future find useful is what survives.

To call the protagonists of these plays "hipsters" is to link them to the American urban counterculture of the late 1950s. One way or another, Mickey of *Are You Lookin'?*, Peter of *Heads*, Matt of *Scar*, and the rest are fugitives from the era of Ginsburg and Burroughs, Miles Davis and Ornette Coleman, the pre-hippie era when cool was equal parts Eros and Thanatos. Their "distress" comes from a deep connection to states of anxiety, intense longing and regret that afflict and harry the soul. Seeking to liberate themselves from habitual stupidity, these characters tap into an awareness that assaults and disorients them. This awareness has an implacable quality, rendering their voices cruel or plaintive depending on whether they embody it or serve as its object.

Staged at Theatre Genesis at the tail end of the Off-Off Broadway movement in 1973, *Are You Lookin'?* is the earliest of these plays. With trenchant lyricism and a minimalist scene structure, this long one-act depicts a junkie (Mickey) in search of a quasi-spiritual score. In *Scar*, completed some ten years later, a songwriter (Matt) seeks to attain the ideal dignity of an Apache sorcerer. *Heads* (1989) depicts an anxious playwright (Peter) expiating the sins of his glory days on the Lower East Side. These uncertain penitents are willing to suffer harsh truths in order to attain wisdom. *Skinwalkers* (1995) takes place in Northern New Mexico, a land haunted by the *brujos* and ghosts of its Latino and Indian past. A highlight of the 1989 Padua Hills Playwrights Festival, *Shatter 'n Wade* has much to say about the recovery movement, a mainstay of modern American culture that has yet to be adequately illuminated. *Switchback*, Mednick's 1994 festival entry, uses the imagery of war and atrocity to mourn the death of a young drug addict. Even the irredeemable *Dictator*, based on Panamanian strongman Manuel Noriega, is attempting to clear his accounts with a pitiless world.

On a more prosaic level, each of Mednick's protagonists has the courage to question the American belief that life can be "won," as if it were a game of some kind. A culture that identifies so completely with winners, these plays suggest, is a culture that is completely deluded. Mortal beings, after all, are by definition "losers" in the end. We die, our bodies rot in the ground or are burnt into ashes. The people we share our lives with die also, leaving no one to remember us. In America, we have become ever more adept at ignoring this inescapably human reality. Our one shared ambition as a people, it sometimes seems, is to become even *better* at ignoring death, as if that would make it disappear. But it is precisely when death is allowed to slip from view that it infiltrates everything and controls our lives.

In Mednick's plays, death is always a part of the picture, but *eros*, the life force, ultimately reigns. These plays can be viewed as full-length dramatic poems, and a strong iambic meter powers the dialogue like a heartbeat. From Shakespeare to Brecht, enduring playwrights have typically been poets, and Mednick's plays illustrate why this remains true today. His rhythms have been painstakingly reconciled with the casual attitude of everyday speech, such that they work their magic from hiding. The sign of this covert musicality is the sense we get, while hearing a play by Mednick or Maria Irene Fornes, or by the many playwrights they have mentored, that each line is bootstrapping itself into existence. Each line is asked to re-create the elements of character and situation that make up the world of the play. When the text renews its claim on reality line by line this way, the strictly narrative elements can never close down the full range of possible outcomes. We in the audience, like the characters on stage, are kept in a state of uncertainty about what might happen next, and this means that revelation and surprise are never far away.

Directors of these plays will discover that they each embody a unique technical challenge involving some aspect of stagecraft, such as the denouement of *Scar*, the blackouts and projections of *Are You Lookin'?*, and the mask work of *Skinwalkers*. Both *Shatter 'n Wade* and *Switchback*, for instance, were written as site-specific events. This latter play, part of the 1994 Padua Festival, is a good example of how Mednick, working as both playwright and director, tapped into a site for inspiration.

Woodbury College in Burbank hosted the festival that year. From the main parking lot you faced a steep, grassy rise with a wheelchair ramp zigzagging up it, and the audience was placed at the foot of this hill. Mednick had written *Switchback* specifically for this site, scripting and staging the play during the four-week workshop period that preceded each year's festival. *Switchback* began with a burst of machine-gun fire. A pair of women appeared at the top of the ramp, running for their lives. One (Brenda, played by Robin Karfo) wore black urban guerilla fatigues; the other (Sharron Shayne as Rita) was costumed as the monocled woman from Sergei Eisenstein's "Odessa Steps" sequence, pushing a 1920s pram. In rhythms that were as staccato as gunfire, and just as compressed, the two women lamented the war and the death of a charismatic young hero. Next came the sound of an airplane overhead, buzzing the audience and then circling back above the field to drop a small parachuting figure that slowly descended, leaving the audience's field of vision. A moment later a soldier (CC, played by Mark Fite) appeared, dragging the traces of the parachute over the crest of the hill. As he ran down the hill the play really began. A bit later this same actor crossed behind the audience and vaulted a chain-link fence, diving into a swimming pool below. One had the strong sense of being in the clutches of a director who'd been at this for a while.

In Mednick's plays the mechanics of stagecraft work in tandem with the poetics of the text to make the action onstage more vivid and complex—more *real*, in fact, than our lives offstage. Each element is geared toward creating an opening where something new can take place. This intensely poetic approach to theatre-making involves Mednick's audience in creative work. It requires that we hold two things in mind simultaneously: each moment as literary and theatrical artifact, and each moment as something with a lurid existence of its own. How the illusory and the real *entail* each other is the spectacle Mednick wants us to witness. The theatrical world conjured in this way is every bit as real as the world offstage. Our entire lives, the aesthetic underscores, emerge moment by moment out of a mosaic of sense impressions and emotional material, interwoven with something finer and more authentic.

As much as any contemporary playwright, Murray Mednick has made the present moment his terrain. To be present is precisely to stand up in the face of mortality. As I noted in the introduction to his *Three Plays*, Mednick's plays are vehicles designed to deliver us collectively into the moment by speaking to a part of us that is unconditioned and radically free. The awareness they embody is full of relevance today, when the destructive tendencies of the species have come to threaten our survival. Today, as always, certain truths can only be expressed via theatre. Hopefully, the beautiful and harrowing plays collected here will help to keep this understanding alive.

Are You Lookin'?

by Murray Mednick

Are You Lookin'? *was first presented at Theatre Genesis, New York in 1973, under the playwright's direction, with Josh Cavastani playing Mickey and Kathleen Cramer as Kay.*

In 1976, the play was produced at the Magic Theatre in San Francisco, under the direction of Robert Woodruff, with John Nesci playing Mickey.

In 1978, the play was produced at the Gene Dynarski Theatre in Los Angeles, under the direction of Darrell Larson, with the following cast:

Mickey: Ed Harris
Kay: Helen Shaver
Peewee: Anthony Gourdine
Robert: Kevin O'Brien
The Venusian: René Assa

The Man On Bench was added in a subsequent draft.

Characters

Mickey *Musician, 28.*

Kay *Actress, 26.*

Peewee *Black man, early 30s*

The Stranger *An extraterrestrial derelict*

Man On Bench *Robert, 20s, a friend of Kay's*

1. In the Dark

In darkness, a silence, then the voices of MICKEY *and* KAY, *stoned.*

Kay	I don't know what you mean. What you were saying before. About history.
Mickey	I was talking about the past. I mean, history is the stuff of the past, right?
Kay	Okay.
Mickey	Well, the past is infinite. (*A silence*) There's always another point backward. In time.
Kay	There is?
Mickey	But it is also true that the past does not exist.
Kay	The past does not exist.
Mickey	No, it's a paradox. Because we can never know what happened then. We'd have to have been there.
Kay	Is that true?
Mickey	I think so. To really know what happened, you'd have to have been there. We only know what happens. And even then...
Kay	What happens?
Mickey	I don't know. This happens.
Kay	This happens?
Mickey	Yeah. This happens, that's all.

Kay	Oh, then what we do is, we make a picture.
Mickey	A picture?
Kay	A picture of what happened. History.
Mickey	Oh, yeah. *(Pause)* I don't know what that would be, though. Exactly. The picture changes.
Kay	Does that mean it doesn't exist?
Mickey	What?
Kay	The past.
Mickey	I don't know. It depends.
Kay	On what?
Mickey	On what you mean.
Kay	History.
Mickey	It exists insofar as it is studied. We study it, so it exists.
Kay	It?
Mickey	History.
Kay	No, the studying is what exists. *(A silence)*
Mickey	More than that which is being studied, yes—namely, the past.
Kay	You mean, "I study" is more real than "I studied?"
Mickey	Maybe. It's doing something. It's an activity.
Kay	*(After a pause)* Oh, I see.
Mickey	I mean, the history book exists. And what exists in the book are pages of words.
Kay	The words exist.
Mickey	Yes. And put together in an orderly way, they make a kind of picture, with ideas.
Kay	Ideas.
Mickey	Well, yeah.
Kay	Ideas exist?
Mickey	Ideas exist.
Kay	In the world.

Mickey	In the world.
Kay	Give me an example.
Mickey	Progress. *(Laughs)*
Kay	A picture in the mind. I'm trying to see that. *(A silence)*
Mickey	It is a matter of opinion, in the long run, what may have really happened. *(Pause)* Based on an accumulation of facts.
Kay	Facts?
Mickey	Yes.
Kay	Facts exist?
Mickey	Well, the written records of the time. *(Pause)* The archeological remains. *(Pause)* And so on. *(Pause)* Yes, these exist. They help to make a hypothesis for what may have happened in the past, relative to...
Kay	Uh-huh.
Mickey	Relative to the context.
Kay	The context of the book?
Mickey	Yes, the context and the premises of the book.
Kay	In the mind of the author. *(Silence)*
Mickey	The book exists. It does exist. For a while, anyway.
Kay	I know it does.
Mickey	And then it becomes something else. It fades away into something else.
Kay	So?
Mickey	So, it no longer exists. Not as a book, it doesn't.
Kay	What about geology? You know, Darwin made up all that stuff about the Pleistocene and Eocene and the ape scene and all.
Mickey	He did?
Kay	Yes, and none of it is true. Boy, that sure pisses me off.
Mickey	Amazing. It comes down to how you decide to divide

	up the time. There's the premise—the division of time. In reality, time is infinite, and relative. *(Pause)* To space. *(Pause)* The relations of time and space are infinite.
Kay	I thought you said "intimate."
Mickey	Yeah, ha, ha.
Kay	It's so big, so vast. I look back into the past, and gales blow, dinosaurs are born and die, the oceans shift.
Mickey	Wow—carbon 14!
Kay	Carbon 14?
Mickey	Fantastic. What they can do is find out how old a rock is. Or a clay pot or something like that. Bones and shit. By virtue of an analysis of its atomic structure. As if the rock were dying, as a rock.
Kay	Too much, the life and death of a rock. I'm interested in the galaxies, man. There's hundreds of millions of galaxies out there! Can you dig that?
Mickey	See, before the rock was a rock, it was something else. Same thing with the galaxies, Kay. *(Pause)* If you accelerate mass, you get...you can transform matter into energy. *(Pause)* Magic. *(Pause)* Something to do with velocity and time. The speed of light. Changes. *(Pause)*
Kay	Wait a minute—how about making energy into matter?
Mickey	Yeah—the Black Hole.
Kay	What?
Mickey	Close your eyes.
Kay	Huh? Okay...
Mickey	What do you see?
Kay	I don't know.
Mickey	You see the infinite.
Kay	Oh, the infinite. Looks like a black hole to me.

Mickey	Yes, right. *(A silence)*
Kay	Is that what you were trying to say before? About the smallest particle?
Mickey	I guess so. There is no smallest particle. If you know the smallest you'd know the biggest. It's like the beginning and the end.
Kay	Is that religious?
Mickey	It's physics, baby.
Kay	Yeah, right. Physics.
Mickey	They'll never find the absolute tiniest unit in the universe, because there's always one tinier. And so on, and so on.
Kay	But there's got to be some practical use for the whole thing. For the search to continue, I mean. Science.
Mickey	Of course. The discovery and harnessing of natural forces.
Kay	What?
Mickey	Nothing. I got a chill. The shit is wearing off already.
Kay	Yeah, funny how the stars turn cold like that, icy. They were looking warm and friendly there for a while.
Mickey	Not any more. It's BLACK and FREEZING out there.
Kay	Do you remember, when we were talking earlier?
Mickey	Yes?
Kay	And I told you about this fear of mine?
Mickey	Yes.
Kay	Well, I've been thinking it over. And it isn't that you have to go, or that I must go, or that I'm going someplace I dislike, or someplace I might be afraid of. When you're gone, I wait for you, and that's what I'm doing, and it passes, it's all right. And when I'm away, I do what I have to do, and that too passes, and it's all right.
Mickey	What is it, then?

Kay	I'm not sure. It'd be a word only, maybe the wrong one. It's a difficult job, to discover what it is. It's so vague, like a substance in the mind, the feeling of dread.

A silence, then a full-color MAP *of the moon, close up, comes into focus.*

Mickey	Look.
Kay	Yes.

They say the words clearly and slowly, in a monotone.

Mickey	The Sea of Showers.
Kay	The Sea of Showers.
Mickey	The Sea of Serenity.
Kay	The Sea of Serenity.
Mickey	Aristarchus.
Kay	Aristarchus.
Mickey	Ocean of Storms.
Kay	Ocean of Storms.
Mickey	The Sea of Vapors.
Kay	The Sea of Vapors.
Mickey	The Sea of Tranquility.
Kay	The Sea of Tranquility.
Mickey	The Sea of Fertility.
Kay	The Sea of Fertility.
Mickey	The Sea of Moisture.
Kay	The Sea of Moisture.
Mickey	Sea of Clouds.
Kay	Sea of Clouds.

A silence; the IMAGE *fades.*

*

2. In the John

A small bathroom, set center stage, well lit. The rest of the stage area is empty and dark. Toilet, tub, cabinet/mirror. Blue-and-white-tiled entrance is through the front, down-stage. KAY *is sitting on the closed toilet, thinking a bit before preparing to leave. A moment, then* MICKEY *appears left, crosses, and enters the bathroom.*

Mickey	I don't know what's wrong. It didn't affect me at all. I feel exactly the same.
Kay	You need another shot.
Mickey	There's no flash. I'd like to get a flash, at least. It's supposed to be pure crystal.
Kay	I know.
Mickey	What the fuck—I don't like speed to begin with—at least there oughta be a—
Kay	Take it easy. Be glad we got that junk to come down with. I am.
Mickey	Yeah? How much we got?
Kay	Enough.
Mickey	*(Contemplating himself in the mirror)* It's a strange thing, the body. You're stuck in it. Stinking meat on aging bones. It's a regular fucking sewer.
Kay	You're so beautiful, Mick.

Mickey	Filthy pipes, infected blood. *(Coming to)* Oh, thank you, Babe. Thanks. *(She becomes sad)* You don't mind doing this, do you? *(No reply)* If you don't want to, I can do it myself.
Kay	No, please. I want to.
Mickey	Okay. *(Cupping her chin)* Give us a smile then, will ya?

She smiles.

I know you like it—otherwise I'd hit myself.

She frowns.

Come on, it's no big thing who hits me—

She smiles.

That's it. Wonderful. Where would I be without you? I'd be lost.

Kay	Really?
Mickey	Yeah, I'd just freak out one day and start screaming and running up and down the street talking to myself.
Kay	No, you wouldn't. You'd find something. Someone. *(Producing a vial of white powder)* How's that?
Mickey	Fine. *(Into the mirror)* I was hoping for something blissful. Orgasmic. Ecstatic. I was hoping to wake up. I feel so tired. And I slept all day today.
Kay	Sit down. *(She rises)*
Mickey	*(He sits)* You're really something, you know? I wanted to get into a low-down, funky, hungry, drawn-out sex binge with you.

Kay	But it wasn't the right time.
Mickey	It was a couple of hours ago, wasn't it? What happened then?
Kay	I could feel that you just wanted to get off on something. It wasn't me you wanted.
Mickey	Yeah, it was. I wanted you, I wanted to get off, too. It's the same thing.
Kay	Okay. I was too tense, then. I don't know why. I'm sorry.
Mickey	No, no, don't be sorry. Really. Who the hell knows what was going on two hours ago? Forget it. *(Pause)* I love you.
Kay	*(Embracing him)* You do? You do?
Mickey	Yeah, I do. Of course, I love you.
Kay	You'll keep me with you?
Mickey	Yeah, I'll keep you with me. What the hell do you think?
Kay	I guess I worry.
Mickey	Don't worry, Babe.
Kay	I'll be anything you want me to be. I'll do anything you want me to.
Mickey	Yeah? Well, give me my goddamn shot then, will you, and I'll keep you with me forever.
Kay	*(Laughing, kissing him)* Coming right up, sir! *(She pours the white stuff into a huge, fire-blackened spoon)*
Mickey	Shit, it's cold in here. And I feel hungry all of a sudden. Can't understand it. Hungry...and tired, Babe. Tired.
Kay	I know. I know how you feel.
Mickey	You do?
Kay	Yes. *(Pause as she drops the cotton)* We haven't been taking care of ourselves as well as we could, Mick...we don't take our vitamins...or eat properly. There...where's the needle?

He points into the cabinet.

	And there's a terrible draft, you know?
Mickey	Yes. Maybe we been travelling around too much.
	(Watching her) You're not having any?
Kay	No.
Mickey	Why not?
Kay	I don't like speed. Ugh. *(Shivers)* It makes me dizzy and sick to my stomach, and I have to be up early tomorrow.
Mickey	What for?
Kay	I have to do my Christmas shopping.
Mickey	Christmas shopping.
Kay	Right. Now, if you get me the outfit, I'll give you a shot.
Mickey	I sharpened the point.
Kay	Good, maybe it won't hurt so much.
Mickey	I hope not. It's in the cabinet.

She opens the cabinet and produces a syringe about five times the standard size. He looks at his badly scarred arms.

My veins, my veins...they're so sore.

He watches her fill the syringe with a green substance from the huge, fire-blackened spoon.

It's a hairy feeling walking around with these punctured veins.

Kay	I'll bet. *(She attaches the needle, puts it down, takes off her belt)*
Mickey	I'm just trying to get into the bloodstream, Babe, get into the bloodstream and effect a change.
Kay	Yes. All right, Honey. Which arm?

Mickey	*(Looking)* Which one...this one. *(The left)* We just shot the other one, didn't we?
Kay	*(Ties him off)* Yes, I think so.
Mickey	They're receding, Babe, running away, almost gone, they don't like it...little blue rivers changing course, Babe, dropping inward.
Kay	I don't blame them.
Mickey	Well, let's get it before it disappears. I need a hit.
Kay	I see it. Flex your arm, it's got to come up more.

He does so.

More.

He does so.

Mickey	That hurts. Cool it, that's as far as it'll go.
Kay	All right, keep your arm straight. *(Takes the syringe)*
Mickey	Give us a smile, Babe.
Kay	*(Smiling sweetly)* I get the creeps sometimes.
Mickey	You love it, though. You love the ritual of it, don't ya?
Kay	Yes, Baby.
Mickey	Come on, then.

She taps the vein.

That's it, that's it. No, further down. Try it a little further down, okay?

She does.

That's it.

It takes a while for the point to penetrate—he grimaces, clenches his teeth, hisses.

Kay   It's in. *(They look)* Should I shoot it?

Mickey   *(In pain)* Shoot it! Shoot it!

Kay   *(Doing so)* Let go!

He lets go of the tie. She withdraws the needle with diffi-cuty. MICKEY almost screams.

There... *(Looks into his face. Helps wipe the blood off his arm)*

Mickey   It *was* a hit, wasn't it? It was a hit.

Kay   I hope so. *(Takes water into the syringe; it turns red)* Sure looks that way. *(Sprays the bloodied water all over the blue tile)*

Mickey   Yeah, wow, I think it is, I think it's a hit. *(He appears suddenly animated and his manner of speech accelerates steadily)* Oh, yeah, Babe. Right on it. Thanks. Thanks a lot. You're too much. You're beautiful. Ah. Yes. Yes, that's it. I know what it is, Babe—it's not anger, it's not just ANGER, Babe—you hear?—it's a question of despair, it's a kind of DESPAIR... based on a... a VISION, yes... of reality, the CONDITION, you know what I mean? I do get angry, Babe—I know that—I get angry—but it isn't at anybody in particular—maybe one time it was, but not any more, not any more—I don't remember, really—it's the whole fucking thing, Babe!

Kay   The species.

Mickey	Yeah, right, that's it—the species! The bird's eye view—the wormy, creepy-crawly crust of earth—worms with big teeth! That's why I have doubts, Babe, about political solutions.
Kay	You do?
Mickey	Sure, I do. Because it's the whole fucking thing—the species, whatever you want to call it, something inside us, given, like a tumor or something, it's screwed up...it'll go wrong no matter what...I don't know...it's a real problem, Babe, because I can see both sides of it...like, I think Mao was a beautiful guy and all, he was a VISIONARY, you know what I mean? A SAINT—he definitely had the best idea of all, which was the idea of hard work and brotherhood and justice and human progress...but I just don't know if the vision is applicable to the human condition, if we could ever make it work.
Kay	*(Finishing up in the bathroom)* Uh-huh. *(Goes to the door and steps out)* I'll be right back, Mickey. *(Goes off into the darkness, left)*
Mickey	Okay. *(Takes down his pants, prepares to relax and take a crap. Lights a cigarette)* Ah. Yes...I'll be walking up and down the room twiddling my chin and I'll be taking a piss every five minutes. And once in a while I'll get hung up on an ice floe, and I'll float so cool on the lovely blue gulf-stream, south...through the Panama Canal into the blue Pacific...yes...riding a dolphin like a feeling on a heartbeat, goin' fast...yes...man on the moon and moon germs and the magical penumbra of my mind. Ah. Thump, thump. Take it easy, heart. Easy does it, shiftin' into third, barroom... Damn, I felt a stab of hunger there, I'm hungry again. Can't stop now, I'm off into the wild blue yonder heh, heh.

Ah. Funny thing about sex, what it does to sex. I do not want to in the immediate present, however, I feel cold. I feel like a hollow tin tube. *(Coughs)* And my throat is getting rusty. Too much smoking. *(Stops. The sound of* RUNNING WATER, *off)* Amazing, but this is it. The pinnacle, the Twentieth Century. The top. The can't be beat. The zenith.

Kay   *(Off)* Are you through in there?

*

3. Casablanca

Scene: a coffee table and chairs, center left. Deep right a sink and a commode. A flickering TV stage center—it is playing the movie Casablanca. *KAY and* MICKEY *sit at an angle facing away from the audience so that they can watch the television and each other. The sound is low. A long wait as they watch the movie.* MICKEY *makes a smiling grotesquerie.*

Kay   What is that?

Mickey freezes, exaggerating the mask, and makes an absurd sound.

What?

He continues.

Goddamn it, Mickey!

Mickey	Nothing.
Kay	WHAT?
Mickey	*(Mockingly foolish)* NOTHING.
Kay	Go to hell.

A long, bitter silence.

Mickey	I was just thinking...how precious these moments are we share together, Kay.
Kay	Where the HELL are you coming from?
Mickey	I went downtown today, to get my medication...and all I could see was bums and dope fiends, dope fiends and bums... *(Acting out)* "You lookin'?" Downcast old ladies hunting for bargains...depressed cops...kids begging... "Hey, can you gimme 26 cents so I can—"

She watches the TV as if not listening.

Kay	*(Speaking of Bergman)* She's too much, she's too fucking much. *(A silence)*
Mickey	In ten years, I'll be forty.
Kay	*(Reproachfully)* Oh, Mickey.
Mickey	Are you listening, or not? *(She mockingly attends him)* People are talking to themselves in the john...perverts showing little girls their crusty dicks...drunken old retired sailors attacking boys on basketball courts...*(Illustrating)* Suicide lunges...
Kay	Suicide lunges?
Mickey	Yeah! Just looking for trouble, right? Trouble and a filthy orgasm someplace dark...ready for anything...fight ya to

the death or suck ya off...it's a bitter ending...lonely old sonsabitches.

Kay I don't feel the least bit sorry for 'em.

Mickey There's a war going on, Kay. It's a goddamed war going on out there.

Kay Where the hell have you been?

Mickey *(Ignoring her)* Murder up 26 percent. Rapes at an all-time high. Murder, rape, prostitution and dope...violence, sodomy and pollution...I never seen anything like it before in my life! *(Laughs)*

Kay I'm watching this right now, if you don't mind.

Mickey Sex and murder, they go together.

Kay *(Watching the TV)* Wow, did you see that?

Mickey No...what?

Kay They're going to arrest Laszlo!

Mickey Huh?

Kay See that car? They're going into Rick's! It's the Fascists!

Mickey What happened to Sidney Greenstreet?

Kay *(Annoyed)* Oh!

A silence. They watch. The commercial comes on.

Shit.

Mickey I would like to get me one of them new Mercury Comets, though.

Kay I'd like a bottle of some expensive shampoo, for my hair— *(Fiddles with her hair)* It's goddamned filthy!

They watch the TV in silence a moment.

Mickey	We've lost it, Kay. We ain't tied into things no more.
	It's a sickness, Kay. We've gone too far.
Kay	What do you mean?
Mickey	There has to be a balance, Kay, between the pollution of
	things and the glory. The beautiful and the diseased.
Kay	Jesus!
Mickey	We've upset the balance. We've gone too far. Too gross,
	too ugly. Too much, too selfish, too many.
Kay	*(Responding to Bogart)* Oh, beautiful!

A silence. Then MICKEY *gets up, goes to the sink, runs cold water over his head, washes, brushes his teeth, returns.*

Mickey	Boy that felt good! *(He looks affectionately at* KAY*)*
	How ya doin'? *(No reply)* You look so fine!

She shifts uncomfortably.

	I think your hair is lovely, Kay.
Kay	It is not.
Mickey	*(Undaunted)* I think it is.

He approaches, leans over, and tries to kiss her. She turns away. He is undeterred.

	You look so sweet to me.
Kay	Cut it out.
Mickey	*(Squeezing her leg)* It's nice...
Kay	*(Annoyed)* Come on...
Mickey	It is...*(He ignores her and squeezes the other leg)*

Kay	Mickey...!
Mickey	*(Grabbing a breast)* I like it.
Kay	Well, I don't!

He freezes, prolonging their shame, which further infuriates her, but she makes a great effort to control herself.

All of a sudden you act like you're in heat or something.

He doesn't move.

What is it? What do you want? *(Gently)* Don't play with me, Mick.

He returns to his chair, wounded and pitiful.

Mickey	Okay.
Kay	*(Singing)* Nobody loves me, everybody hates me, I'm gonna eat some worms...
Mickey	Forget it, Kay.
Kay	I'm sorry, Mick...I just...I don't know...
Mickey	Forget it. *(A seething silence)* I ain't going out there no more. I'm through with it. I can't stand it. I ain't going out there ANY FUCKING MORE.
Kay	Good.
Mickey	It's not worth it. It's degrading. They'll cut your throat for a dollar. Thank God they don't know I'm white.
Kay	*(Slight snicker)* How do you know they don't?
Mickey	*(Exploding)* I AIN'T GOING OUT THERE AGAIN. I'M NEVER GONNA COP FOR YOU AGAIN.

Kay	Don't blame me, Buster.
Mickey	They're dogs. They're nigger dogs. It's humiliating. To be at the mercy of dogs. Like an animal. FOR JUNK.
Kay	Race don't have nothing to do with it.
Mickey	Did I say race? *(Screaming)* YOU THINK I DON'T KNOW THAT? YOU THINK I DON'T KNOW? CAN'T I TALK STRAIGHT TO YOU? IT'S A QUESTION OF STYLE. NOT RACE. UNDERSTAND? THE WORD NIGGER IS A QUESTION OF STYLE. IT'S A DIFFERENT THING.
Kay	Oh.
Mickey	You wouldn't know. You don't go out there. You don't have to deal with it.
Kay	There are plenty of places to cop. You picked your own scene.
Mickey	*(Subsiding, after a pause)* You're right. I did. Why? Why?
Kay	I don't know. Maybe you're identified with the poor and the downtrodden.
Mickey	Well, that's it. I'm through with it. I can't do it no more.

For a moment the sound of another COMMERCIAL *rises painfully.* KAY *relents and goes to him.*

Kay	It's all right. Don't do it. *(Caressing him)* I'm glad. I don't want you to.
Mickey	I'm not. That's it, Babe.
Kay	I'm so glad. *(Bursting suddenly into tears)* I'm glad. Oh, Mickey! I hate it. Let's put it down! Let's do it!
Mickey	*(Consoling her now)* We will. I swear we will, Babe. We will. We will. We will.

They get quiet. Finally she leaves his embrace and goes back to her chair. They watch the television—more COMMER-

CIALS, *the banality of which should be absolutely horrible now—and quickly grow restless.*

Kay	*(Speaking of an Alka-Seltzer commercial)* My God.
Mickey	Comes the revolution, they'll be shot. Tortured and shot.
Kay	They give you no rest! Every minute they want you to be taking something! They treat us like worms, Mickey. Worms!
Mickey	I know. *(A pause as they watch)*
Kay	*(Giggling hysterically)* The quick relief of neuritis and neuralgia. *(Pause)*
Mickey	*(Blurting)* You want to use up the rest of the dope?
Kay	*(After a pause)* Yeah, I do.

They brighten up considerably. MICKEY, wielding a fly swatter, goes after flies with zest and abandon.

Mickey	I got one! That makes eight I killed today. The rest are disguised, or clinging to the ceiling.
Kay	They're smart little fuckers.
Mickey	They're on the run. Death is all around them. They can smell the corpses of their fellows and friends.
Kay	*(Enticingly)* Come here. *(He hesitates)* I just want to talk to you.
Mickey	What about?
Kay	Don't you want to talk to me? Don't you like me?
Mickey	*(Facetious)* No. *(Pause)* Yeah, sure I do. I like you a lot. *(Pause)* You know that. *(Pause)* Come on, let's get off. Then we'll talk, okay?
Kay	Promise?
Mickey	Yes.

Kay	(Eagerly) Let's go.

They cross to the bathroom, where MICKEY assembles the imaginary paraphernalia, preparing a fix. KAY watches him closely from the toilet seat.

Mickey	This is it, Kay. We got to stop after this. I just can't make that shit on the street anymore. It isn't worth it, you know what I mean? It isn't worth getting cut up, or killed, or time in the joint, you know what I mean? It's exciting, sure, when everything is everything and you're on your way to the cooker…
Kay	(Angrily) What are you doing?
Mickey	Huh?
Kay	That's too much, Mickey!
Mickey	No it isn't. I measured it.
Kay	Put some back!
Mickey	I measured it, Kay. It's equal!
Kay	You do this to me every time! You cheat!
Mickey	I do not! You were sitting right there!
Kay	You cheat! You ALWAYS have more than me, ALWAYS!
Mickey	(Placatingly) You'll see. Just wait, I'll bet you.
Kay	You're just a cheap, lying, sneaky sonofabitch, Mickey!
Mickey	Come on, tie me off will you?
Kay	I better have the same amount as you in there, Mickey; or I'm through. This is the last time.
Mickey	It will be. I swear. (Frantic) Come on, Kay. Please.

She belligerently starts to tie him off, then explodes and grabs the tie and the outfit away from him.

Kay	I'm going first! I'LL measure it!
Mickey	*(Rattled)* All right...okay, then put the shit back into the cooker and measure it.
Kay	What's the matter, Mickey? Huh? You know you have more than me, don't you? You rat bastard. Don't you?
Mickey	No, I don't.
Kay	THEN WHY SHOULD I PUT ANY BACK, GODDAMN YOU!
Mickey	I just think you ought to do what you say you're going to do, that's all.
Kay	*(Furiously)* Okay, man.

She squeezes the stuff back into the cooker and re-measures.

Mickey	You must be kidding.
Kay	What? What the fuck is that supposed to mean?
Mickey	I'm doing just like you do, Kay.

She squirts a bit back into the cooker, then ties off angrily. The process is painful and bloody—she has trouble making a hit.

Kay	There. Thank God.

A pause. She feels a slight rush, puts on a disappointed look. Hands the outfit back to MICKEY.

Mickey	Thank you. *(He cleans the hypo...prepares his fix)*
Kay	How come you don't say anything? Because you got more than me, you sonofabitch. Every fucking time. You do it every fucking time.

He fixes in a hurry. Waits. Nothing, or very little, happens.

	You feel it? *(A silence)*
Mickey	*(Bitterly)* No. Nothing.
Kay	Come on, you got all of it, didn't ya?
Mickey	Nothing. Absolutely nothing.
Kay	Not even a buzz?
Mickey	Yeah. I don't know. That sonofabitch. That treacherous piece of shit. I could kill him, I swear.
Kay	Not a buzz even, eh?
Mickey	*(In a rage)* I'll kill him.
Kay	You got any more money?
Mickey	Are you kidding? That's it.
Kay	That's it, huh?
Mickey	That's it.
Kay	Shit.
Mickey	Oh, God!
Kay	What're you crying about? At least you didn't have less than half of nothing.
Mickey	Get off it, will you.
Kay	I will not.
Mickey	*(Frenzied)* Okay, don't then.
Kay	What are you doing?
Mickey	I'm going.
Kay	What for? Where are you gonna go?

He loses control, hauls off and belts her across the face. Starts wild-eyed for the door. Blackout.

*

4. In the Cold

A few moments of blackness, then a CHRISTMAS TREE *lit up with a string of blue lights comes on upstage right. It flashes on and off throughout. A half dozen flashes, then* KAY *enters left and proceeds to light some candles on a white stool down left. The candles and the tree provide the only lights.* KAY *is wearing a beautiful orange fur coat.* MICKEY *is revealed in a white wicker chair, slightly upstage from the stool. He is all bundled up in blankets, etc., unshaven, hair long and wild, wearing dark sunglasses.*

Kay	Hi. How are ya?
Mickey	*(Speaks in a strange, high-pitched monotone)* You get anything?
Kay	How do you feel?
Mickey	I'm cold. It's freezing in here.
Kay	I know. There's no heat coming up.
Mickey	I can't move.
Kay	Well, it's worse outside, believe me.
Mickey	What did you get? Did you get anything?
Kay	No, nothing. I couldn't...*(A dead silence)* I hate it out there. I couldn't do it. And especially in this weather. *(Another surly silence)* I just can't hang around in the street, Mickey! I'd get killed! I don't know those guys.
Mickey	Forget it. Don't go anymore.
Kay	I tried, Mickey...I'll try again, if you want me to.
Mickey	No, don't. *(Withdraws angrily)*
Kay	All right. You're not feeling any better?
Mickey	It's my heart. My heart hurts.

Kay	Take a deep breath.
Mickey	Yeah, I do that anyway. It happens by itself. *(Takes several deep breaths)*
Kay	Okay. I was only trying to help.
Mickey	It's the Harpies. The're eating out my heart and my liver. The pain is here, right here under the rib cage, here.
Kay	The Harpies, eh?
Mickey	Yes, the Harpies. The Harpies are a bunch of spacey chicks from a doll's audience, with jagged blue masks, black eyes, and large yellow teeth.
Kay	Where are they?
Mickey	They're quite sentient now, in this room, in a bright light.
Kay	Sentient?
Mickey	I mean, visible. Can't you see them?
Kay	No, I can't. I do feel for you though, Honey. I know how it hurts.
Mickey	Do you? It's the white light of the Buddhists, the one that passeth understanding. *(A silence)*
Kay	God, how I hate it down there on the street.
Mickey	If my liver wasn't being torn away and eaten alive, blood three inches deep in this room, you'd think I was getting closer to becoming enlightened. Enlightenment is the obliteration of the self. They can have my stupid liver. *(Pause)* Some warrior I am, hunting my own sick death. Invisible Harpies. Stuck in a chair. *(A silence)*
Kay	*(Desperately)* Would you like something to eat?
Mickey	No, I wouldn't. Are you kidding me? How could I EAT anything? *(Pause)* I wanted to be a warrior, a fighter. ...
Kay	How about some tea?
Mickey	Yeah, awright...

Kay	And an orange?
Mickey	Yes, an orange. *(She goes off)* In quarters, please.

A silence. He tries to move about in his chair. Moves his head from side to side. Gives up, becomes rigid. Seems to be regarding the audience from behind the shades. His eyes turn on faintly...PINK. KAY returns with an orange in quarters and a cup of tea.

Kay	*(Cheerfully)* Here you are!
Mickey	Thank you.

A silence. He continues to regard the audience. His eyes are still faint, pink dots. KAY impulsively kisses him on the mouth.

Kay	Merry Christmas, Darling.
Mickey	*(Stonily)* Merry Christmas to you, too, Sweetheart.

A silence. He eats a quarter of the orange. Kay sits on the floor at his feet.

I love it when the wind blows. When it swoops in on you and stands you up inside out and makes you move like you're going someplace. Blowing the snow around, like a frozen mist...that raw feeling of cold force coming against you, telling you that you're alive and trying to get warm, get warm...

Kay I know what you mean, Honey. I just can't get used to it. It's twenty degrees out there and it's murderous on top of that. Where I come from it's warm all the time. I mean, people are crazy anyway, but when they insist on being insane killers even in this unholy freezing weather, I can't take it. I don't even have the clothes for it, you know? Mickey? We've got to move, Mickey! This is an ice age, I can feel it. I don't want to become like one of them frozen dead in a glacier...ice moving down on us... Mickey...?

Mickey   I remember it well. The cold and the snow and the sheer fun of it—sleighriding, snowball fights, ice skating and all. I was the first one up, you know, when I was a kid, the first one—right there ahead of everybody, ready to get out and do things. I don't know what happened to me. ...I have a lot of nice memories you know, more than you'd think...

Kay   I know you do, Mick. ...*(No reply)* I'm not surprised. I can see you when you were a little boy, running around and stuff. I'll bet you were real cute, huh?

Mickey   *(Rasping)* Yeah, real cute. *(A silence)*

Kay   Can I get you something else?

Mickey   No, nothing. Thank you.

He stares. A silence. Then, as if approaching from a distance, we hear MUSIC: *Big Brother and the Holding Company's "A Piece of My Heart."* KAY *gets up, goes to the window, right, looks out. The sound gets louder; a moment; she closes the window, the music fades.*

Kay   Wow, that was a group of carolers, Baby, singing in the street...and they were all black people!

Mickey   Weird. *(A silence)*

Kay	*(Eagerly)* Did you ever hear Little Stevie Wonder? A twelve-year-old kid, man. He ate Ray Charles up one time, in the Cow Palace, San Francisco. Years ago.
Mickey	Yeah. He's a lot older now.
Kay	Very hip.
Mickey	Very.
Kay	The good old days.

She rises aimlessly. He reaches for her but misses, his attention still riveted toward the audience.

Mickey	Jesus, I wish they'd give us some goddamned fucking heat. Check out the radiators, will you? *(She goes into the dark, left. Radiator sounds)* Maybe they're clogged or something.
Kay	*(Returning)* No, they seem okay. I think the furnace is broken.
Mickey	God. *(By now his EYES are glowing a bright pink.)* Radiators. *(Strident)* Radiators.
Kay	Drink some of the tea. It'll warm you up.
Mickey	There's something I have been trying to express. For years now I've been trying to express it.
Kay	About radiators?
Mickey	Yes! Radiators! Machines! Bodies!
Kay	Go ahead and express it, then.
Mickey	Listen to me, will you?
Kay	I am listening to you.
Mickey	It starts with the heart, with the heartbeat. Call it a feeling, only it isn't exactly a feeling. Wait, if it is a feeling, it is not sayable, not in words—it—*(Stops, as if atrophied)*
Kay	Go on, go on. I'm listening.

MICKEY'S voice has risen in pitch and his eyes are now
flashing on and off in unison with the Christmas tree.

Mickey   It's in the heart, the heart. Between the beats. Under the beats. When you hold your breath. Something like drowning. No, emptiness. Nothing, a hopeless nothing. Not to be thought, not a thought. A feeling, a feeling of space. Dread?... You can't fuck around with it...it holds you up, like an invisible wire, through the flesh...freezing you...in space, empty space, empty space. Around the heart, the heartbeat... the heart...

Kay   Breathe. Breathe in and out. Take a big, deep breath. In and out. In and out.

Mickey   No, I can't do that. *(Panicking)* I can't do that!

Kay   Just breathe.

Mickey   If I THINK about it, it gets worse!

Kay   Lie down, then. Lie down!

Mickey   No, I can't lie down.

Kay   Okay, then don't think about it. Just breathe easily, in and out, and don't think about it.

Mickey   That's what I'm doing. I'm sitting here breathing and trying not to think about it.

Kay   Good! Good, now what about your music? Do you want to play some music?

Mickey   *(Smiling madly)* Yeah, I feel more normal now.

Kay   Thank God. Do you want your horn? *(No answer)* How does your heart feel now? Mickey?

Mickey   Stopped. It's stopped.

Kay   Stopped?

Mickey   *(Rasping)* Stopped cold.

Kay	Huh? What do you mean?

MICKEY'S CHAIR begins rolling very slowly down the incline of the stage toward the audience.

Mickey	Something has sprung loose, Kay! My heart is flowing now! *(Pause)* I feel a whole lot better, Kay. I feel fantastic!
Kay	Please eat your orange. Drink some tea, at least. Please.

We notice the CHAIR moving now. Accompanied by the SOUND of rusty wheels and pulleys, as his EYES FLASH ON AND OFF in synch with the Christmas tree.

Mickey	Don't bother me! I have no time!
Kay	Oh, God!
Mickey	*(Frantic)* Put out the light, will you? Put out the light!
Kay	Oh, my God!
Mickey	Put it out! Put it out!
Kay	*(In tears)* All right, all right! *(Blows out the candles)*
Mickey	*(Loud, rasping, hysterical)* YEAH! GOOD! ALLELUJAH! GET ME MY HORN! QUICK! I FEEL POWERFUL! I FEEL INSPIRED! I FEEL LIKE A GOD!

KAY stifles a scream and rushes away. The tree LIGHTS go out. MICKEY'S eyes continue to flash. The SOUND of rusty pulleys and wheels builds to a crescendo—a moment, then a tremendous metallic crash...the eyes go out. DARKNESS.

*

5. On the Street

PEEWEE, a young black addict, and MICKEY. The stage is bare.

Peewee	Hey, Mickey. How are you, man?
Mickey	All right. What's happening?
Peewee	Out on the prairie, Mick. Out on the prairie.
Mickey	Yeah.
Peewee	You lookin'?
Mickey	Uh...yeah...but it's cool. You know. I could let it pass on by, you know.
Peewee	That's good. Right on. Yeah, I'm going into the hospital next week myself.
Mickey	You are? What for?
Peewee	I'm gonna kick it, man. I'm gonna go through the change.
Mickey	Good. Glad to hear it.
Peewee	Twelve days. I'll be in there twelve days. Beth Israel.
Mickey	How about your teeth? You going to get your teeth fixed?
Peewee	No, fuck my teeth. I'll do that later, man, once I get it all together. I'm going to make me some money.
Mickey	You better take care of your teeth.
Peewee	They ain't bothering me lately. It's all them sweets. When I get the bread, man, I'll BUY me some teeth. *(Dances, laughs; they slap hands)*
Mickey	Nothing like your own teeth, Peewee. Once they gone, they gone.
Peewee	I know that. You think I don't know that?
Mickey	I wish I had all my teeth. You need a lot of money to get teeth put in.
Peewee	Well I'm gonna get me what I need. I got a lot going for

me, man. I ain't one of these jive niggers out here.

Mickey   I know you're not.

Peewee   I don't pull none of that low shit, brother. Passing dummies, taking people off. And I don't let myself get sloppy. I keep my respect.

Mickey   I know.

Peewee   You can trust me. *(A silence)* Can't you?

Mickey   Yeah, Peewee.

Peewee   I plan to get straight with you, too, Mick. I'm going to be righteous with you, brother. You wait and see.

Mickey   Okay.

Peewee   Maybe you don't believe me, Mick, but you been real nice with me and I'm not the kind of dude which takes advantage of a friend. You dig where I'm coming from?

Mickey   Yeah, sure. What happens in the hospital?

Peewee   They detoxify you. It's the methadone treatment. Then if you don't make it they put you in the program. What I'm going to do, see, is I'm going to clean up. I'm going to stop taking that methadone, because it's dope, it's dope. And it's worse than smack, you know that, it gets into your bones. Not me, I'm afraid of that shit man, but I'll still be in the program, so I'll sell it and straighten myself out. Do some coke, drink a little, everything'll be everything. You understand what I'm trying to say?

Mickey   We'll see what happens, Peewee.

Peewee   You're not still down on me, are you?

Mickey   What can I tell you, man?

Peewee   *(Fake outrage)* Don't tell me nothin', man. Nothin'! You sure it was ME your old lady said had took her off? *(No reply)* Because I ain't even SEEN your old lady.

Mickey	Come on, Peewee. She knows damn well who you are, man.
Peewee	At NIGHT, man? In the DARK?
Mickey	Yeah, Peewee. *(Disgusted)* Forget it, man.
Peewee	All I know is, you shouldn't be judging peoples guilty without no proof. You know me, Mick. I wouldn't do that shit.
Mickey	The whole fucking scene sucks, Peewee. It ain't just you. People acting like fucking animals, man.
Peewee	I know what you trying to say, Mick. These niggers out here, they ain't got no pride, man. No pride, no morals, no respect. I don't know what it's coming to, when folks start burning their friends.
Mickey	*(Sad)* I gotta stop this shit, man.
Peewee	You and me both, Babe. I ain't going to be doing this much longer. I'm going to put it down, man.
Mickey	*(Dubiously)* Yeah. *(A silence)*
Peewee	You're not sick are you?
Mickey	A little. It's just starting to come on.
Peewee	What time did you last get off?
Mickey	This morning.
Peewee	Yeah, I know what you mean. Ain't had nothin' myself, since last night. My damn wife comes visiting with the kid— you know my son Michael, don't you?
Mickey	Groovy kid.
Peewee	He's beautiful, I'm telling you. He's something else, that kid. Wasn't for him I'd have nothing, Mickey. He's the light of my life, he's my heart.
Mickey	I know it. You're really into that kid. Too bad you can't get together with your family.
Peewee	Don't think I don't know what you're talking 'bout, Mick, but it ain't easy. I been trying.

42

Suspicious look from MICKEY.

Peewee   I have, man! Me and her was like daytime lovers, bro, we
never had enough of one another, man, it was something.
She put up with a lot from me, Mick.

Mickey   I understand that, Peewee.

Peewee   I fucked up, and I admit it, I fucked it up good. The more
she hassled me about stuff, the worse I got. It was some
kinda—I dunno—some kinda craziness, man, you know?
You're an educated cat, you know what I'm talking about.

Mickey   Education ain't got nothing to do with it.

Peewee   Man, I wish I had me some. I KNOW things'd been a lot
brighter for me, because I ain't no fast nigger who don't
want to amount to nothing. I ain't no pile of shit in the
morgue, man. Least ways, I'd make something of myself,
Mickey, if I had me a CHANCE. I'd like to go to college,
man, and learn how to be an architect. Yeah, that's what
I'd like to be, an architect. Right on, man, building me a
project of my OWN.

Dances, laughs, slapping of palms.

Mickey   Too much. A project named for Peewee. The PEEWEE
PROJECT.

More dancing and laughter.

Peewee   Anyway, my ma and her's in the bedroom watching Flip,
and I'm playing with Michael, and they find my wallet,
which was in that blue suede jacket of mine.

Mickey	Poor Peewee. They took all your dope and all your money.
Peewee	How'd you know? I musta told you, huh?
Mickey	Yeah, you told me.
Peewee	I been out all night, man, trying to scrounge me up a taste. Can you believe it? I had twenty dollars and six bags! My wife throws the stuff away and my mother takes the twenty dollars!
Mickey	*(Aside)* A likely story.
Peewee	I had to beat her, Babe. I give her a black eye and I tells her to get.
Mickey	I thought you wanted to be back together with your family.
Peewee	I do! But you got to have your respect! Ain't no use in being home if you ain't got your dignity and your respect. Not me, Jack, when I get ready to deal with my family, I want it to be together. I got to deal with my family, I wants it to be together. I got to feel proud like a black man should! You're a white boy. You don't necessarily know what I'm talking about, do you?
Mickey	I think I do.
Peewee	Yeah, you're all right. You're straight up with me, Mick. You're all right!

Dances, slapping of hands.

Mickey	Thanks a lot.
Peewee	Most of the niggers out here, man, they just lookin' to beat a white boy ever chance they get. They got no sense. I ain't like that. To me a man's a man, and you're a stand-up dude, Mick. I don't go for them Black Panthers or nothing, man.
Mickey	Why not?

Peewee	Cause they're crazy! Walkin' around with rifles, man, who they think they kidding? Ain't nobody digs 'em, man, they bring the pigs down on us, give us a bad name, act like a bunch a commies.
Mickey	You ought to find out more about them. I think they're outasight people.
Peewee	Oh, what you talkin' 'bout? I know what's happening!

MICKEY *shrugs, gives up.*

	Ah, it's all bullshit, ain't it, Mick?
Mickey	Where is everybody?
Peewee	There's nothing out here, man, nothing for the money.
Mickey	Yeah, but there's nobody on the street. It's weird.
Peewee	It's hot, the avenue is HOT. People are being wiped out.
Mickey	Every time I come down here you say the same thing. "It's hot! Hot."
Peewee	I got no reason to put you on. See for your own self.
Mickey	Yeah, looks very quiet...I can't hang here much longer.
Peewee	Well, come on, if you're lookin'. I know where there's something nice.
Mickey	Where? Where is it?
Peewee	You don't know the dude.
Mickey	No, I'll just go on...
Peewee	It's a SMOKER, Mick! I swear it. I had some myself last night. I only hope he's still holding, 'cause there ain't nothin' that good here, man. The dude is a friend of mine.
Mickey	Yeah? I don't know, Peewee.
Peewee	What's the matter? You're lookin', aren't you?
Mickey	Yeah, I'm looking. I told you I wasn't feeling good.

Peewee	Then let's get it ON, man!
Mickey	Just hold it, will you? *(He looks around anxiously)*
Peewee	There ain't nobody out here, man. I'm tellin' you!
Mickey	Isn't that Uptown Joe across the street?
Peewee	Where?
Mickey	Coming out of the project. *(Pointing)* There!
Peewee	No, that ain't him.
Mickey	You sure?
Peewee	Yeah, that ain't Uptown. He don't walk like Uptown.
Mickey	*(Hesitating.)* Shit...
Peewee	He ain't got nothin' anyway, man. Doesn't make no sense to hang out here for Uptown. Even if he does come out, you know his stuff ain't been up to standard.

MICKEY mumbles and turns his back, scanning the opposite direction.

You're sure acting spooky.

PEEWEE steps away and appears interested in something down the block. A long silence.

Mickey	*(Desperate)* You got any money, Peewee?
Peewee	Shit, I had some money I'd been on my way to the cooker a long time ago!
Mickey	Figures.
Peewee	I take you to the man, you give me a bag, right? You always gimme a bag.
Mickey	Yeah, but I can't keep doing it.
Peewee	Come on, Mick. The last time, I swear to God.

Mickey	I can't.
Peewee	*(Pleading)* Come on, Mick. You can do it, man.
Mickey	I can't, Peewee. I'm sorry.
Peewee	*(After a silence)* Listen, I got five dollars. Just gimme a dollar, will you? Okay?
Mickey	*(As if he hasn't understood)* What's that?
Peewee	Just gimme a dollar so I can get me one.
Mickey	Well, where is this guy? I don't want to go too far.
Peewee	He's right around the corner on 4th Street.
Mickey	You sure it's there? I don't want to go through any badass changes man.
Peewee	I was out there myself earlier, man! That's why I want to get back before he runs out!
Mickey	How do you know he's home?
Peewee	Where else is he gonna be? What's the matter with you, Mickey?
Mickey	*(Thinks, submits)* Okay.
Peewee	Let's go!

They start walking toward the audience, PEEWEE excitedly, MICKEY resigned.

	Man, I sure hope he's still got that same stuff I had before! It's a smoker, Jim! *(Conspiratorial)* I shot two bags! Two! You KNOW I got a five or six bag jonesie!
Mickey	*(Enthusiastic)* The shit's really good, huh?
Peewee	Man, I shot them two bags up just figurin' to get the nut off, you know what I mean? And I went DOWN, my good man, I was DOWN for the COUNT. They had to pour me outta that crib and walk me home, Jim, 'cause I could not stand UP.

Mickey	*(Eagerly)* No shit? That's good, Peewee, I appreciate it.
Peewee	*(Stopping)* How many'd you say you wanted?
Mickey	Uh...three.
Peewee	You sure you don't want no more? Like you ought to get as many as you can, you dig where I'm comin' from?
Mickey	Uh...yeah. No, I just want three. *(Pause)* Maybe four.

They continue offstage, entering the audience; stop.

This the building? *(Frightened)* This it, Peewee?

Peewee	Come on.

He maneuvers MICKEY, *who is clearly scared, in front of him, and follows close behind as they go further up the aisle. After a few steps,* PEEWEE *throws his left arm around* MICKEY'S *neck, holding his head tightly by the chin, and, all in the same smooth motion, clicks open a small switchblade, pressing the point against* MICKEY'S *throat.*

Okay, gimme the money, Mick.

Mickey	Hey, Peewee? What are you doing? What are you doing?
Peewee	*(Tightening his grip)* Just gimme the money and I won't hurt you.
Mickey	Hey, come on, Peewee! Please! What are you doing? Turn me loose, will you?
Peewee	*(Drawing blood)* Gimme the money. All of it.
Mickey	*(Starting to cry)* I ain't got any money Peewee! I ain't got any money! Come on, Peewee! What the fuck are you DOING?

PEEWEE cuts a bit deeper, MICKEY yells.

Oh! SHIT!

Peewee Gimme the money. *(Blood is spilling over his hand)* Blood is pouring all over me you sonofabitch!

Throws MICKEY away from him, but holds the knife ready a few inches from MICKEY'S chest. They look at each other, MICKEY, pitiful, "how could you do this to me" and PEEWEE "gimme the money."

I'm uptight. I'm not fucking with you much longer.

Mickey Okay, man. *(Hands PEEWEE a handful of money and makes a reproachful face)*

Peewee *(Counting)* That's the way it is, Mick. I'm sorry. Is this all you got?

Mick *(Bitterly)* It's all I have, Peewee.

Peewee You sure? Turn out your pockets.

Mickey *(Outraged)* I gave you all my goddamned money, Peewee!

Peewee Turn 'em out.

MICKEY does so, trying to maintain his dignity, and produces a surreptitious ten dollar bill.

(Taking it) Okay, now go on down the hall and don't turn around.

MICKEY hesitates.

Go on, start walking.

MICKEY *walks away up the aisle as the lights* DIM OUT.

*

6. Are you lookin'?

Scene, a lower east side kitchen. KAY *is sitting at the table holding her head in her hands. A moment, then* MICKEY *enters.* KAY'S *guitar lies near her against the table.*

Mickey	Hi!
Kay	Hello.
Mickey	Whatsamatter?
Kay	Nothing.
Mickey	You were crying. *(A silence)* Why?
Kay	I don't know.
Mickey	Why were you crying?
Kay	No reason.
Mickey	What happened? Where were you?
Kay	I went to the poetry reading.
Mickey	I was there. Didn't you see me?
Kay	It was embarrassing.
Mickey	Yeah, I was there.
Kay	It was unbelievable, man. It was death...and Gregory—
Mickey	Everybody acting so pious.
Kay	—It really made me upset.
Mickey	Is that why you were crying?
Kay	Wasted, washed up drunk. *(Mimicking)* "Allen, Allen, right, Allen?"

Mickey	Pathetic.
Kay	Were you there? Did you see?
Mickey	Well, part of it.
Kay	Like a dried out piece of old cake, man.
Mickey	It was boring.
Kay	People listening to that sorry motherfucker, methadone fat hanging all over him, teeth falling out.
Mickey	What do you mean?
Kay	Sallow and fleshy as a rotten banana.
Mickey	What are you trying to say?
Kay	Shit, man.
Mickey	You mean me? *(She starts picking on her guitar)* You don't mean me, do you?
Kay	*(Sings) O sump mother, she's sump fine,* *She likes the hard stuff, won't touch wine,* *Ain't nobody match the way she works her pump,* *Make all the little boys in the factory jump—*
Mickey	I ain't him. Me and him don't have nothin' to do with each other.
Kay	*(Sings) O sump mother you sure sump fine,* *If that pump break down, you gotta use mine—* *Sump mama's no dummy the way she use her head.* *Workin' nine to five, don't hafta leave her bed—*
Mickey	I'm going to a gymnasium, soon's I get the money I'm getting off this shit. I ain't no methadone addict. *(Gets down and starts doing pushups)*
Kay	*(Sings) Sump mother what's the secret of your success?* *"Ain't no secret boy, it's all over my dress."* *O sump mother, she's sump fine,* *She likes the hard stuff, won't touch wine.*

Mickey	*(Collapsing)* In the meantime, I'm gonna work out... play some ball...go swimming...take a sauna...
Kay	I was talking about Gregory Lifeboat, not you.
Mickey	You were, eh?
Kay	I'm sick of the poetry con, man. You could throw up from it. Sloppy lifestyle. Discredited ideas.
Mickey	But that's not my scene, Kay.
Kay	Sanctimonious, sentimental assholes. People eat that shit up. Pretentious bastard.
Mickey	Who?
Kay	All of 'em! Little faggot egos climbing over one another to get to "Allen"...goddamn panty-waisted audience going ga-ga...and all those liberal cliches, man! How can you stand it?
Mickey	It's got nothing to do with me!
Kay	Methadone lush freaks, you seen one, you seen 'em all.
Mickey	Everybody on methadone I suppose is an alcoholic too, right?
Kay	Well, what did you expect? They'll do anything to get off, anything! They're junkie juicers, man!
Mickey	It ain't true, Kay.
Kay	It ain't?
Mickey	No, it ain't. Besides, it's better than being out on the street and geezing in hallways.
Kay	Shit, I'd rather be a junkie any day.
Mickey	No, you wouldn't.
Kay	Yeah, I would! Look at you—you're fat suddenly, you're out of shape, you got chubby gills, and a big ass, and a swollen liver, you oversleep and you're groggy all day, and you're always sucking on a bottle or a candy bar! *(A silence)* Well, aintcha?

Mickey	I'm gonna detox, babe. I told you I was.
Kay	And you don't make love anymore. You ain't even interested.
Mickey	That's a temporary side effect, Kay.
Kay	What good are you? *(A silence)*
Mickey	What do you want?
Kay	What do I want?
Mickey	Yeah. What are you hitting on me for?
Kay	Nothing.
Mickey	What?
Kay	Nothing, I told you!
Mickey	Come on, Kay.
Kay	*(Shouting)* I don't know! Something! Anything!
Mickey	*(Subdued)* Okay.
Kay	Okay, WHAT? Don't you FEEL anything? You're fucking narcotized, man, that's what's wrong with you. You don't even get bored.
Mickey	Yeah? Well, it's better than being a lousy dope fiend, sneaking around with sores on my arms, feeling ashamed of myself, throwing up in taxi cabs. At least I feel like a person again. I can look people in the eye...and I don't have to spend all my time on the street trying to score.
Kay	All right, Mickey.
Mickey	What do you mean?
Kay	*(Screaming)* I mean ALL RIGHT. *(A silence, she quiets herself)* Really, Mick, forget I said anything.
Mickey	I just ain't ready yet, Kay. I've come a long way, I really have...only I can't take a chance right now.
Kay	Right.
Mickey	I don't like it anymore than you do. I feel fat, and groggy. And constipated.

Kay	Ha!
Mickey	I'm outta shape. And I ain't got my freedom yet—that hurts. And my health ain't together.
Kay	Nope. *(Sings) You ain't no high roller if you can't handle the dice—*
Mickey	I'm hip to myself, Kay. I am—I won't be a free man 'til I can make it on my own again.
Kay	*(Sings) If you ain't got the engine, baby, don't ride me down the pike—*
Mickey	I got to be patient, Kay. I'll do it when it'll be just another sickness, you know what I mean?
Kay	*(Sings) Don't crease my fender, honey, don't hang onto my side. Don't set me up with money, baby, if your motor has died!* Ha!
Mickey	When I won't be thinking about going out for a fix no more to get well.
Kay	What did you say?
Mickey	Forget it, Kay.
Kay	No, seriously, Mick. I didn't hear you.
Mickey	Nothing.
Kay	Hey, Robert, what's happening?

Sighs. An agonized silence. ROBERT enters. KAY jumps up.

Robert	Uh, nothing much. How you doing, Mickey?
Mickey	Awright. How're you?
Robert	Good. I was just passing by, thought I'd see how you all was feeling.
Mickey	Fine. Doing real fine.
Robert	That's good.

Mickey	Yeah.
Kay	How's the family?
Robert	*(Depressed)* Okay, I guess.
Kay	Anything wrong?
Robert	No, no, everybody's all right. You know...
Kay	What?
Robert	Nothing. Everything's groovy.
Kay	Well that's good. *(A silence)*
Robert	You still on the thing, Mick?
Mickey	What? You mean the stuff, the methadone?
Robert	Yeah.
Mickey	Yeah, sure. Sure I am.
Robert	*(Unconvincing)* That's good.
Mickey	Yeah... *(A pause)* So, what are you into, Robert?
Robert	*(Working it up)* Oh, I been writing a great piece, man. Fantastic. It's subtle, you know. There's three black guys, and there's a couple of white revolutionaries, you know. And they get together on Mt. Rushmore, you know. And there's a gang rape, and a murder, some weird shit, man, you know. It creeps up on you, you know. It has a powerful impact.
Mickey	Sounds terriffic.
Kay	Very interesting.
Robert	Yeah, it is. It's interesting.
Mickey	Uh-huh. *(An awkward silence)*
Robert	Uh, you seen Peewee lately, have ya?
Mickey	Nope. *(Silence)*
Robert	Yeah, well, I was just wondering.
Mickey	Why?
Robert	*(Defensive)* No special reason, man. I was just wondering if you saw him.

Mickey	Why, you looking?
Robert	Well, yeah, I just wanted to pick up a few, man.
Mickey	Yeah...I guess he's out there, Robert. I haven't seen him myself, but I'm sure he's out there. Doing his thing. *(Laughs derisively)* If he hasn't been popped or something, you know, iced.
Kay	You know Robert can't go out there and cop by himself, Mickey.
Mickey	So?
Robert	That's okay.
Mickey	I ain't gonna cop for him.
Robert	Forget it, man. I wouldn't want you to. I don't blame you.
Mickey	I don't want nothing to do with that shit, or Peewee neither.
Robert	It's cool, Mick. Really. *(Gets ready to leave)*
Kay	*(To ROBERT)* How many were you gonna get?
Robert	*(Checking MICKEY)* Uh, just a couple. Three or four...
Kay	How much money you got?
Robert	I don't know. Twenty, twenty-five dollars maybe.

Heavy silence. MICKEY is staring hard at KAY.

Mickey	What the fuck you doing, Kay?
Kay	*(Ignoring him)* Why don't you and me split a half load then, Robert?
Robert	*(Watching MICKEY)* Uh, I don't know, Kay.
Kay	I'll help you score, man. I can get it.
Mickey	*(Pleading)* Kay...?
Kay	*(Defiant)* What, man? *(To ROBERT)* I got my own connection.
Mickey	You know *what*, Kay.

Kay	I do what I want, man. It's my money and I'll do what I want with it.
Mickey	Do whatever the fuck you want to do, Kay. You go get yourself some dope, but don't come back here with it.
Kay	*(To ROBERT)* You ready to go?
Robert	*(Hesitating)* Hey, Mickey...
Mickey	*(Hostile)* What?
Robert	*(Wormy)* Listen, I ain't doing nothing. I didn't mean to, you know...
Mickey	*(Contemptuous)* Fuck it, man.
Kay	Let's go, Robert.

Kay and ROBERT start to leave.

| Robert | I'll see you, man... |

No response. MICKEY turns away.

| Kay | Come on, Robert. |

ROBERT exits ahead of her, she turns to look back at MICKEY, then follows excitedly, calling after ROBERT down the hall. DIM OUT.

*

7. The Venusian

Scene, a subway station platform. MICKEY *enters, talking to himself.*

Mickey   Billions of young, giant starts...cooking...we're on the spiral edge, fighting the cold...our small, dying sun. *(Stops)* The relations of time and space are intimate. *(Takes a step or two, stops)* Farther than we can see is the beginning of time. On the other side...the universe expands, and contracts... *(Breathing in and out)* expands, and contracts...Right...deja vu!...a feeling in the heart...Far away on the most distant star, my past is coming to meet me. *(Laughs)* The sensation of having been this way before...right here...this...*(Closes his eyes and concentrates with all his might)* It's gone. *(Looks around)* It's the sense of Fate...a feeling in the heart, full of consequence...of time...time passing. Sad, a moment choking with blunders, wrong things said...broken promises...lies...delusions...desperate moves...lunges...loudness...drunkenness...paranoia... *(Moves on, disgusted)* If I could just get OUT THERE! Get it going fast enough—beyond the speed of light—burning like the sun—exploding and falling inward—deep, deep, diving downward into the BLACK HOLE...

Stops, crouches into a ball, concentrating his energy as if trying to wrench himself into another dimension, collapses onto the floor from the effort, and a pause.

Space travel. *(Laughs, rises, walks quickly across the darkened area offstage left, from where we hear him shouting)*

I SAID I'M TRYING TO GET TO VENUS. IS THIS THE STATION
FOR THE VENUSIAN SPACESHIP? *(Pause)* IS THERE A LAW
AGAINST IT OR SOMETHING? LEMME ALONE.

*He comes flying back on stage as if thrown. LIGHTS come
up, revealing a subway bench up center with a beat-up black
man on it, hidden under his coat, his worldy goods scattered
around him, obviously in desperate shape.*

Fucking fascist assholes. *(Observes MAN ON BENCH)*
That's some act he's got there. *(Crosses, a spasm from the
MAN ON BENCH)* Let's see… he comes to the station, he
buys a token, he puts the token in the turnstile, walks
down the stairs…

*Another spasm on the bench, MICKEY approaches, looks
closely.*

What we have here is a state of terminal self-hate and
humiliation. *(Walks back downstage)* A drug-addled idiot.
(Looks for the train) They get on, the doors close…they
get on, the doors close…

*The subway train—SOUND—approaches and passes by—a
flash of light—and a weird-looking STRANGER is standing
down left.*

Stranger	How do you like that? Went right by us!
Mickey	A Venusian!
Stranger	*(Startled)* Don't say things like that, kid.

Mickey	I've seen you guys around before, but I never met one.
Stranger	Uh-huh. Well, that's nice.
Mickey	My name's Mickey. *(Shaking hands)* How are ya?
Stranger	It's cold down here.

A spasm from the bench.

Mickey	He's dying.
Stranger	I can tell.
Mickey	I think he pissed in his pants.
Stranger	Yes. That was ill-advised, wasn't it?
Mickey	*(Laughing)* You talk funny.
Stranger	We have different kinds of heads on Venus.
Mickey	*(Watching him)* Yeah. You breathe air, the same as us?
Stranger	No. Nitrous oxide, actually. *(A silence)*
Mickey	I figured it was something like that.

Spasm from the bench.

	You think we should do something?
Stranger	Like what?
Mickey	I don't kow.
Stranger	No. Leave him be.
Mickey	He's scary. What's it like on Venus?
Stranger	*(Considering)* Warm. Real warm.
Mickey	Yeah. Sure wish I could go there.
Stranger	Me, too. I'm sick of this cold. I'm tired and cold all the time. *(Thinking)* It's the wind, see? We ain't got the human defenses against the wind...also, any little exertion, and we get tired, very tired.

Mickey	That's too bad.
Stranger	I know. And I'm sick of waiting for this godforsaken train. You understand what I'm saying?
Mickey	Yeah, sure. There was one, but it didn't stop.
Stranger	I know that. *(Pause)* You got someplace to go? Warm? Warm, and nice, and cozy? Eh?
Mickey	Uh, no. Isn't there something you can do? I mean, while you're on this planet, to get warm?
Stranger	One thing, amigo. Just one.
Mickey	What's that?
Stranger	Now, remember the quarter-pieces you could get up in Harlem for a hundred bucks? Enough dope for a week... guaranteed count...scrambled, of course...the .38 snubby... warm, nice...
Mickey	*(In a reverie)* Yeah, riding up the East Side Highway in my Mustang V-8, pocketful of money...
Stranger	Tying off...heroin bubbling, hissing in the cooker...fill the dropper, get the vein, blood popping up...the warm rush...
Mickey	*(Doubling up)* Ow! Cut it out!
Stranger	Speedballing is what I dig the most...first that shock of pure pleasure across the top of your brain and into your chest, from the coke, then the warm wave of smack coming up underneath it...you lay back and you ride it...up into the head... mmmmmm...nice...
Mickey	Stop that!

Spasm from the bench.

Stranger	Hey, check him out.
Mickey	What?

Stranger	Check him out, maybe he's holding.
Mickey	No, he don't have nothin'.
Stranger	Come on.
Mickey	You want to? Okay...

They approach the bench. MICKEY *examines the man's pockets.*

	Jesus, he stinks... *(Recoiling)* Shit, he's already been cleaned out. He don't have a fucking thing.
Stranger	All right, it was just an idea. Forget it.
Mickey	I will. *(Looking him over as they come back downstage)* Hey, why don't you go back where you came from?
Stranger	*(Laughing)* I can't.
Mickey	Why not?
Stranger	It's my metabolism. See, it's been altered. No way back, no way. Whole biology's changed. I couldn't make it there anymore. It's a one-way street for guys like us.
Mickey	It's too late now, huh?
Stranger	Yup. Later for that, amigo. Wish I was in the jungle. In Asia. Where it's warm. Little yellow boys on motor scooters with vials of brown Asian junk. Shit is practically pure.
Mickey	*(Blurting)* You got some pure?
Stranger	No, no, no. I was just riffing, son.
Mickey	You shouldn't do that.
Stranger	You can't beat a man from Venus when it comes to wishing for warm. No, no. *(Laughs)* Junkies. Blah, blah, blah, you heard one story, you heard them all.
Mickey	Ain't it the truth, though? *(Suddenly abstracted)* Same heads.
Stranger	Heads?

Mickey	The flyboys...the P.O.W.'s. Same heads when they came down from the sky as when they went up...the flyboys, the good guys.
Stranger	Junkies...they're repulsive. No sense of honor. No shame, no remorse. Stone killers, everyone of 'em.
Mickey	Heroes when they went up, heroes when they came down.
Stranger	*(Shivering)* Hey, we got to get it on...make some dummies... take somebody off, anything...come on, kid.
Mickey	Yeah...burn somebody...dummies?...with what?
Stranger	What difference does it make? Borax...rat poison...what's the diff? Come on.
Mickey	Huh? No...I don't want to...You got a knife?

Rumble of train approaching, etc. BLACKOUT and a FLASH OF LIGHT. THE VENUSIAN is gone. A spasm from the bench. MICKEY whirls around, sees the man's wasted face.

Man On Bench	You lookin'? *(Lurches to his feet)* Are you lookin'?

The MAN lunges forward—MICKEY recoils in horror, rushes off—MAN falls dead, LIGHTS go dim—MICKEY reappears.

Mickey	*(Freaked, as if talking to someone close by)* Keep going... get it on...through the ether. *(Breathes in and out)* Oxygen... photosynthesis...green plants...polluted...earth's crust...in the flat ring of galaxy, far from the center...where it's cold... *(Stops)* He was a greaser, a monkey. He oiled the machines, the moving parts. Got the rockets up, the planes flying. Little yellow boys with brown Asian junk riding motor scooters. They had dead little pink eyes. I have some-

thing good, something nice. A smoker. *(Pause)* Mickey's gonna get something. If he says he's gonna do it, he'll do it. Be home soon. Ah, the Sea of Serenity. *(Pause)* Wow, he thought he was black for a while, he was hanging black. You listening?...Boiling, bubbling heroin hissing in the cooker...get the vein...the blood jumps...the warm rush... *(Bends over with a cramp)* Gimme your dope, Mick. Gimme your dope and all your money. *(Like a young black man)* I know what's happening. I'm gonna get my shit togethah... do you know what that is? It's political GRACE...gonna put some ice on my balls and get to some of my own peo-ple....Battle ain't even half started...lines still being drawn up. Time, time speeded up. The speed of flight. It was inti-mate. *(To his invisible friend)* Let me tell you about genetics. There are an INFINITE number of possibilities, but it only happens ONE way...over and over again, ONE WAY.... The creation of LIFE, step by step. in the stream of things. In time. Stress. *(Pause)* But why the poppy? Why that funny flower? *(Pause)* I scored 37 points in one game, best night I ever had. I was 19 years old. Annapolis, Maryland...with this guy, Mickey, a friend of mine...*(illustrating)* I was shooting one-handers, jumpers around the key! They come up to you, and you go around them, swish! *(Near the exit now, sees "SOMEONE" off-stage)* Hey, come 'ere!... How you doin'? You lookin'?

BLACKOUT.

The End

Scar

by Murray Mednick

Scar *was first produced at the Magic Theater of San Francisco, in 1985, directed by the playwright. The same production moved to the Met Theatre in Los Angeles.*

Scar *was produced a second time by the Met Theatre in 1992. It was directed by Darrell Larson, and starred Ed Harris.*

Stevie: Steve Hartley
Matt: Ed Harris
Molly: Amy Madigan
Ralph: Rene Assa

Characters

Stevie *A famous musician and rock star; athletic, charismatic; rugged good looks; favors Western clothes and a Western outlook; in his mid-thirties.*

Matt *Was once a musician and friend of Stevie's and is about the same age; has a strange walk; dressed neatly but in rough clothes; carries a leather-thonged bedroll within which is wrapped a flute, a gourd rattle, and his personal medicine bundle.*

Molly *Stevie's wife, a beautiful, sexy actress in her early thirties; solid, straightforward.*

Ralph *Business manager for Stevie and Molly; sly sense of humor; fastidious and neurotic.*

Scene

Night, about two in the morning. The interior of a large, rustic but well-furnished cabin in the Sangre de Cristo Mountains about fifty miles out of Santa Fe, New Mexico. Dominating the room, stage rear, is a huge, sliding glass-paneled door with a view of the mountains. The area beyond the door should be at least three yards deep. Up left is a short stairway leading to the bedroom. The entrance is down right. Down left is an opening into the kitchen. Navajo rugs, musical instruments, bookcases, leather chairs, a cabinet housing a collection of shotguns, mounted antlers, photographs of STEVIE *and* MOLLY, *ropes, bridles, and other equestrian artifacts. To the right is a couch, and on it is* RALPH, *apparently asleep, under a blanket. Off, the* HOOTING *of an owl. It calls two or three times, then a silence. Then a sudden* LOUD KNOCKING *on the door, down right.* RALPH *sits up and switches on a* LAMP.

Act One

Ralph	What? *(More knocking)* What is that?

RALPH puts on robe and slippers and goes to the door.

	Who's there?
Matt	*(Off left)* It's me!
Ralph	Who?
Matt	*(Off left)* It's me! Matthew!
Ralph	Matthew?
Matt	*(Off left)* Matt! Stevie invited me for dinner!
Ralph	Stevie invited you for dinner?
Matt	*(Off left)* Yeah!
Ralph	Just a minute. Stevie!
Stevie	*(Off upstairs)* What?
Ralph	Get up! There's somebody here!
Stevie	Where?
Ralph	At the door!
Stevie	Who?
Matt	*(Off left)* It's Matt!
Ralph	It's Matt! He says you invited him for dinner!
Stevie	*(Off)* Dinner? You know what time it is?
Ralph	What should I do? *(Pause)*

Stevie	*(Off)* Ah, fuck. Let him in!
Ralph	*(Opening the door)* Come in.
Matt	*(Entering)* Thank you.
Stevie	*(Off)* I'll be right down!
Ralph	Stevie will be right down.
Matt	Okay. *(Awkward silence)* I'm Matt.
Ralph	I know.

They shake hands.

	You know what time it is?
Matt	Uh, no, not really.
Ralph	It's two o'clock in the morning.
Matt	Is it?
Ralph	Yeah, we had dinner exactly seven hours ago.
Matt	That's all right.
Ralph	I know it's all right. *(Pause)*
Matt	Your name is Bernie, right?
Ralph	No. It's Ralph.
Matt	Oh. Sorry. I thought it was Bernie. I heard some people down at the polo field calling you Bernie.
Ralph	That wasn't me. My name is Ralph.
Matt	Ralph. Right. *(Silence)* How you doin'?
Ralph	Great. *(Pause)* I was sound asleep.
Matt	Sorry. How long you in New Mexico for?

Bored, RALPH shrugs but doesn't answer. We hear the voices of STEVIE and MOLLY, off. MATT tries again.

Uh, you on vacation, or what?

Ralph	I'm in business with Stevie and Molly.
Matt	Oh, I see.
Ralph	The music business.
Matt	Sure. You like it here?
Ralph	Great.
Matt	Yeah, the air, the light.
Ralph	Air's thin.
Matt	Elevation seven thousand feet in Santa Fe. Up here you got to figure it's close to eight. It's wild up here. (*Pause*) Undeveloped. *(Pause)* Indian country.

RALPH ignores him. MATT looks around, checks out the cabinet.

	Nice guns. Shotguns.
Ralph	Stevie collects shotguns.
Matt	They work?
Ralph	They work fine.
Matt	Yeah, he's got horses too, huh?
Ralph	He's got horses, he's got houses, he's got cars.
Matt	Boy, I never thought I'd run into Stevie like that, right there in Santa Fe, New Mexico.
Ralph	What do you mean?
Matt	Well, ya know, after all the years that have gone by, and the events that have happened.
Ralph	Events?
Matt	To come together like this, in this place, each in our own lives. *(An uncomfortable pause)* I'm not trying to be poetic about it. I'm just saying.

MATT walks to the door and exits abruptly.

Ralph   Jeeziz.

Enter STEVIE, barefoot, in jeans and Western shirt.

Stevie   Hey. Where'd he go?

Ralph   He left.

Stevie   You're kidding?

Ralph   No. He's standing there talking to me and then he walks
         out the door.

Stevie   Matthew.

Ralph   The fucking guy is weird, Stevie.

Stevie   *(Opens the door, calls out)* Matthew? *(Waits a moment;
         closes the door)*

Ralph   What the hell did you invite him over for?

Stevie   I don't know. I was getting off my horse and there he was.
         He's okay. He's an old friend.

Ralph   He witnessed you in your glory, so you had to invite him
         for dinner.

Stevie   I didn't think he'd show up.

Ralph   This kind of guy always shows up.

Stevie   Well, that's okay. He's gone. I'm going back to bed.

Enter MOLLY, a robe over her nightgown.

Molly   What happened to your friend?

Stevie   I guess he left.

Molly   He wakes us up at two in the morning and then he leaves?

Ralph   I think he got embarrassed.

Stevie	He's easily offended.

A KNOCKING, off left.

Molly	What's that?
Ralph	Uh-oh.
Stevie	*(At the door)* Who's there?
Matt	*(Off, left)* It's me again! Matt!
Stevie	Holy shit. *(More knocking)*
Molly	Let him in, honey.
Stevie	Damn. *(Opening the door, right)* Matthew? *(Pause, then a rattling, left)*
Ralph	He's at the kitchen door.
Stevie	*(Shuts the door, crosses left)* Oh, for chrissakes.
Matt	*(Off, left)* It's Matt!
Stevie	*(Off, in the kitchen)* I hear ya! *(Opening the other door)* Matt?
Matt	*(Off)* Hiya, Stevie! I wasn't sure which door was the real entrance!
Stevie	*(Off)* It's the other one, but come on in this one.
Matt	*(As they enter)* Sorry. I was looking around outside, and then I forgot which way I came in. Hi, Ralph. *(RALPH nods)* I was just looking around the place. Nice. Storm's coming, though. Lots of electricity.
Ralph	We thought you'd left.
Matt	No, I was just taking a look around.
Ralph	Don't you think it's odd?
Matt	What?
Ralph	Your behavior. It's odd.
Matt	Sorry. *(Looks at MOLLY)*

Stevie	Oh, this is Molly.
Molly	Hi.
Matt	Pleased to meet you, Molly. *(They shake hands)* What a beautiful woman. *(Startled at himself, he laughs)*
Molly	Thank you.
Stevie	Sit down, Matthew.
Matt	*(Sitting)* You keep your horses here, too, Steve?
Stevie	I keep two of them here.
Matt	Two, huh?
Ralph	*(Holding up two fingers)* Two horses.
Stevie	I keep the others in California.
Matt	This is something. As I was saying to Bernie, I mean Ralph, earlier, this is amazing fate. I mean, I'm downtown, and somebody says, "You ought to see the polo match today we have down at the polo field. It's a hell of a spectacle." And there you guys were, and my old friend Stevie is right there riding in the polo match itself!
Stevie	Ah, I couldn't get into the game.
Matt	I enjoyed it very much.
Stevie	Did you?
Matt	Oh, yeah. Especially the horses.
Stevie	Really?
Matt	Full tilt from one end of the field to the other!
Stevie	That's it. Those horses are trained for polo. They know what they're doing.
Matt	I don't know much about horses, personally, but I've tried to ride, and I can see what I lack on a horse, which is authority. *(Sigh)* No authority.
Stevie	Listen, Matt, it's a little late for dinner, we've already eaten, but maybe we can rustle something up for you.

Molly	Are you hungry?
Matt	No, that's all right.
Stevie	*(Relieved)* You sure?
Matt	Positive.
Molly	It's no trouble.
Matt	No, thank you. I'm really not hungry. *(Pause)*
Molly	Excuse me a minute.

A pause as the three men watch her exit up to the bedroom.

Matt	I thought you played good today, Stevie.
Stevie	I didn't. Couldn't get into the game. No rhythm, and I never got next to the ball, and then one of my stirrups broke. Let's have a drink. I got tequila gold.
Matt	No, nothing for me, Steve, thanks.
Stevie	Ralph?
Ralph	*(Impatiently)* No.
Stevie	I guess I won't either, then. *(Awkward pause)* So what have you been doing, Matt? I haven't seen you in years.
Matt	Right now I'm getting ready to go back into the mountains.
Stevie	Whereabouts?
Matt	Up in the Jemez.
Stevie	Oh, that's beautiful country. God's country.
Matt	Yes, it is.
Stevie	You playing any music?
Matt	*(Uncomfortably)* No, I gave it up, Stevie. Professionally, commercially. I carry this around, though. *(Takes a bamboo flute out of his bag)* Once in a while I'll play on it for myself, or for friends.

Stevie	Nice flute.

He hands it to RALPH, who looks at it and hands it back to MATT.

Matt	Yeah.
Stevie	Where's it from?
Matt	Mexico. I traded for it with an old Indian I know down there.
Stevie	You writing any songs? We're always looking for songs.

RALPH gives STEVIE a dirty look.

Matt	Here's one. It's short.

Removes an old rattle from his bag and accompanies himself with it as he sings:

I live, but I will not live forever,
Mysterious moon, you only remain,
Powerful sun, you alone remain,
Wonderful earth, you remain forever.
(Laughs shyly)

Stevie	That's nice.
Ralph	What kind of song is that?
Matt	That's a Kiowa song. I didn't write that. It's a Kiowa death song.
Stevie	Yeah, I thought it was some sort of Indian thing.
Matt	Yes.
Ralph	We're in the rock and roll business.

Matt	I know.
Ralph	Rock and country. Songs for white people.
Matt	That's all right.
Ralph	*(Irritated)* I know it is.

STEVIE *laughs affably at* RALPH, *who impatiently wanders left into the kitchen.*

Matt	God, but your career has taken off, Stevie. I mean, you were always a star, you were always the greatest, but now you're in the movies, you're a leading man in the movies, you're a star in the movies, too—and you can act!
Stevie	Hell, that's not acting.
Matt	Yeah, you're good! You can act! I was amazed!
Stevie	It ain't much different than putting a song over.
Matt	No, I guess not, but you're playing real characters up there on the screen. There aren't many who can do that.
Stevie	Things just happen.
Matt	No, this is real interesting, Steve. How do you do it?
Stevie	It's just like with a song. I try and stay out of the way of it. Molly is the real actor in this house.
Matt	I saw you in, uh, uh, I forget the title—something about a military man.
Stevie	*A Question of Honor.*
Matt	That's it, *A Question of Honor.* I thought you were really good in that picture.
Stevie	I didn't see it.
Matt	*(Astonished)* You didn't see it?
Stevie	No. I'm not much interested once it's done. Hollywood. It's a good thing Molly and me have this place here.

Matt	Sure.
Stevie	Where you can breathe.
Matt	Jeez, she's something too, Steve. I just had a glimpse of her down at the polo field, and I could tell then how special she is. She is special.
Stevie	Yes, she is.
Matt	You look great together. *(This irritates STEVIE)* She is even more beautiful in person than she is on the screen.

RALPH wanders back in, obviously anxious for MATT to leave. STEVIE puts his hands on his knees as if to stand for the conclusion of the visit.

Stevie	Well...so...*(MATT doesn't move)* So, you getting by all right?
Matt	Yes, thank you. I get by. *(Smiles)*
Stevie	So, uh, you spend most of your time up in the mountains, do you, or, what?
Matt	I work with Scar.
Stevie	Scar?
Matt	Yes. You never heard of Scar?
Stevie	No.
Matt	Well, some folks around here know of him. Indians, mostly.
Stevie	Scar? *(Shakes his head)* No...
Matt	It's like an Indian name. It was given to him.
Stevie	By whom?
Matt	By life.
Ralph	Let me ask you something.
Matt	Yo. *(Smiles warmly at STEVIE)*
Ralph	Why should we give the Indians all that fucking land we gave them?

Matt	I don't know. I suppose it's because it's their land.
Ralph	How is it their land?
Matt	I don't get it.
Ralph	We beat them for it and now we're paying them reparations.
Matt	I see what you mean.
Ralph	We beat them for the land and then we give it back to them!
Stevie	Ralph.
Ralph	What?
Stevie	Take it easy. *(To MATT)* We own a lot of land out here. Some of the young bucks are going around cutting roads and blowing up power lines and shit.
Ralph	They should just let go of the land. They don't do anything with it anyway. They should let it go.
Matt	What would you do with it?
Ralph	Whatever you do with land is what I'd do. I wouldn't sit on it out of spite. I'd put buildings on it. I'd dig for oil. I'd plant a few seeds, for chrissakes. I'd do something.

MOLLY re-enters, freshened up, but still in robe and nightgown.

	People are trying to make a buck and those guys are still whining about getting beat.
Molly	I'll sit for a second and then go back to bed.
Stevie	Good, honey. *(To MATT)* We didn't just walk in here and take this country for a sack of beads and a jug of whiskey.
Ralph	Damn right. This country was earned and paid for. This country was fought over and won by some very tough individuals.
Matt	Cowboys?

Ralph	I'm talking about men who could live as hard as the Indians, who got up into these mountains and survived, trapping and trading and living off the land.
Stevie	They were fierce, independent white men. They opened this country up.
Ralph	Damn right. *(Exits into the kitchen)*
Matt	We can't understand this country. We won't understand this country until the dust of our forefathers is in the air we breathe.
Stevie	I understand this country.
Matt	Only then, Stevie.
Stevie	I don't agree with you. I understand and love this country, and I got as much right to own it and live on it as the Indians. That right, Moll'?
Molly	I think so.
Matt	Indians don't own it. Indians don't own land, they live on it.
Stevie	Well, you got a point there, Matt. So. Thanks.

STEVIE *waits.* MATT *doesn't move. An impasse.*

Molly	Was that you I heard singing earlier?
Matt	Yes. I was singing a Kiowa death song.
Stevie	Matt's doing some work with an old Indian up in the Jemez mountains.
Molly	Oh, that sounds very interesting.
Matt	He's not old and he's not Indian.
Stevie	Oh. I thought you said he was an old Kiowa Indian.
Matt	No, I didn't.
Stevie	Oh. What is he?
Matt	He's white, and he's in his forties.

Stevie	Oh. What did you say his name was?
Matt	Scar.
Stevie	Right. Scar.
Molly	What work do you do up there with Scar?
Matt	He's teaching me. He's my teacher.
Molly	I see. Is he teaching you survival? Survival in the wilderness? Stalking and trapping? Plant life? Things like that?
Matt	Those subjects are a part of it. Actually, he's teaching me an Indian life-way, a warrior's way.
Molly	Sounds interesting, eh, Stevie?
Stevie	Interesting, very interesting.
Matt	It's not easy to explain, of course.
Molly	No, of course not.
Matt	It is about learning how to live in the natural world, how to be with nature, how to see and hear the movements, the energies, the spirit of nature. Quietly.
Molly	I see.
Matt	It's about putting one foot down in front of the other one, without disturbing the environment. No noise. It's about deciding to meet up with yourself, face to face. It's about death.
Molly	Death?
Matt	Yes. A warrior gets his death song ready for the moment of his death.
Molly	Sounds hard.
Matt	It is. It's hard. *(Pause)* But it's not that hard. *(Laughs)* I've got nothing better to do.
Stevie	Occupies the time.
Matt	Yes.

Another awkward silence.

Molly	Well…*(Rising)* Good luck with your studies, Matt.
Matt	Thank you.

MOLLY *looks at* STEVIE *for guidance.*

Stevie	I'll be up soon, honey.
Molly	Okay. *(To* MATT*)* Good night.
Matt	Good night.
Molly	I'm glad to have met you.
Matt	Same here.

MOLLY *exchanges another look with* STEVIE, *then exits to the bedroom.*

Stevie	So. It was good to see you, Matt. Glad you could make it over. *(Stands)*
Matt	We want your horses.
Stevie	What?
Matt	We want your horses.
Stevie	Who does?
Matt	Scar does. Scar and me.

Silence. STEVIE *can't believe it. He sits down again and laughs. re-enter* RALPH.

Ralph	*(Pointedly)* Oh. Did Molly go to bed?
Stevie	Sit down, Ralph.
Ralph	What's the matter?

Stevie	Tell him what you just told me, Matt.
Matt	Okay. My friend—my benefactor, my teacher, his name is Scar—he's a veteran of the war, what they call a bush vet. He lives alone, in the mountains, because he can't be around people. He's afraid he'll hurt somebody. He lives by hunting and fishing. He is the most feared predator out there.
Ralph	Yeah? And?
Matt	Sometimes he'll go on a raid.
Ralph	A raid?
Matt	Yes, like for Stevie's horses. That's his way of life.
Ralph	Stevie's horses?
Matt	Yes. I was real impressed with them, the way they raced across that green field after the little white ball.
Stevie	Those aren't mine. I borrowed those. Those are polo horses. I keep my Appaloosa and my Arabian here. The quarter horses are on the ranch in Santa Clara.
Matt	Fine. We'll take the Appaloosa and the Arabian.
Ralph	You got to be out of your mind. *(Looks at STEVIE and laughs. To MATT)* I think you'd best go on back where you came from.
Matt	I was wrong to call it a raid. It's more like a polite request.
Ralph	A polite request?
Matt	Yes.
Stevie	Then why doesn't he come and ask me himself?
Matt	Because he's my teacher, and I'm his apprentice, and he's sending me for them.
Ralph	Who? Who is sending you?
Matt	Scar. His name used to be Ron something, but now they call him Scar.
Ralph	Who is "they"?

Matt	The ones that know him—Scar, that is. I mean, the people that know him.
Stevie	*(Putting his boots on)* I don't know what you're trying to do, Matt. I don't know what you're up to, as usual. But what ever it is, it isn't going to work. *(To RALPH)* I'll be right back. *(Exits, right)*
Matt	He's going to look at his horses now. *(Laughs)*
Ralph	What's so funny?
Matt	They'll still be there, is all, of course. We're not prepared to take his horses. We want him to give them to us.
Ralph	Fuck off, man—he's not going to give you his precious horses. Why should Stevie give away his horses?
Matt	Because Scar has a lot of respect for them horses.
Ralph	Respect?
Matt	He's a warrior.
Ralph	I don't know what you're talking about. That's no reason for anyone to give anybody anything.
Matt	Then it's up to Scar what happens.
Ralph	Where is this guy, Scar?
Matt	*(Gesturing)* Out there.
Ralph	What does that mean?
Matt	That means out there.
Ralph	Where?
Matt	Out there.
Ralph	What did you say your name was?
Matt	Matt.
Ralph	You're an idiot, Matt.
Matt	Suit yourself, Ralph.
Ralph	If it was up to me, I'd kick your ass out of here now.
Matt	It's not up to you.

Ralph	Listen, friend, what's good for Stevie and Molly is good for me. And what's bad for Stevie and Molly is bad for me. You understand?
Matt	Sure do.
Ralph	Good. *(Pause)*
Matt	They're not your horses.
Ralph	You didn't understand what I said.
Matt	Yeah, I did. Stevie's giving up them horses is going to be good or bad for you, too, depending.
Ralph	Depending? How could it be good?
Matt	Depending on your attitude.
Ralph	Forget it.
Matt	Okay.
Ralph	You're not right mentally, friend.
Matt	You can have it be any way you like it, Ralph.

Re-enter STEVIE.

Ralph	You see anything, Steve?
Stevie	No. Horses are a little spooked, though. There's a storm happening to the north of here.
Ralph	What do we do with this guy, Steve?
Stevie	I don't know.
Ralph	He's a nutcase. Let's get him out of here and go to bed.
Matt	You remember the Motherfuckers, Stevie? *(To RALPH)* This was when Stevie and I were hanging out together, playing music years ago, in New York City.
Ralph	Yeah, so, what's the point?
Matt	No point. I was asking Stevie if he remembered the Motherfuckers.

Stevie	No, I don't.
Matt	They were a bunch of guys we knew, anarchists, always talking about going into the woods and living on horseback like the Indians.
Stevie	I was never into any of that shit, Matt. *(Exits to bedroom)*
Matt	True, he wasn't. *(Chuckling)* Now he's going to look at his woman.
Ralph	What's funny about that?
Matt	She sure is fine, too. Exceptional. Stevie did well for himself.
Ralph	Did you hear what I said?
Matt	It's not funny.
Ralph	Why Stevie's horses?
Matt	Stevie is a star. He's in the movies, he's in the papers, his picture is in the magazines. And so he got Scar's attention. Mainly, he's here. And he's an old friend of mine. So Scar thought he might be reasonable.
Ralph	He did, eh?
Matt	Yes. So when Stevie invited me for dinner, it worked out good.
Ralph	Fell right into place, did it?
Matt	Yes, it did.

They stare at one another.

	And here I am.
Ralph	*(Going for his billfold)* Tell you what, Matt, here's a couple hundred bucks. Get yourself a motel room, take a shower, have a warm meal, buy some clothes, find a job, and start a new life. Okay?
Matt	No, thanks.
Ralph	Take the money, Matt. It'll give you a new perspective.

Matt	Keep your money, Ralph.
Ralph	Your perspective is way off line.

MATT doesn't answer.

	You know, in Latin America they shoot people with funny ideas. It's a wise course of action. They just keep the bullets flying until things quiet down.
Matt	You like that funny idea?
Ralph	My ideas are not funny. There's two ways of looking at wealth: one, you're glad you got it; two, everybody ought to have it. I'm glad we got it, because it's impossible for everybody to have it, and I don't care who does the killing so we keep it.
Matt	That's right.

Re-enter STEVIE and MOLLY. She is dressed now in jeans and a flannel shirt.

Ralph	That's right?
Matt	Yes, so this civilization of ours can survive.
Ralph	You've eaten too many buttons or something, friend.

STEVIE, upstage, switches on the outside LIGHT.

Matt	I'm not your friend.

MOLLY sits where she can study MATT.

One time a party of Mexican traders was crossing towards California with their families. They were well-armed and well-prepared. A band of Apaches followed them for a while and then attacked, but the Mexicans put up a stout resistance. Finally the Apaches signaled to the Mexicans—"Okay, you guys, fair fight! Let's talk it over! We'll trade a bit and then go our separate ways! What do you say?" Well, the Mexicans fell for it. The Apaches killed all the men but the two strong leaders and took the women and children captive. Then they strapped the two leaders to wagon wheels upside down, so that their heads were about six inches from the ground. Then they built fires under them and watched as their skulls cracked and their brains popped. *(Chuckles)* Fuckin' Apaches.

RALPH angrily gathers his clothes.

| Stevie | Who asked you, Matt? |
| Matt | Just a story, Stevie. The Apaches had, uh, religious beliefs that we can't understand. |

RALPH goes upstairs to change.

Stevie	Okay, Matt?
Matt	Yo.
Stevie	Let's talk about this man, Scar.
Matt	Okay. He's originally from Philadelphia. He is a veteran of the war. They said he had P.T.S.D. That's "Post Traumatic Stress Disorder." But he knew he wasn't crazy. He was depressed, but he wasn't crazy. He walked out of the V.A. hospital and he went to a lonely mountaintop where he screamed and cried his heart out. Then he became a bush vet, because he can't be in society, around people. He can't

look at that stuff anymore. The faces. The fear. The violence and ugliness. And the noise. He's got no tolerance for the noise. And he'd be at an intersection, for example, or a red light, and he'd break into a sweat. And then he'd panic. He can't work or strive or be ambitious. He can't eat shit anymore for a paycheck. And he don't want to hurt nobody. After what he's been through over there, he don't want to hurt nobody, not if he can help it.

Stevie   So why does he threaten me about my horses?

Matt   Scar says he has no confidence in the way of being with people. He has to live alone with nature. With the horses, he can move about easier and have good company. He says he'll take excellent care of the horses.

Stevie   What makes him think that I'll give him my horses?

Matt   Scar says he sees a warrior in you. He says you have integrity, sensitivity, and power. He has a lot of respect, like I was saying to Ralph.

Stevie   And?

Matt   He says you're capable of a "give-away." A "give-away" is a common practice among many native peoples. One gives away what is precious. Robes and skins, weapons, horses, even a woman. Well, sometimes. It was, it is, a sign of leadership, manhood, grace.

Stevie   So, I'm a candidate for a "give-away."

Matt   Yes, according to Scar.

Molly   How would he know?

Matt   He knows. Like he knows your horses.

Stevie   He knows my horses?

Matt   Sure. He senses them. And they sense him. He can talk to them horses. He can be a hundred yards away and be talking to them horses. And he ain't opening his mouth, either. He does it with his mind, with the power of his mind. He's trying to teach me—about mind. But those kinds of powers are beyond me, Steve. Now Scar, though, he's way up there, Steve, way up there. He can do—Me, I'm just a... an apprentice.

Silence. STEVIE and MATT stare intensely at each other.

Molly	Scar's a white man?
Matt	Yes. He met some people, I guess. Indian people.
Molly	Where?
Matt	Up in the Jemez. After the war.
Molly	And before that?

MATT doesn't answer.

Like what did he do for a living?

MATT still doesn't answer.

Stevie	Scar. What was his line of work?
Matt	Oh. Machinist. Toolmaker.

RALPH, dressed, re-enters from the bedroom.

Stevie	Where was this again?
Matt	This was in New York, and Detroit. He was good, real good. I don't know much about that particular trade, but Scar says he had a talent for it. And you can see it, of

course, back at his camp, in the mountains. You can see the talent there. He's got like a plumbing system he put together, with running water. He's got rigs he made for meat drying and skin tanning, and rigs for cooking. And he's great with his weapons, the way he maintains them and improves on them. You can see the talent there, the ability.

Ralph Weapons?

Matt Yes.

Stevie What are his weapons?

Matt Knife. Bow and arrow. Rope. Sling shot. Club. Spear. Poison. Traps. You name it. Plus a pistol, a .45, on his hip, and a submachine gun on his back. And he's got defenses around his camp. See, what he'll do is, he'll find a secure spot, and he'll dig in, and watch. Then he'll set up his perimeter, so he can cover it, and no one gets in. You cross his lines and you're in the shit, you're food for the dead-eaters. But mainly he's a master, a warrior.

Ralph Where is he now?

Matt Like I said, he's out there.

Ralph Out there where?

Matt Outside.

Molly Steve?

Stevie I think I'll take a look around.

Ralph I'll come with you, Steve.

STEVIE and RALPH exit, right. A silence.

Molly Tell me, how well do you know Stevie?

Matt He never told you about me?

Molly No. We never talked about you. He's never mentioned you.

A pause as MATT digests this.

Matt We were musicians together years ago, and friends. This was way back, before the war. I'm surprised he never mentioned me.

Molly No, he never did.

Matt He went his path and I went mine, I guess.

Molly Is there someone outside who wants his horses?

Matt 'Course there is.

Molly Is it true?

Matt I believe it is true, yes, I do. It's true. I believe it is. *(Pause. He clears his throat)*

Molly Well, if we feel that there really is someone out there, Matt, we'll call the police.

Matt 'Course you will. You can go on ahead and do that. Call the police, if that would make you feel more secure. There'll be no trouble. But they won't find Scar. He's too good. He's too wary. And he'd only wait. He'd wait for another time, and then he'd come back and ask again. He's got a whole other sense of time than we do. Stevie should just give us those horses. He's got no real right to sole possession of those horses. That'd be the least troublesome way, I believe.

Molly I don't believe he'll do that.

Matt Scar says that some day the horses will be wild and free again. He says there'll be herds and herds of them roaming the plains. He says that some day the people will be free and healthy, too.

Molly I don't care what Scar says. What do you say?

Matt *(Considers)* I say what Scar says.

Molly	What are you, his slave?
Matt	I'm his pupil, his apprentice. He's trying to teach me what he's learned—how not to be a slave. He's a real man, Scar is. He's self-reliant, independent, and close to nature. He doesn't say, "I this, I that." He owns nothing, not even his flesh. He walks the earth like a warrior, with his head clear and straight, one step at a time.
Molly	Self-reliant, independent, and close to nature.
Matt	'Course he is.
Molly	There's a lot of people would like to have what Stevie's got.
Matt	'Course they do.
Molly	Like you, for instance.
Matt	Scar, you mean. Mainly his horses. But not for me. For Scar.
Molly	I think you're lying.

MATT starts to cough, but controls it quickly.

	Are you sick?
Matt	No.
Molly	Does that offend you?
Matt	No.
Molly	Would you like some water?
Matt	No, thanks. I can see that you are a person of strong convictions.
Molly	That's right. I am.
Matt	I used to be also, locked into my way of thinking. But Scar has shown me the true value of my convictions.
Molly	Good for you.
Matt	'Course, it's true what you say. There is a side to me that envies Stevie's amazing gifts. I'll have to admit to that.

Molly	Good. What is it then, drugs?
Matt	Is what drugs?
Molly	That would make you try something like this.
Matt	I haven't taken any kind of drug for five years or more. I'm stone cold sober. Sober as a bear in the woods. Not a pill, not a toke of weed, not a drink of whiskey, not a whiff of crank, not a line of coke, not a hypodermic needle of the hard stuff—not nothing at all.
Molly	Congratulations again.
Matt	And I fast and walk long distances.
Molly	And again.
Matt	Thanks. And Stevie?
Molly	He smokes once in a while, and drinks his tequila.
Matt	He's slowed down some, has he?
Molly	So I've been told.
Matt	Well, you're good for him then.
Molly	I am, thank you. And Scar?
Matt	Scar?
Molly	Does he have a wife?
Matt	No. I guess he did have one, once, when he came back from the war, a while ago, after he had dismissed himself from the V.A. hospital—because all they were doing was giving him medication to numb out the problem—so then when he got out of there, he got married. He wanted to be normal and make a go of it, but he couldn't adjust. He couldn't compete. He couldn't stay on the job. And he would slug his wife in his sleep or ass-kick her out of bed. So, she left him, finally, and moved to another city.
Molly	What was her name?
Matt	I don't remember now. It was something like Ellie, or Kelly.

Molly	Ellie or Kelly.
Matt	That's right. He can't have no family, he can't have a tribe. That's how they got Crazy Horse. Crazy Horse had to come in because it was winter, and his people were with him, and they were starving. He had to bring them in, and they got him, they got him! They stabbed him in the back! Scar stays alone.
Molly	And you?
Matt	What?
Molly	Do you have a woman?
Matt	The Apaches, when they went on a raid, would stay chaste two, three, four months at a time. Occasionally, a few women would go along, but mostly they stayed chaste. It was part of the Way.
Molly	Don't tell me about the Apaches, Matt. Tell me about yourself.
Matt	I'll tell you what Stevie used to say. "Men are to be dominated and women seduced," that's what Stevie used to say.
Molly	He's not like that anymore.
Matt	Scar might like you, too, you know. He might have a thought or two about taking you with him. As a matter of fact, he might want you instead of them stupid horses.

Re-enter STEVIE, right.

Molly	I'd kill him first, of course.
Matt	Hi, Stevie. We were just talking. *(To MOLLY)* I didn't mean what I said.
Stevie	*(Picking up a rope, to MOLLY)* What did he say?
Matt	I was saying Scar might want her instead of them stupid horses.

STEVIE becomes menacing with the rope.

| | I shouldn't have said it. A woman's not possible for Scar no more. Scar is chaste. And he's shy, besides. Scar says that he never will get over his fear. *(Pause)* That's quite a rope, Stevie. |
| Stevie | How did you get out here, Matt? |

RALPH appears upstage beyond the glass door. He KNOCKS and MOLLY opens the door for him.

	For chrissakes, Ralph.
Ralph	*(Entering)* What?
Stevie	Why can't you come in the front door?
Molly	You startled us, Ralph.
Matt	*(Friendly)* How is it outside? Felt like rain earlier. Felt like a storm coming. I love that musty smell after a rain. But Scar says it reminds him of the war. Makes him nervous.
Ralph	Is that so? *(To STEVIE)* How did he make it out here?
Stevie	*(Swinging the rope)* He didn't say.
Matt	You look real handy with that rope, Stevie.
Stevie	I am.
Matt	I heard about it. Folks say you're a rodeo-class roper.
Stevie	That's probably right.
Matt	They say you're buying your own calves now, to practice on.
Stevie	I do. It's great sport.
Matt	I guess you sure like having your toys around.
Stevie	I guess I do.
Matt	And fuck those who are poor and needy.
Stevie	Fuck 'em.
Matt	I guess that's one attitude to take.

Stevie	I got one life.
Matt	I guess that's how you earned Scar's attention. A warrior requires a worthy opponent.
Stevie	Fuck Scar.
Matt	Stevie, you throw that rope on me and I'll find a way to strangle you with it.
Ralph	Throw it on him, Stevie.
Matt	I won't be played with like some damn toy of yours.
Molly	Stevie! Stop it!

STEVIE stops.

	Did you see something?
Stevie	No, nothing out of the ordinary, but we don't know how he came out here.
Matt	I walked.
Ralph	You walked?
Matt	I walked.
Ralph	Fuck this, Stevie. Rope the sonofabitch.
Matt	No need for that. I'll go any time. *(Stands)* Nice seeing you again, Stevie.

MATT offers his hand; STEVIE doesn't take it.

Stevie	So long.
Ralph	Don't come back.
Matt	Don't worry, you won't see me no more. *(Starts for the door)* 'Course, I can't speak for Scar on that.
Molly	Wait a minute.
Matt	Yes?

Molly	You want the horses?
Matt	I do, yes. For Scar.
Molly	*(To STEVIE)* Give him the horses.
Ralph	Are you serious?
Molly	Give Scar the horses.
Stevie	Tell you what, Matt. We'll give Scar the horses.
Ralph	Why?
Molly	We can buy more horses. I'm tired. I want to go back to bed.
Ralph	You would sacrifice the horses for a night's sleep?
Molly	I would, yes.
Ralph	It's all right with me.
Molly	They're Stevie's horses.
Stevie	Yeah, we'll give Scar the horses.
Matt	Good deal, Stevie. *(Offers his hand)*
Stevie	*(Not taking it)* Tell Scar to come and get the horses. *(Silence)*
Matt	No.
Stevie	No?
Matt	No. Scar ain't gonna show himself. He wants for you to give *me* the horses. He isn't going to come out. You give *me* the horses. And then I'll take them to Scar.
Stevie	I'll only give the horses to Scar, personally.
Matt	You don't just go up to Scar and say, "Hi." He won't let you come near to him.
Molly	So what do you do?
Matt	There has to be an appointment, at a certain time and place, set up way in advance. Then you truck in there, into the bush. You bring your water and food, and then you wait until he feels it's all right to come out. And even then, you might not see him. He's shy, like I told you. You know how it might be, when you want to keep your head down.

	You don't want to look up, you don't want to see the faces, the fear in people's eyes, the doubt.
Stevie	No way.
Matt	No?
Stevie	No. I'll only give the horses to Scar, personally, like I said.

A shaft of LIGHTNING, *and the sound of* THUNDER.

Matt	Listen, why don't I communicate to Scar how you don't want to give him the horses. I know you don't. You just want him to come out so you can shoot him or lasso him or something. He can smell that shit a mile off. So I'll tell Scar your answer is "No." *(Again starts for the door)*
Stevie	Sit down, Matt.
Matt	What for?
Stevie	Sit down.
Ralph	Let him go, Steve.
Matt	I'll tell Scar, "No."
Stevie	Sit down, Matt.

STEVIE *suddenly tries to throw the rope around* MATT, *but misses and hits him with it instead.* MATT, *outraged, grabs the rope.*

Matt	Don't you fuck with me, Stevie!
Stevie	Who is fucking with whom here, Matt? You walk into my fucking house in the middle of the fucking night and ask for my fucking horses!
Matt	*(Dropping his end of the rope)* Sorry. It's not up to me.
Stevie	Asshole!

STEVIE slams the rope to the floor. MOLLY quickly picks it up. A pause as she stands between MATT and STEVIE.

Okay, let's start over again.

Matt	Sure.
Stevie	There's a man out there who wants my horses.
Matt	Right.
Stevie	He was a soldier in the war.
Matt	Right.
Stevie	He's armed.
Matt	Always.
Stevie	He's crazy.
Matt	He's not crazy. He'd just rather kill a rattlesnake than line up for a hamburger in McDonald's.

He tries to laugh; STEVIE cuts him off.

Stevie	How did you get out here, Matt? There's no car, and it's fifty miles to town. *(No answer)* What did you do, park somewhere down the road?
Matt	No car. I wouldn't bullshit you, Stevie, we're friends. I walked.
Stevie	We're not friends. I haven't seen you or talked to you in seven years.
Matt	Nine. You always did have a lousy head for memory, Steve.
Stevie	What's he look like?
Matt	Scar?
Stevie	Yeah, Scar!
Matt	He's a big man, heavy set, maybe six-four, six-five. Played ball in high school—football, basketball, baseball. He was

a star, to hear him tell it. Like you, Stevie. Agile, athletic. Walks like a bear, but light-footed. Bearded. Wears a pair of those rimless glasses. Wears leather and fur. Army boots. Army hat. Cartridge belt. Canteen. Forty-five. You'd take notice of him if you saw him. He don't look ordinary. *(Pause)* I'm glad we're getting a chance to talk finally, Steve.

Stevie   Talk?

Matt   I want to own up to something. I owe you an apology.

Stevie   Listen, forget about the horses, and Scar, and I'll take you to town, and this whole thing never happened.

Matt   I don't mean that. Scar needs the horses. I mean a personal apology. All these years I've harbored envy and resentment towards you and I'm sorry for it.

Stevie   You can harbor whatever you want to, Matt. It makes no difference to me at all.

Matt   *(Hurt)* Okay.

Stevie   Just tell me one thing.

Matt   What?

Stevie   You think you have a moral right to the horses because I have them and you don't?

Matt   Not me. Scar.

Ralph   That's sick. Everybody could go around taking whatever they want.

Matt   The American soldiers came home and got fucked over and those assholes they were fighting for over there get three percent loans from the United States government to start up businesses.

Ralph   So what?

Matt   So Scar says he has a moral right.

Stevie   But what's it got to do with me?

Matt	Because he's calling on you, Stevie! He's calling on you for help!
Stevie	Where is he?
Matt	Through me. He's doing it through me.

The HOOTING *of an owl, off;* MATT, *listening intensely, starts to tremble badly.*

Ralph	*(Of* MATT*)* What is it with this bozo?
Molly	It was an owl.

LIGHTNING *and* THUNDER.

Stevie	Matt is a trembler from way back. We'd be up there on stage in the middle of a number and all of a sudden there's Matt, shaking in his boots like a Dervish.
Matt	That's a fact.
Stevie	Overstimulation and hypersensitivity.
Matt	Afraid so.

More LIGHTNING *and* THUNDER.

Stevie	We'd have to quit and start over.

Suddenly a tremendous crashing EXPLOSION, *as though the house were hit by a huge battering ram. The* LIGHTS *go out.* MOLLY *yells:*

Molly	Stevie!
Ralph	*(In the darkness)* What the hell was that?

Stevie	The lamps! The kerosene lamps, Molly!
Ralph	What WAS that?
Stevie	I don't know. Let's get some light in here! *(Fumbles his way off, left)*
Ralph	*(Of MATT)* Where is that sonofabitch?
Molly	Here's one lamp.

She lights it; STEVIE returns from the kitchen with a flashlight.

Stevie	Try the phone, Ralph.
Ralph	Where is it?
Stevie	It's around, Ralph.
Molly	Here's another one.
Stevie	Great.

MOLLY lights the other LAMP. MATT is revealed on his knees, trembling badly and gasping for breath.

	Jeeziz.
Ralph	The phone is dead.
Stevie	What do you mean the phone is dead?
Ralph	What the fuck is the matter with you, man? Dead means dead!
Molly	Okay! Okay!
Stevie	Come on, Matt—get up.
Molly	He's frightened, Steve.
Matt	It's the noise...I...can't take the noise...picked it up from Scar...Scar hates the noise...*(To RALPH)* Don't come behind me like that! Please.

RALPH moves away.

	I can't handle that...I don't walk on sidewalks. You can't hear anyone...coming up behind you...on a sidewalk...
Ralph	What WAS that?
Stevie	Could have been lightning.
Matt	It was Scar...Scar...
Stevie	Damn! I've got to check on the horses.
Molly	Do you?
Stevie	*(Opening the shotgun cabinet)* Yeah, I do.
Molly	Do you really need those?
Stevie	Just in case, Molly.
Ralph	What do you want me to do, Steve?
Stevie	*(Handing him a shotgun)* Here. Go around the north side of the cabin. Take a look.
Molly	Shouldn't you stay together? That way you won't shoot each other in the dark.

MATT can't help but laugh.

Ralph	(To *MATT*) You be quiet.
Stevie	Okay, we'll go together.
Molly	Good.

STEVIE heads for the kitchen.

Ralph	Where you going?
Stevie	I'm locking the kitchen door, Ralph. *(Goes off)*
Molly	*(To RALPH)* Be careful with that thing.
Stevie	*(Returning)* We'll leave the shotgun with you, Molly.
Molly	I won't need it, Steve.
Stevie	*(Giving it to her)* It's loaded. *(To RALPH)* Ready?

Ralph	Yeah.
Molly	Don't get too far from the house.
Stevie	We're just going to check the barn and the power line.

They exit, right. A long pause. MATT is still trembling.

Molly	Would you like a blanket, Matt?
Matt	Yes, please.

She lays the shotgun aside, takes the Indian blanket from the couch and drapes it over him.

Molly	Here you go.
Matt	Thank you. *(Pause)* When I kill, all I feel is the recoil...all I feel is the recoil.
Molly	Who says that?
Matt	Scar...it was Scar.

BLACKOUT.

End of Act One

Act Two

Moments later, as before.

Molly	*(Softly)* Are you afraid of Scar?
Matt	No. Not Scar. You can't be afraid of Scar. Scar is gentle and quiet. He's shy.
Molly	Then why is he armed?
Matt	He won't be interfered with. And he has to eat.

A long pause as MOLLY adjusts and rearranges the lamps, one of which she places on the floor near MATT, who remains on his knees.

	It's a thin thread.
Molly	What is?
Matt	My heart is beating. I'm breathing. I'm talking. I'm looking out at you. It's like a pool cut, you know, a thin cut. *(Gesturing)* A thin cut, they call it. Stevie is an excellent pool player.
Molly	I know.
Matt	We used to play all the time, him and me. He always won. He always beat me.
Molly	He beats most people.
Matt	Yeah.

Molly	Do you want to lie down?
Matt	No.
Molly	Do you want to stand up?
Matt	No.
Molly	Something to drink?
Matt	No, thanks.

A silence; MOLLY finds a cigarette, lights it, takes one drag and puts it out.

	I was followed on my way from the polo match today by a strange little man. He looked like an Aztec Indian, but he was wearing grey sneakers and a Los Angeles Dodgers baseball cap. He's trailing me, and he's looking at me like he wants to ask me a question, like he needed to ask someone an important question. Here was this little old Aztec wandering about, lost in America, trying to ask a question.
Molly	What was the question?

MATT shrugs and shakes his head.

Matt	Which way is Mexico? *(Laughs)*
Molly	I have a question.
Matt	Yes?
Molly	When was the last time you took a bath?
Matt	Oh. Sorry. I was in the bush. No bathtubs in the bush. I was walking. You start out, you know, and after a while you get there, but it's hard to keep your mind on it.
Molly	On what?
Matt	On the walking. *(Silence)*

Molly	Why do you want to steal Stevie's horses?
Matt	I'm not stealing them, I'm asking for them.
Molly	Stevie loves those horses.
Matt	I think it would be a good thing for Stevie to give Scar those horses, especially because he loves them. It would be a payment, a way of balancing the scale for all the good things in his life.
Molly	It's not Stevie's fault that he's rich and famous.
Matt	No, it all comes to him from the Creator, and here's a way to help pay the debt, by giving the horses to Scar, who really needs them in order to survive.
Molly	We're not responsible for Scar's survival.
Matt	No. That's what they say. And maybe it's true. They're not.
Molly	What?
Matt	Responsible.

He takes a deep breath and appears to be checking a sort of inner gauge.

Molly	Matt, the war has been over a long time now. We have to go on with our lives. We can't help but live our lives. The same with you and Stevie. He's got to live his life, you got to live yours.
Matt	Scar says there'll come a time when we'll all share in the sorrow.
Molly	When?
Matt	When the time comes, we'll all share in the sorrow.
Molly	Don't you think it's time for him to adjust?
Matt	Scar has made his adjustment.
Molly	And you?

Matt	Me? I'm making mine. I'm making my adjustment. See?

He shows her his hands, palms up.

Molly	You've stopped trembling.
Matt	I can control it. Takes time, but a person can acquire the ability to control the body with the mind. You can close it down, if you want, shut it off, in parts. The nervous system, the circulation, the pulse.

RALPH enters, right. He goes directly to MATT and holds the shotgun to his head.

Ralph	What do you want here?
Molly	Ralph, what are you doing? Where's Stevie?
Matt	You know what I want. I want the horses for Scar.
Ralph	You're not getting shit from us.
Molly	Stop it, Ralph.
Matt	Sooner or later, he's going to receive those horses.
Ralph	Get up.
Matt	No.
Ralph	Get up.
Matt	No.
Molly	Where is Stevie, Ralph?
Ralph	Stevie's with the horses. *(To MATT)* Come on, we're gonna meet this friend of yours.
Molly	There is no "friend," Ralph. *(MATT scoffs)*
Ralph	What do you mean, no friend? Somebody blew up the power line!
Molly	That happens around here sometimes.

Ralph	Then who did it, Molly? Who blew it up?
Molly	I don't know. Disgruntled Indians. Relax.
Ralph	Relax?
Matt	Go round up Stevie.
Ralph	Fuck you!
Matt	He should be here now.
Ralph	What for?
Molly	Go get him, Ralph.
Matt	We have to talk.
Ralph	We're going to throw you into the fucking truck and see that you're locked up, you hear me? I'm going to personally see that you spend the next ten years of your life in jail, you fucking prick! *(Heads for the door)*
Matt	Okay, Ralph.
Molly	Get Stevie. We'll talk.
Ralph	There's nothing to fucking talk about! *(Exits)*
Matt	I didn't know he'd be here. If I'd known, I might have waited. Might have been easier with Stevie, one on one. But Scar said now was the time.
Molly	I don't think it would have been any different. Did you imagine that Stevie would just give you his horses?
Matt	In the war, Scar was regular infantry, a grunt. What they'd do over there, in the bush, they'd keep within their perimeter, and they stayed stoned all the time. If a gung-ho officer came along who wanted to go out on patrol or something, they'd blow him away. They'd shoot him in the back or frag him with a grenade while he was asleep in his hooch.
Molly	You were never there.
Matt	No. Me and Stevie, we both were just old enough to miss it. But Scar was right on time...right on time...

Tears come to his eyes and he coughs.

Molly   Lie down, Matt. You're sick and exhausted. Forget about
          the horses and rest.

Matt   I'd be standing at a corner looking at a red light and I'd
          panic. I'd freeze. I couldn't move forward, or right, or
          left, and someone was coming up behind me, someone I
          couldn't hear.

Molly   Matt? When was this, Matt?

MATT doesn't answer.

          You just said, "I."

Matt   "I"?

Molly   I couldn't move, I couldn't hear.

Matt   I meant Scar.

Molly   You did, eh?

Matt   Yes, I did. *(Smiling)* Where you from, Molly?

Molly   Chicago.

Matt   Chicago. Never been to Chicago. Always wanted to go
          there, but never have. Did walk by it once, though.

Molly   On foot?

Matt   Yes. Then I got a ride to Omaha. The Indians tried to
          associate a name with a personal quality. What would
          your name be?

Molly   How about "Strong-legged Woman?"

Matt   Good! Good name! Feet on the ground, in touch with her
          ancestry!

Molly   Solid Irish stock.

Matt   Mine would be Snow Eagle.

Molly	Snow Eagle.
Matt	Yes, I like it high up, where it's clean, bright, crisp. I'd like to soar above the snow line.
Molly	I can see why Stevie was fond of you.
Matt	Did he say that?
Molly	No, but I can tell that he was.
Matt	Ah, here comes Stevie now. I know his walk. It's a confident walk, a walk with body to it. Not like mine. My walk is all for show. It's a walk plagued with doubt.

Enter STEVIE.

Stevie	*(To MOLLY)* Hi. *(They embrace)* You all right?
Molly	Fine.
Stevie	The power line was destroyed.
Molly	I figured.
Stevie	Could have been an accident.
Molly	Where's Ralph?
Stevie	I left him in the barn with the horses.
Molly	Good.
Stevie	What's going on?

She nods toward MATT.

	What do you want, Matt?
Matt	Want?
Stevie	Yeah, WANT.
Matt	I want to fulfill my mission, and bring the horses to Scar.
Stevie	*(To MOLLY)* It's useless to talk to him.
Matt	My last assignment.

Stevie	Ralph thinks we should get in the truck and take him to the police in Santa Fe and have him arrested.
Molly	And the horses? We leave the horses?
Stevie	We'll bring the horses with us. We'll load them in the van and bring them with us.
Matt	Won't work.
Stevie	Why not?
Matt	Truck won't work. Scar's not stupid.

STEVIE storms out the door.

Molly	Why are you doing this, Matt?
Matt	Doing?
Molly	You heard me.
Matt	I'm tired. Caught up with me. Lots of walking. I could sleep now, right here on my knees. But I've got to—
Molly	Answer my question.
Matt	I told you, Molly. I've been given an assignment.

Off, TRUCK noises. They listen as the engine refuses to turn over.

Molly	You'll never get away with it, Matt, you'll never pull it off.
Matt	Yes, we will.
Ralph	*(Off)* What's the matter with the truck?
Stevie	*(Off)* I don't know! Try it again, Ralph!

SOUNDS of the engine trying again to turn over.

(Off) It's fucked! Distributor's ripped out!

SOUND of hood slamming.

Matt	Sure.
Molly	You didn't know?
Matt	Scar amazes me.
Ralph	*(Off)* What do we do?
Stevie	*(Off)* I don't know.
Ralph	*(Off)* Shoot him, Stevie.
Stevie	*(Off)* You shoot him, Ralph.
Ralph	*(Off)* Okay. Bring him out here! I'll shoot the fuck!
Stevie	*(Off)* Ralph, do me a favor and keep an eye on the horses. I'll talk it over with Molly.

Pause, re-enter STEVIE.

	The truck is out, Molly. I'm not sure of what to do now.
Matt	You'd better get that shotgun away from Ralph, before he hurts somebody with it.
Stevie	Shut up, Matt. *(Taking MOLLY aside)* I don't know how all this happened. *(Of MATT)* He's a sick man.
Molly	Maybe he only wants to be friends.
Stevie	Friends?
Molly	Friends, Stevie.
Matt	You're talking about me like I'm not here.
Stevie	What do you WANT?
Matt	I want the horses for Scar. I want the debt paid. I want the slate clean.
Stevie	I don't owe you! I don't owe you anything! You hear me? Your problems have nothing to do with me!
Matt	This is the hardest thing I've ever had to do in my life. To

	come here like this, and face you, and own up, and ask for the horses.
Stevie	I don't feel sorry for you.
Matt	I don't want you to.
Stevie	I don't feel sorry for you.
Matt	That's not why I'm here.
Stevie	You're a psychopath, Matt.
Matt	You don't know what's out there. You don't know what kind of blood is simmering out there, ready to pop, ready to burn your house down.
Stevie	The world is full of sick people.
Matt	Full. And they're equipped. They got knives and guns. They got tanks. They got submarines and bombs.
Stevie	You're crazy, Matt. You're deranged.
Molly	Don't say that.
Matt	(To MOLLY) I told you all about Scar and you didn't listen.
Molly	I heard every word of it.
Matt	You don't believe me. You didn't hear me.
Molly	Is to hear you to believe you?
Matt	It's the truth.
Stevie	Damn, I can't leave Ralph alone out there.
Matt	Why can't you let go of the horses? What are you afraid of? You afraid it's a trick? You afraid of being humiliated? No one will know outside of this house but Scar.
Stevie	There is no Scar. He did it all, the power line, the truck, the whole thing. The entire war was on television, Molly. Television and the newspapers. Everything he would need to know to make up Scar.
Matt	You're talking about me like I'm not here again.
Stevie	You're not. As far as I'm concerned, you're not here, Matt.

Matt	That's nothing new. You never could hear any voices but your own.
Molly	Then what does he want from us?
Matt	I want you to hear me. You think you've come to something, an understanding of something, but all it is is success, the energy of success.
Stevie	Oh come on, Matt.
Matt	And now you have the glib idea that there's no Scar. But there is. There is a Scar. Flesh and blood. Out there, waiting. You're stubborn and you're smart, but you don't know anything except how to achieve and maintain success, which is a gift in the first place.
Molly	And you, Matt?
Matt	Listen, I could play and sing as good as anybody in America. Ask Stevie.
Molly	Was he any good?
Stevie	Yeah, he could play.
Molly	And his songs?
Stevie	His songs? They were sad and mean. But I thought they were good songs.
Matt	You bet!
Molly	What happened?
Matt	I walked.
Stevie	One day we finally got a gig. We had been working together for almost two years and we finally got a job in the city. It was a very good group.
Matt	Excellent. We had Eddie and Pete, and Rhonda, and some first-rate original material.
Stevie	It was okay.
Matt	I wrote most of the lyrics.

Stevie	He didn't show up that night and we couldn't find him. We got somebody else and that was that.
Molly	Why?
Matt	I walked.
Stevie	He could never stand the business end of it. He couldn't take the idea that he might succeed. He wouldn't join the so-called establishment.
Matt	I got tired of feeding my face, so I took a hike. Are you listening? I'll tell you.
Molly	I'm listening.
Matt	I walked right out of New York City. I had nothing with me but what I was wearing and a small army-issue canvas bag I got in a surplus store. Every time the thought came to stop I wouldn't listen to it, I'd keep going, down the street, down the road, across the field, through the woods. First it was hours, then it was night, then it was a day, then two days, then a week, and then, gradually, I'd gone over. I was out there.
Molly	Where?
Matt	There. Out. One of the homeless, one of the vagrant.
Stevie	What good did it do you, Matt?
Matt	I became very sensitive to the weather. *(Laughs)* And I got a good look at the country. Lots of noise and garbage. Beefy people slaughtering the animals. Petty tyrants roaming the highways.
Stevie	Life is tough and then we die.
Matt	In the old days, when a warrior went off like that, alone, with his pain, they called it "Crying for a vision." Scar did that when he went up on the mountain. He was crying for a vision.

Stevie	You just went off the deep end, Matt.
Matt	True.
Molly	How did you live?
Matt	I scavenged.
Stevie	Jeeziz.
Matt	It was a game I played. It was one of the games I played with my mind. Everything becomes precious, you know, every scrap, anything found, like a can opener, you know, precious. A whole orange, a pair of socks, a towel, an old hat, a knife. I couldn't get that kind of story out of my mind. Like finding a nice place to sleep was—I was ingenious about that. I'd make a little nest, you know, with whatever, with cardboard, newspapers, whatever. I couldn't get that sort of worry out of my mind. I was always making a little home, always taking care of my little bundle of possessions. Everything depended on what I did with my mind. It was everything, all in the mind. I'd make up a destination. I'd say, "I'm gonna get up to that stone wall today, I'm gonna make that wall, and I'll be next to that apple orchard." Or, "I'm gonna follow this stream, I'm not gonna leave this stream until it ends into a lake or a river." And if something got in my way, like a swamp, or brambles, or a fence, or if the name of a street changed on me, I'd get so frustrated that I'd cry. It was too much. I'd be walking along bawling like a baby.
Molly	You didn't walk all the time.
Matt	You have to do something. Listen, it's really simple, it all becomes very, very simple. You only have one concern, which is, "What am I going to do with my mind?" For the next minute, the next second, what? You have to invent new rituals, rituals for the mind. "Don't take three left turns

in a row. Always have matches in your pocket, matches and a knife, and you'll be okay, Matt." You do a lot of counting. Steps. Trees. Sidewalk squares. Railroad ties. Telephone poles. Stones. People. I hardly ever spoke. You don't hear the sound of your own voice much. It's a shock when you hear it. It's a shock when someone speaks to you. Who are they referring to? Who can answer for you? Eventually I met Scar, who taught me how to walk like a man.

Stevie   Great. *(To MOLLY)* I'd better see how Ralph is doing.

Molly   Tell him to come on up to the house, Steve.

Matt   At any time out there, someone might come along and cut your throat.

Stevie   I don't want to hear about it.

Matt   It's a side to vagrancy I wouldn't want to forget.

Stevie   We don't want to hear any more about it.

Matt   There are people who will kill you just for the experience, for the fun of it, the thrill.

Stevie   Best to stay out of their way, Matt, and not go wandering around the country on foot. You're so naive, Matt. I always thought you were an idiot that way.

Matt   I know you did.

Stevie   A naive idiot. You think me and Molly are living in some kind of magic bubble where the world is less dangerous.

Matt   It is.

Stevie   It isn't, Matt. It's dangerous. You could slip and fall, or get lost on the mountain. Or you could get kicked in the head by a horse. Or you could get hit by a car on the road. Or you could get shot by an Indian. Or you could get invaded by an old friend who blows up your house. All kinds of things happen around here. And now I got to go find Ralph.

Matt	Stick around, Stevie. Nothing is going to happen to Ralph. You're doing great. This is the first time I've ever seen you stay in a room this long when you weren't the sole object of discussion. *(To MOLLY)* Stevie thinks everybody wants to hit on him for a piece of his action.
Molly	They do, actually.
Matt	Just give me the horses, Stevie, and I'll get out of your light.
Stevie	No.
Matt	Why?
Stevie	Nobody gets my horses, Matt. Least of all you.
Matt	Why, Steve?
Stevie	You're a little crazy, Matt, and a scavenger, a tramp.
Matt	Soon there'll be a whole new class of people, a class of marauders, like the Apaches of old. They'll give no quarter. They'll be in the cities and in the countryside. Scavengers, thieves, marauders. They'll take everything you have.
Stevie	I regret I said hello to you in Santa Fe. And I should have never let you into my house, because now you won't leave.
Matt	You fucking snob, you wouldn't have invited me if I didn't walk up on you as you're getting off your stupid polo horse. And I'd never have done that if it wasn't for Scar! Never!
Molly	Scar?
Matt	Stevie is fed so much from the table while others are going begging, like Scar, and then he has the attitude of fuck 'em, keep 'em away from me, get 'em out of my path.
Molly	That's not his attitude, Matt. You got it wrong. And I resent what you're trying to do.
Matt	I'm sorry.
Molly	I feel sorry for you, Matt.
Stevie	Where you going?

Molly	I'm cold. *(She exits)*

STEVIE chuckles.

Matt	I apologize, Steve. She's right, of course. I guess we took a wrong turn there.
Stevie	You took a wrong turn fifty miles back, Matthew.
Matt	You've got to keep personal shit out of the way of a thing like this.
Stevie	You must be kidding. If this isn't personal, then what is it?
Matt	It's an impersonal request from a solitary warrior to a great man of wealth, through an intermediary, for a give-away of horses.
Stevie	Okay, Matt.

STEVIE looks at his watch, starts off right, then changes his mind and goes up toward the bedroom.

Matt	You have any idea of the pain that Scar is walking around with, Steve?
Stevie	I thought he was a master.
Matt	He is.
Stevie	Then he should be out of his pain.
Matt	It's the pain of remorse, the remorse that comes from being a stupid grunt, killing and maiming, and the hatred and anger that festers in you because of it. On the other hand, he's got a great sense of humor right along. Just when you least expect it he'll start whistling a cowboy song and dance around like a big old happy bear. *(Whistles a tune)*

Stevie	I'm not interested in the kind of pain you're walking around with, Matt.
Matt	Not me. Scar.
Stevie	I'm talking to you now.
Matt	What kind of pain, Steve?
Stevie	You know what kind. The troubled kind. The confused kind. The kind that gets in the way, that stops the enjoyment of life. I feel sorry for you, I guess, and you feel sorry for yourself, Matt.
Matt	I apologize. I don't mean to do that, but I'm talking about Scar.
Stevie	It's too bad, really, because you could be having a good time up here.
Matt	True.
Stevie	I enjoy my horses. I enjoy the desert. I enjoy the mountains and fresh air.
Matt	Scar does, too.
Stevie	I don't have to think about it or apologize for it. And I do like my music.

MOLLY re-enters, wearing a warm serape.

Molly	You ought to go and get Ralph, honey.
Stevie	I know, I will in a minute. *(To MATT)* It's good stuff and it's fun.
Matt	I know it is, Stevie, and I admire you for it. Used to be I harbored resentment, like I was saying to Molly over here, but not since I been working with Scar, not anymore. I think you'd be amazed at what you've got in common with Scar, Stevie. You're both such good craftsmen and excellent athletes.

Stevie	*(To MOLLY)* I give up.
Matt	The only difference is that Scar is in pain, because he cares.
Stevie	Bullshit! Cares about what? The starving millions? My horses? You? What? Pussy? Sunlight? What? What does he care about?
Matt	I explained already.

Suddenly the LIGHTS come on again.

Stevie	What the hell!
Matt	Oh, he's a trickster, Scar is!

The LIGHTS go out.

Molly	The cable?
Stevie	I think so. It's the cable, Molly. I'll get Ralph.
Matt	Wait, Stevie.
Stevie	No more talk, Matt.
Matt	For old time's sake, Steve, about the giving away. Molly?
Molly	Stay for a minute, Steve.
Stevie	All right. Hurry up, Matt.
Matt	This is supposed to be a true story that happened over a hundred years ago. At that time there was a young warrior by the name of Snow Eagle. This was a beautiful young man, much loved by his people. His benefactor, his spiritual teacher, was a renowned old medicine man. The old man was trying to get a sign from the Great Spirit to tell him what to do about the crazy white people who were coming into their country. A dream came to him saying that he had to send someone directly, in person, the flower of his

	tribe, his favorite pupil, Snow Eagle. And Snow Eagle gladly fulfilled his assignment.
Molly	What was the assignment?
Matt	He had to die and go to the Creator and ask the question. And that's what he did.
Stevie	He intentionally died?
Matt	Yes, so they say. Snow Eagle fasted and purified himself over many months, and made his farewells to family and friends. And then he went out into the high desert and sat down and sang his death song.
Molly	Go on, Matt.
Matt	Snow Eagle said to his organism, "Now you will shut down." Not all at once, but in parts, over time. First the extremities, the nervous system, and then inward, the circulation, the pulse, toward the breathing. He was trained in the ability to accomplish such a task. A man who dies in this way is Wakan, holy. His body is not to be touched. And the place where he dies is then a sacred precinct, not to be trespassed.
Molly	What was the result?
Matt	The old medicine man received the Great Spirit's answer to Snow Eagle in a vision.
Molly	And the answer?
Matt	The Great Spirit said, "The sacred mountains are still there above you, the waters of life are plentiful before you, the dust of the fathers remains in the earth below you."
Stevie	Come on, Matt.
Matt	The Great Spirit said, "But the mountains are wounded and the waters are poisoned and the air is foul. Many must die if the earth is to live."

Molly	How do you interpret that?
Matt	Means you have die a good death. Means we'll have to give it all back. That's Scar's interpretation.
Molly	Back to the land?
Matt	Yes. To the land. To the horizon. To the sky. To the water. To the sun and moon. The thoughts, the hatred, the demands, the envy, the lying, the feeding of the face. We'll have to give it all back, back where it came from. *(Pause)* This spread here is a good place for it. These grounds around here been known about for hundreds of years. Generations of Indian dead, dust of the fathers.

The report of a SHOTGUN BLAST, off. MATT starts trembling again.

Stevie	That was Ralph.
Matt	That man should never have had a weapon in his hands.
Stevie	Quiet!

Another SHOTGUN BLAST, off.

	I'd better get down there.
Molly	Wait, Steve.
Stevie	What for?
Molly	Please wait. We don't know what happened.

STEVIE goes upstage, looks out the glass door.

Stevie	You can't see anything from here.

They listen intensely, then sudden NOISES *at the down-right door.* STEVIE *freezes, his shotgun at the ready.*

Who's there? Who's at the door?

Enter RALPH.

	What the fuck, Ralph?
Ralph	What do you mean, what the fuck?
Stevie	What the hell were you doing? We heard shots!
Ralph	That's right.
Stevie	What were you shooting at?
Ralph	I don't know.
Stevie	You don't know?
Ralph	No. I'm not sure.
Stevie	What were you doing?
Ralph	Shooting.
Stevie	Why? What happened?
Ralph	I don't know what happened, Steve.
Molly	What were you shooting at?
Ralph	I don't know what I was shooting at, Molly.
Stevie	For chrissakes, Ralph. How are the horses?
Ralph	*(Testy)* How should I know? I don't understand horses.
Stevie	Where are they?
Ralph	Where I left them. In the barn. They're fine. They stand there and look at you.
Stevie	Is the barn door locked?
Ralph	The barn door is locked.
Stevie	Are the horses tied?
Ralph	They're tied.

Stevie	Maybe that's not such a good idea.
Ralph	Why not?
Stevie	If something happened, they wouldn't be able to get loose.
Ralph	You tied them up, Steve. You put the bridles on them and tied them up.
Stevie	I know I did. I'm saying maybe it wasn't such a good idea.
Ralph	Then go down to the barn and untie them.
Stevie	I don't understand what you were shooting at if you don't know what you were shooting at.
Ralph	Might have been a man.
Stevie	A man?
Ralph	Or it might have been an owl.
Matt	That's bad. Bad luck to shoot an owl.
Stevie	Go on, Ralph.
Ralph	I just got tired of hanging out in the barn with the horses. I went outside for some air. I was looking at my watch. A fine precision instrument, this watch. Made in Japan. It reassured me. It comforted me to remember that there was high technology in the world. Modern industry. Civilization. A healthy economy. I don't care what happens so long as the insurance companies and banks and pension plans survive into the next century.
Molly	What were you shooting at, Ralph?
Ralph	I saw something move. I was ready to see something, so I thought I saw something. Might have been a bear.
Matt	Bad luck to shoot a bear.
Ralph	If he says another word, I'll shoot him.
Stevie	Good thing I didn't go down there. Might have been me.
Ralph	I knew it wasn't you, Stevie. *(Pause)* It was crouched over,

low, moving very fast, and not coming from the direction
of the cabin.

MATT chuckles.

Stevie	What's funny, Matt?
Matt	*(To RALPH)* Wasn't there a sound?
Ralph	What kind of sound?
Matt	Like a growl?

RALPH doesn't answer; MATT laughs.

Ralph	*(To MATT)* Shut your mouth.

MATT stops.

Molly	Why were you laughing?
Matt	Not another word.
Molly	You're not concerned?
Matt	You mean worrying that it was Scar out there getting himself shot at?
Molly	Whatever.
Matt	Ralph was spooked, is all.
Molly	By?
Matt	By something that growled.
Ralph	What do we plan to do, Steve?
Matt	He saw his enemy. Growling, snarling, hungry, brushing past him in the night, brushing his leg.
Ralph	Steve?
Stevie	Right now we'll have some coffee.

Ralph	Coffee?
Stevie	Coffee.
Ralph	Then what?
Stevie	I don't know, Ralph.
Matt	The next round belongs to the Chinese, Ralph, the Chinese and the Mexicans.
Ralph	Is that so?
Matt	Yes. Stands to reason.
Ralph	Not if we kill them all first.
Matt	All of them?
Ralph	All of them.
Matt	We could do that.
Ralph	Right. We'll start here with crazy people like you, who don't understand the facts of life.
Matt	Who understands the facts of life?
Ralph	Howard Hughes understood the facts of life. There used to be two of us who knew, and now there's only one.
Molly	I'll make some coffee.
Ralph	Yeah.
Molly	Stevie?
Stevie	Please.
Molly	Matt?
Matt	No, thank you.

MOLLY exits.

Ralph	See what nice people we are, Matt? All celebrities aren't bad. You drop in on us for a little game and the three of us oblige politely. The woman even offers coffee.
Matt	I appreciate it.

Ralph	Sure you do. What a guy.

MATT removes his flute from the bedroll.

Matt	You feel like playing a little music, Stevie?
Stevie	No.
Matt	Last chance we'll have.
Stevie	I really don't feel like it, Matt.

MATT begins playing a melody on his flute.

Ralph	I've had enough, Steve.
Stevie	Hang on, Ralph.
Ralph	I've had enough.

A pause, then RALPH suddenly springs at MATT with a vicious kick that knocks the flute from his mouth.

Stevie	What the hell did you do that for, Ralph?
Ralph	I've had enough.

MOLLY re-enters as STEVIE retrieves the flute.

Molly	What's going on? What happened?
Stevie	He kicked him.
Molly	Damn it, Ralph!
Ralph	I've had enough!
Stevie	*(Handing MATT the flute)* You all right?
Matt	Yes, thank you. *(Sitting up straight)* Pray for your relatives, Ralph.

Ralph	What's that?
Matt	I said pray for your relatives.

RALPH makes a threatening move, but STEVIE and MOLLY intervene.

Molly	Ralph!
Stevie	Leave him be.

RALPH turns away. MATT plays another few notes on the flute and RALPH charges again, stopped by STEVIE and MOLLY. A pause. RALPH drops it.

	Bring the coffee, Molly. I need a cup of coffee. *(She goes)* Soon as it starts to get light we'll be leaving here, Matt.
Matt	Suit yourself.
Stevie	You come with us and he's going to have you arrested or something. Isn't that right, Ralph?
Ralph	Absolutely. After I kick his head in.
Matt	I'm not coming with you.
Stevie	What are you planning to do then?
Matt	I appreciate your love of horses, Steve. Scar is the same way. But I'm like Ralph here, I don't understand them either.
Stevie	You didn't answer me.
Matt	I'm answering you, Stevie. I'm on an assignment for Scar, which I've done. I've asked for the horses. But I've also got an intention of my own.
Stevie	What is it?
Matt	It's not violent. I didn't come here to hurt you.
Stevie	Okay. What is it then?

MOLLY comes back with the coffee.

Stevie	Why did you come here, Matt?
Matt	Why not? Why not be near to an old friend?
Stevie	You can't go around expecting friendship, demanding friendship.
Matt	No. You're right. One must be thought worthy. And you don't think I'm worthy.
Stevie	I didn't mean that. We just got nothing in common anymore, Matt.
Matt	Time was we could talk like brothers.
Stevie	That was in another life.
Matt	No matter. It all evens out in the end.
Stevie	What does?
Matt	I don't have anything more to say, Steve.
Stevie	*(To MOLLY)* Get ready to leave. First light.
Molly	How we going, Steve?
Stevie	On the horses. Ralph can ride the mare, and you and me can double up. We'll ride out.
Molly	I don't know, Steve. Shouldn't we wait?
Stevie	No, it's time to go.
Matt	You can't run from Scar. You have to face his power.
Molly	His power?
Matt	Yes. It's the power of vengeance not taken; of the torment of an oppressed people, living and dead.
Stevie	I've thought it over, Moll'. That's what we'll do.
Molly	And Matt?
Stevie	Matt can stay, or do what he does, go where he goes.

MOLLY looks at MATT, who smiles reassuringly.

Dress warmly. It's cold out.

MOLLY hesitates, then exits to the bedroom.

I'll go down for the horses.

Ralph   *(Stopping him)* Steve?

Stevie   Yeah?

Ralph   What about him?

Stevie   He can stay here, do what he wants.

Ralph   You really intend to leave him here?

Stevie   I do, yeah.

Ralph   We're not taking him?

Stevie   No.

Ralph   No?

Stevie   No. Leave him be, Ralph. We'll find a phone, call the power company, come back for the truck. *(To MATT)* After we're gone, you can stay here awhile. Then probably it'd be best if you disappeared.

Matt   Thanks, Steve.

Stevie   *(At the door)* Stay cool, Ralph. *(Exits)*

Ralph   *(To MATT)* You're not off the hook yet, my friend. You've got me to contend with. I'm going to file charges against you. I'm going to make sure there's a warrant out for you. I'm going to put you in jail or in a hospital. And if I ever see you—

Matt   You won't see me, Ralph.

Re-enter MOLLY.

Molly   Where's Stevie?

| Ralph | He went for the horses. |

Off, the HOOTING *of an owl; it calls twice, stops.* MATT *struggles painfully to his feet.*

Ralph	Hey, what are you doing?
Matt	Jeez. Legs hurt. Circulation's gone.
Ralph	Answer me.
Matt	Time to go, Ralph.
Ralph	Where to?
Matt	Just outside. I want to sit down and watch the sunrise.

A tense silence. MATT *looks to* MOLLY.

| Molly | Sure. |

First LIGHT *begins to break.*

| Matt | Thanks. When it's all over, what's left? Bones. |

He steps painfully to the upstage sliding door.

| | *(To* RALPH*)* Okay? |
| Ralph | Okay. |

MOLLY *opens the door for him.* MATT *smiles and offers her his flute, which she accepts.*

| Molly | Thank you. |
| Matt | You take care of ol' Stevie, now, you hear? |

She nods. MATT *goes through the door and upstage a few feet, where he falls to his knees on the beat of a drum.* MATT *arranges himself into a good posture, then carefully removes his medicine bundle and rattle from his bedroll. He is facing away from the audience. Very carefully, precisely, he withdraws an eagle feather from the bundle and prays silently with it to the four directions. Replaces the feather. Picks up the rattle and starts playing a strong, steady rhythm. Re-enter* STEVIE.

Stevie	I've got the horses. Let's go. *(Seeing* MATT *upstage)* What's he doing?
Molly	He wants to watch the sun come up, Steve.
Stevie	Fine. Shut the door and lock it, and we'll go.

MOLLY hesitates.

Matt	Remember, Stevie, it ain't all yours! Ain't none of it belongs to you! It all goes back where it came from!
Stevie	You settle down somewheres and write some tunes, Matthew! *(To* MOLLY*)* Are you ready?
Molly	Yes. I'm ready.
Stevie	Ralph?
Ralph	Yeah.
Matt	*(Chanting) I live, but I will not live forever.* *Mysterious moon, you only remain,* *Powerful sun, you alone remain,* *Wonderful earth, you remain forever!*
Stevie	Let's go.

RALPH exits, but MOLLY lingers.

Molly	Wait, Steve.
Stevie	It's a long ride down, Molly.

MOLLY starts to move. The rattling stops. MOLLY freezes, staring at the figure of MATT.

	What is it?
Molly	He's stopped.

Re-enter RALPH.

Ralph	Steve, are we going or not?
Molly	Something's wrong.

They look at MATT. He is absolutely rigid. MOLLY goes to the upstage door and calls:

Matt!

No response. MOLLY unlocks and opens the door.

Matt?

Stevie	Leave him be, honey.

MOLLY tentatively opens the door and approaches MATT. He doesn't move. STEVIE starts upstage.

Molly?

Molly	Stevie, he's dead. He's not breathing.
Stevie	Can't be.

Molly	He's not breathing, Stevie. He's dead.

STEVIE goes to MATT.

Stevie	Matt? Stop it, Matt. Come on now, Matt, get up.
Molly	He's dead, Steve.
Ralph	*(Joining them)* How do you know?
Stevie	Look at him.
Ralph	Damn. Sonofabitch.
Stevie	What the hell did you do, Matt?

RALPH approaches MATT.

Molly	Don't touch him.
Ralph	*(Stopping)* Oh, for chrissakes.

The LIGHT continues to change as dawn breaks.

Molly	He knew he was going to die, Steve.
Stevie	First time I met him, we passed each other on the side-walk before an audition. I said to myself, "That guy has got a walk that could cut through concrete." One time I asked him, "Where'd you learn to walk like that?" "That ain't my real walk," he said, "that one is a front. Sooner or later I'm going to have to learn what my real walk is."
Molly	Don't touch him. Let's not touch anything.

She moves away, downstage.

Stevie   We won't. Come on. We'll leave the horses. We'll walk. We'll show respect. We'll leave the horses. For Scar. For whoever wants them. We'll show respect. Let's walk.

RALPH exits. MOLLY retrieves the Indian blanket, goes upstage to MATT and, careful not to touch him, drapes the blanket over him and returns. STEVIE takes a last look at MATT and leaves as MOLLY lingers to blow out the lamps. Then she follows, closing the door. A very long wait as the LIGHT continues to change with the sunrise. Off, the HOOT-ING of an owl. It calls four times and stops. In the changing light, MATT begins to look like an old Indian sitting before a desert sunrise. After a while, he looks like a part of the desert. Off, the SOUNDS OF HORSES being led away by someone whistling a cowboy tune.

BLACKOUT.

The End

Heads

by Murray Mednick

Heads was first produced at the 1991 Padua Hills Playwrights Festival/Workshop under the direction of Steve Albrezzi and with the following cast:

Peter: Norbert Weisser
Tom: William Dennis Hunt
Ella Mae: Nancy Mette
Illiterate Daughters: Karole Foreman, Gina LaMond

Subsequent productions include Push Push Theater of Atlanta and the Omaha Magic Theatre.

Characters

Tom *50. Long hair. Forceful, charismatic. Raspy voice, slight Southern (West Virginia) drawl.*

Ella Mae *His wife. 40. Worn, but still quite pretty; sensuous.*

Jeanine *20. Daughter of Ella's from a previous liaison, brought up by Tom. Ethereal, heavy-set blonde woman. Conceals a bright, unengaged mind.*

Peter *45. A black man. A long-ago live-in friend of the family.*

Amy Lou *Another daughter. Mulatto. An extremely smart, angelically beautiful teenager.*

Scene

Interior of a small house—a shack, really—on the outskirts of Woodstock, New York. Furnished poorly, but clean and neat. We face (right to left) a living room-lounge area, a combination TV and sleeping room (JEANINE'S place), and a section of the kitchen. This could be a small loft built above, or the lounge can be divided from Jeanine's place with a curtain. A thin, makeshift wall separates the kitchen. Lots of evidence of impromptu carpentry and mechanics, especially the stove apparatus TOM has rigged up in the kitchen, having adapted a gas-burner into a wood-burning heat source. Jeanine enters and turns on the black-and-white television set upstage, leaving the sound off. A pause, then ELLA enters.

Ella	Jeanine? Jeanine?
Jeanine	Yes, Mom.
Ella	I was looking at the night.
Jeanine	What, Ella Mae?
Ella	The stars. What are you doing?
Jeanine	I'm watching a story now, Mom. Did Dad go out?
Ella	*(Big sigh)* Your father went out.
Jeanine	Yeah.
Ella	He felt a pull.
Jeanine	Mom?
Ella	Something...a pull...
Jeanine	Is Amy Lou coming back?
Ella	The End of Days, Jeanine.
Jeanine	What?
Ella	The End of Days.
Jeanine	Mom?

SOUNDS, *off.*

Ella   Here comes your father. *(Jumping up)* Someone's with him. He's got someone.

TOM *walks through the door, right, with* PETER *in tow.*

Tom   Look what I found, Ella Mae!

Ella	Oh! Peter! Peter! Hi!
Peter	I was wandering in the Safeway and I heard a voice.
Ella	Peter! *(They embrace)*
Peter	Went right through me.
Ella	What are you doing here?
Peter	Well, I'm visiting with friends, actually. I mean—
Tom	Good thing I went out, Ella.
Ella	Yeah.
Tom	Didn't know what I'd see, but I followed me the feeling, eh, Ella Mae?
Ella	We both did, Tom.
Tom	Hey. Voice drove me into the Safeway for a quart of milk, said, "Buy the family milk, Tom."
Ella	Did you look for Amy Lou, Tom?
Tom	I sniffed around the depot for her.
Ella	*(To PETER)* That's our daughter. Amy Lou.
Peter	Amy Lou?
Tom	I saw no sign of her. Worrisome child. *(Snorts)* Independent.
Ella	Oh, Tom. She left without supper. Goes where she wants, when she wants. Why didn't you let us know you were coming, Peter?
Peter	Well, I didn't know you were here. I mean, I didn't know you lived here.
Tom	It's Providence.
Peter	Actually, I should get going—
Ella	You should stay in touch, Peter.
Tom	Been here for years.
Peter	Do you have a phone?
Ella	But I'm glad to see you anyway.

Peter	My friends will be looking for me.
Tom	No phone.
Peter	That's okay. I ought to get back—
Tom	Can't afford a phone.
Ella	Amazing. I didn't think you could live without one.
Tom	Easy as pie.
Peter	I really should—
Ella	Stay, Peter. You just got here.
Peter	Okay, for a minute, then I gotta go.
Tom	Relax, man. What's it been, fifteen years?
Peter	Yeah, I guess.
Ella	God, I can't believe it. You look the same, Peter.
Peter	You, too.
Ella	I can't believe it.
Tom	You've gotten some gray, Peter.
Ella	But he looks the same.
Peter	So do you. You both do.
Tom	Hell, we do.
Peter	You do.
Ella	Nothing changes.
Tom	Yeah. You got any grass, Peter? Ella's been after me for some grass.
Peter	No. I don't smoke.
Tom	Grass?
Peter	I haven't for years.
Tom	I'll be damned.
Peter	My friends might have some.
Tom	Oh, yeah? You wanna go get some?
Peter	Well, I'm not sure they do. They might.
Ella	Oh, that's all right. Sit down, Peter.

Peter	*(Hesitant)* Uh...well.
Ella	How 'bout a cup of coffee?
Peter	Okay.
Ella	You remember Jeanine?
Peter	*(Amazed)* Is that Jeanine?
Tom	Yeah, she's grown some. *(Snickers)*
Ella	Say hello to Peter, Jeanine.
Jeanine	Hello.
Peter	Jeez, I remember, we used to wrestle, she and I...
Ella	You remember playing with Peter, Jeanine?
Jeanine	Uh-huh.
Ella	What do you take in it, Peter?
Peter	Uh, black.
Tom	You missed the other one.
Peter	The other one?
Ella	Amy Lou.
Peter	Amy Lou. Right. You said that—
Tom	She's out somewheres rockin' and rollin' and gettin' laid.
Ella	Oh, Tom!
Tom	She's an eyeful at seventeen, Peter.
Peter	I didn't know you had another girl.
Ella	Looks just like her father. *(Pause)*
Peter	Where'd you say she was?
Tom	She comes and goes as she pleases. I don't rule her.
Ella	She's wild. *(Hands* PETER *the coffee)*
Peter	Thank you. *(Takes a sip, puts it down)*
Ella	I don't know what will become of her, Peter. *(Sighs)*
Tom	She's untamed, is all.
Ella	And unschooled.
Peter	Unschooled?

Tom	I took her out of that mess when she was seven. Both her and Jeanine.
Peter	You took them out of school?
Tom	Damn right.
Ella	They can't read or write, Peter.
Tom	I'm the Father!
Ella	*(To PETER)* I tried. *(Sighs)*
Tom	I didn't want all that shit in their heads.
Peter	What shit?
Tom	You wouldn't know it lessun' you're outside of it. *(Snickers)*
Peter	Try me.
Ella	Don't get started, Tom.
Tom	Money and the state shit. All that mind-fuckin' which forces people to hire themselves out to the economy. *(PETER nods agreeably to avoid conflict)* I'm the Father! *(Cackles)*
Peter	You're the father.
Tom	Yeah. *(Grins)*
Peter	Is that a big 'F' or a little 'f'?

ELLA chuckles.

Tom	Any kinda 'F' you want, son. Don't mean a snail's prick to me. *(Snickers)*
Peter	Isn't it illegal to keep kids outta school?
Tom	Hell, man, who cares? I am illegal. I am totally illegal. I'm outside the pale. What're they gonna do to me?
Peter	How'd you manage it?
Tom	I fought 'em, son. I took on the town, the county and the state.
Ella	He wore 'em out.
Tom	What are they gonna do? *(Snickering)* Arrest me? They

	send me shit in the mail—I burn it! They send people to
	my door an' I yell at 'em!
Ella	They finally figured it wasn't worth the trouble he was
	causing. Amy Lou did start attending after a while, so she
	could make some friends.
Peter	They can't read or write?
Tom	Nothin' to stop them from learning if they want to.
	Jeanine here don't mind. All she's interested in is watching
	the funny box. Ain't that right, Jeanine?
Jeanine	Uh-huh.

TOM snickers.

Ella	You're not drinking your coffee, Peter.
Peter	Oh. I'd really best be going, Ella. Thanks.
Tom	Hang on a minute, Peter, and I'll run ya over in the Buick.
Peter	Okay, but we ought to get moving pretty soon then.
Tom	Relax, Peter.
Peter	I am relaxed.
Tom	Hell you are. You're so tense your back neck is stiffer 'n a
	concrete post. *(Touching his neck)*
Peter	It's always like that.
Tom	Too bad.
Peter	I'm working on it.
Tom	Are you? How?
Peter	Uh...
Ella	What do you think of his car?
Peter	Seems to run all right.
Tom	That there is a fifty-three Buick. It'll run forever.
Ella	He rides around in it like the King of the County.

Peter	I noticed.
Ella	Fifteen miles an hour.
Tom	Hell, what's the rush? Where we all headed?
Ella	Drives me crazy. I won't ride with him if I can help it.
Tom	So you don't smoke, eh, Peter?
Peter	Well, I smoke cigarettes.
Tom	No more of the weed, eh?
Peter	Nope.
Ella	Well that's a wonderment.
Tom	Ain't it, though? Why's that, Peter?
Peter	No big deal. I just stopped enjoying it. I don't know if I ever did, really.
Ella	*(Flirtatious)* I find that hard to believe.
Peter	I don't like what it does to my head. Paranoid and fuzzy. I will have a toke now and then, but that's all.
Tom	Time was when we'd all be dipping into ol' Peter's stash, eh, Ella?
Ella	I guess that wasn't very nice.
Tom	The hell it wasn't. It was part of the deal, right Peter?
Peter	*(Uncomfortable)* Sure was, Tom.
Tom	You lived with us, and we all shared the cookies, eh Peter?
Peter	Can we get going now, Tom?
Tom	*(Ignoring him)* I thought we had a emergency joint hid away here, Ella.
Ella	We already had the emergency, Tom.
Tom	We did? When?
Ella	Last night.
Tom	That was the one, eh?
Ella	Remember?
Tom	Oh, yeah.

Peter	Tell you what. You run me over to where I'm staying, and I'll see if I can round you up some grass, okay?
Ella	That sounds good. Will you come back then?
Peter	Well, I'm supposed to be in this poker game, but later, later on I'll come back. How'd that be?
Ella	You promise? It's been thirteen years, Peter.
Tom	Oh, what is it you have to be in a poker game for, Peter?
Peter	I don't HAVE to, Tom. It's a social thing.
Tom	Well, finish your coffee, then.
Peter	They won't know where I've gone to.
Tom	They'll realize you're a grown man now, Peter.
Peter	That's not the point, Tom.
Tom	Did you know I called to your California number a couple of times, Peter? *(No reply)*
Ella	We had a phone then.
Tom	Yeah, I called a few times. Talked to your machine. Guess it got erased or something. *(Pause)* Yeah, and back a couple years we read in the *Record* how you'd be doing a reading and a lecture of sorts down in Middletown and we almost rode down for that, weren't I was worried the Buick might not like a long trip in cold weather.
Ella	That car wouldn't 've made it.
Tom	Did you show up for that?
Peter	Yes. I was there.
Ella	Oh, Peter! You should have called!
Peter	I had no idea you were living up here.
Tom	Yeah, I heard on the grapevine you were doing real well in California, making lots of money.
Peter	Not true, Tom.
Tom	Heard you were making money working in the film business.

Peter	It's not true, Tom.
Tom	Hmmm.
Peter	I don't know how these stories get started.
Ella	What do you do, Peter?
Peter	I teach. I get by.
Tom	Who are these folks that are putting you up? I know everybody in this town, or they know me, heh, heh.
Ella	For sure.
Peter	Man's a doctor who lives here, works as a radiologist in Poughkeepsie.
Tom	What's his name?
Peter	Weiss.
Tom	Weiss. Don't know him.
Peter	I'm here visiting with his son, a very old friend of mine. *(Pause)* He'll be looking for me, Tom.
Tom	Don't know where he lives, Dr. Weiss.
Peter	I can find it. It's over on the north end of town, near a big stream.
Tom	Oh, yeah. Rich folks' section.
Peter	Let's go, Tom.
Tom	What's the son do?
Peter	Name's Michael. He's a television producer.
Tom	You hear that, Jeanine? Peter's friend here is a TV producer! Jeanine's an expert on TV, heh, heh. What show's he produce?
Peter	Oh, he does different things, in the business.
Tom	You hear that Jeanine? Peter's friend does TV shows! *(No reply)* Jeanine? You wanna contribute to this conversation Jeanine?
Jeanine	*(After a pause)* No.

Ella	Leave her alone, Tom.
Tom	Who's bothering her? She hasn't seen Peter in how many years? And the two of 'em used to be tighter 'n two bugs in a rug!
Ella	That's the truth. I can hear that.
Tom	Remember, Jeanine? *(JEANINE nods)*
Ella	I was even jealous of her in those days. *(An awkward silence. PETER stands by the door. TOM snickers)*
Tom	I let her stare at the damn thing, but I won't have sound. I won't have it. Picture's bad enough.
Ella	You watch it yourself, Tom.
Tom	*(Caught)* Hell, it's the only way to keep her company.
Ella	You watch it anyway, Tom.
Tom	Yeah, it's like having a telescope on Mars. *(Snickers)*
Ella	What does that mean?
Tom	Means I'm watching the earth slugs spreading their dumb viruses around, heh, heh.
Peter	Tom, I gotta go. I just wanted to see you...and, uh...say hello...
Ella	He's waiting to go, Tom.
Tom	I know he is.
Peter	I'll come back later.
Tom	When?
Peter	Maybe tomorrow. We can have breakfast or something.
Ella	It would be nice to smoke some grass.
Peter	I'll try to get you some. I think I can. I know Michael smokes.
Tom	I usually have a nice stash around. Hell, it's the easiest thing in the world. Caught us at a bad time, is all.
Peter	I don't smoke.
Ella	*(Bitterly)* We're broke, Peter.

Peter	Listen, I can loan you a little money, Tom. My checkbook is over at Doc Weiss's place.
Tom	Hell, I don't want no check. What would I do with a check?
Peter	I'll get you some cash, then.
Tom	Fuck it, Peter, and sit down! Let's have a fuckin' conversation! You been here, what, fifteen minutes?
Ella	Stay awhile, Peter, the poker game can wait.
Peter	*(After a pause, with foreboding)* Okay.
Tom	There you go. Want some more coffee?
Peter	No, thanks. Where's the john?
Tom	*(Pointing)* It's in there.

PETER goes. ELLA sits across from TOM. They stare at each other. TOM snickers. ELLA goes back to the kitchen. TOM goes to the front door and quietly locks it, putting the key in his pocket. Re-enter PETER, who stops to look at the stove apparatus in the kitchen.

| Peter | What is this, Tom? What did you do here? |

ELLA giggles.

Tom	That there is a wood-burning stove, Peter.
Peter	Does it work?
Tom	Damn right it works. I smashed a hole in the roof, hitched up a pipe through it, and got us a heat source independent of the gas company.
Peter	Why?
Tom	Why? Because I got tired of dealing with the gas company bureaucracy, that's why. Bunch of fuckin' airheads.

Ella	We didn't pay the bill for twenty-eight months, so they went ahead and disconnected us. I thought it was cruel.
Tom	The heating bill got higher than the rent! That gas there in the ground belongs to all the people! It don't belong to the gas companies! Next thing is, I'll put a fireplace in the living room here.
Ella	Sure you will, Tom.
Tom	I'll be working on that.
Peter	This is quite an apparatus, I'll say that for it.
Tom	It works.
Peter	In the winter?
Tom	We just sorta shift the center of family activities into the kitchen.

ELLA sighs.

Peter	What about the landlord?
Tom	*(Snickering)* What about him?
Peter	What's he think of the hole in the roof?
Tom	It's sealed. Anyway, I ain't asked him.
Ella	We haven't paid rent in years. *(Laughs, sighs)*
Peter	How'd you manage that?
Tom	Squatter's rights. Onliest way for him to get us outta here is the sheriff and the fire department. I guess he don't feature the trouble and the publicity.
Ella	You never know, Tom. One of these days.
Peter	Do you play at all, Tom?
Tom	Sit down.
Peter	*(Sitting)* Do you?
Tom	Play? It's all play. It's all play. *(Grins)*

Peter	I mean the guitar.
Tom	I bang on it once in a while.
Ella	That's the truth.
Tom	Playin' a guitar is old shit, man. I BANG on my guitar. It's around here someplace. I bang on it when I want to shout out a song.
Ella	That's what he does all right, he shouts his songs. He screams them at you.
Tom	Otherwise, it don't get through. Maybe I'll shout one at ya later, Peter.
Peter	I can't wait.
Ella	You guys used to make such beautiful music. Remember, Peter?
Peter	Yeah, sure.
Ella	I just loved it. *(Awkward silence)*
Peter	We were stoned day and night in those days.
Ella	Do you still play?
Peter	No, I'm no musician.
Ella	Your stuff sounded good to me.
Peter	You were stoned.
Tom	So you put it all down, eh, Peter?
Peter	Yeah, I have no training, no chops, and no interest anymore.
Tom	Is that right?
Peter	That's right.
Tom	And you don't smoke the weed?
Peter	Hardly ever.
Tom	Do you take anything at all?
Peter	I like a couple drinks before dinner.
Tom	No acid? Mushrooms? Peyote?
Peter	No, none of that.

Ella	Oh, Peter.
Peter	Can't take it anymore.
Tom	Can't take what?
Peter	What I see.
Tom	I can.
Peter	Bully for you.
Tom	I get way up there.
Peter	Where?

Tom snickers.

Ella	He's looking down at it all.
Tom	What about narcotics?
Peter	Never.
Tom	Coke?
Peter	Hate the stuff.
Tom	I thought you were on the methadone program.
Peter	I kicked it eleven years ago.
Ella	But that's supposed to be impossible.
Peter	It very nearly is.
Tom	Well, at least you're off the government shit.
Peter	I'm off it all, Tom. *(Pause)*
Tom	All?
Peter	I drink. You got anything to drink?
Tom	*(Studying him)* Like what?
Peter	I don't know. Vodka? Just a beer would be fine.
Tom	No. You an alcoholic?
Peter	*(Startled)* What?
Tom	New York?
Peter	Pardon? The answer is no, Tom.

Tom	Okay. I went down to New York a while ago just to see for myself if it was still there and what was going on in it. *(Whistles)* I'm standing at a corner on Fifth Avenue and I must've seen a hundred thousand guys with the same suit on and carrying the same briefcase. Robots. Waves of robots rollin' down the avenue. I had me a vision that day. *(Pause)* Bunch of 'em buyin' crack an' shit by the library. *(Snorts)* Eh, Ella?
Ella	Ain't it the truth, Tom.
Peter	*(Recovering)* Did you go, too, Ella?
Ella	Yeah. I waited for him in the park while he took his walk. You know I hate the city, Peter. *(Pause)*
Peter	*(Trying to be casual)* I guess I ought to be heading on back... *(Yawns, rises)* Maybe we'll talk some more tomorrow.
Tom	Sit down, Peter. You're more restless than an amphetamine freak.
Peter	I've got people waiting for me. Let's go.
Tom	What for?
Peter	I don't need to give you a reason, Tom. It's been nice to visit with you. Now it's time for me to go. *(He looks at ELLA, who looks back at him silently)*
Tom	Kids got fuckin' crank factories in the woods out here. Don't they, Ella?
Ella	They do, Tom. A horror.
Tom	*(To PETER)* You can't go.
Peter	I'm going. I'll find my own way.
Tom	I don't see why we can't set around and have a relaxed conversation.
Peter	This is not relaxed.
Tom	Why not?

Peter	So long, Tom. I'll see you around. *(Goes to the door)* Bye, Ella. *(Tries door)* Is it locked? *(Tries again, in disbelief)* It's locked. *(Long pause as he looks at* TOM*)* Open the door, Tom.
Tom	No.
Peter	Open it, Tom.
Tom	I won't.
Peter	Why not?
Tom	Not till we've had us a talk.
Peter	I don't have any more to say.
Tom	Sure you do, son. Sure you do.
Peter	I'm not your son.
Tom	I'm the Father.
Peter	Oh, horseshit.
Tom	I'm the Father.
Peter	Ella?

She shrugs.

	Tell him to open the door, Ella.
Ella	I can't.
Peter	Why not?
Tom	Relax.
Peter	Fuck you. You relax. *(Crosses resolutely left)*

ELLA and TOM *look at each other.*

Ella	Tom...?
Peter	*(Returns)* Where's the back door?
Tom	Ain't no back door.

Peter	No back door?
Tom	Had to seal it up. Keep the cold out.
Peter	This is bad shit, Tom.
Tom	Hell, man, this is nothin'. The bad shit is what's comin' down out there.
Peter	Where?
Tom	Where? Right here in Woodstock and in the rest of the country coast to coast.
Peter	Like what, Tom?
Tom	Like the citizens goin' for theirselves, sayin' it's the natural way, beatin' each other down—eat up the minerals, the trees, the grasses, killin' off the animals, an' no thanks to nothin'! Look what happens—preachers rippin' off the dummies! *(Snickers)* Pourin' filth into the waters! Coast to coast! Whole families out on the streets wandering the countryside! Got enough NUKE-LEE-ER CRAPOLA in the silos of the heartland to poison the whole solar system FOREVER. THAT'S THE BAD SHIT, PETE. *(A pause)* Just fuckin' sittin' there, man! Out on the prairie! Warheads! *(Guffaws)* And for no goddamned reason! Fuck, man, they got holes ten miles deep just for the fuckin' waste!
Peter	Tom?
Tom	*(Suddenly reflective)* And hell, that ain't nothin', that's just politics.
Peter	Tom?
Tom	Yeah?
Peter	I don't want no trouble. *(TOM snickers)*
Tom	Hell, I know all about that.
Peter	What?
Tom	Your poor insecurity.

Peter	What?

ELLA giggles.

	Open the fucking door. Open the door and let me go on with my business. *(Pause)* This is crazy, Tom. *(Pause)* Ella?
Ella	We're just glad to have the company.
Peter	You can't force people to be company, Ella!
Ella	I'm not doing anything. Am I?
Peter	Come on!
Tom	Twelve, thirteen years go by, you'd expect an old friend 'd want to sit down and catch up and reminisce the old times.
Peter	I told you at the Safeway, Tom, I only had a minute. I only came by to say hello. It was a shock to run into you.
Tom	I could see that.
Peter	I mean, it's nothing personal. If I'd known you were here, I'd have set something up in advance. As it is, I'm pressed. I've got people waiting on me and things to do.
Tom	What things?
Peter	Things.
Tom	Like what?
Peter	None of your fucking business!
Tom	Have it your way.
Ella	Are you hungry, Peter?
Peter	*(Incredulous)* Hungry? For God's sake, Ella!
Ella	I could fix you a peanut butter and jelly sandwich.

PETER looks at her, horrified. She smiles.

Peter	Open the door, Tom, and let me go.

TOM snickers. A silence. PETER is frozen to the spot.

Tom.

Tom	I ain't gonna hurt you none.
Peter	Tom.
Tom	Sit down. Have a sandwich.
Peter	I don't want a sandwich.
Tom	Then sit without one.
Peter	What are you doing, Tom? What is this about?
Tom	Hell, I'm playing it by ear, like I always do.
Peter	By ear?
Tom	I do whatever feels right. I'm the Father.
Peter	I don't understand what that means.
Tom	Means I got responsibilities.
Peter	Give me an example.
Tom	I got responsibilities to my children.
Peter	Like what?
Tom	See, you don't understand 'cause you ain't got none yourself.
Peter	I can see what a great job you've made of it, Tom.
Tom	You don't see shit.
Peter	You got two illiterate kids, Tom. And one of 'em is staring at the television set with the sound off. Don't she have anything to do? Doesn't she have any interests at all? Jesus Christ, Tom, she was a wonderful three-year-old kid!
Tom	Jeanine!
Peter	Forget it, Tom. Open the door, and that's it.
Tom	Jeanine!
Peter	Please let me be on my way, Tom.
Tom	Jeanine!
Ella	Oh, leave her be.

Tom	Jeanine!
Jeanine	All right.
Tom	Come over here and talk to your old friend, Peter.

JEANINE slides away from the TV and sits with the others. She and PETER look at each other, at a loss.

	Go on, talk to him, Jeanine.
Jeanine	We only got two channels. *(A silence)*
Ella	That's all she can think of saying.
Tom	Talk to the man, Jeanine. Don't you remember cuddling with Peter?
Ella	Oh, shut up, Tom.
Peter	That's all right, Jeanine.
Jeanine	Channel two and channel four. It's all black, white, and grey. If we had cable, we could get more channels, probably channel seven and public TV. That would be good. I get tired of two and four all the time. I know what's on every hour of the day, every day of the week. Sometimes they change it and then I'm surprised. They change the programs in the summer, to give people a rest. I like all the stories, and the stories in the commercials, too. I like every kind of story. I don't mind the sound being off, because I can tell what the characters are saying.
Ella	How can she do that?
Jeanine	I can hear what they're saying, because I can hear the story. I follow the story right away.
Tom	Does that make sense to you, Peter?
Peter	Of course it makes sense.
Ella	Not to me. It's beyond belief.

Jeanine	Where the stories come from, is what I don't know.
Tom	They come from Hollywood, Jeanine.
Jeanine	Yeah.
Ella	Some people write them, then other people film them. You know that. And those people you see are actors. I've told you a hundred times.
Jeanine	Not all of 'em. Some of 'em are real people.
Tom	Peter here lives in Hollywood, don't you, Peter?
Peter	No, I don't.
Ella	Where do you live, Peter?
Peter	Uh, in Silver Lake.
Ella	I lived in Silver Lake!
Peter	Did you? Where?
Ella	Gee, it was on…on…near Glendale Boulevard. I can't remember.
Peter	That's right near my home.
Ella	Oh, it was lovely there. That was when Tom sent me out there, you know, to get me away from Jeanine's father. Remember?
Peter	I didn't know you then.
Ella	But I told you about it.
Peter	Uh, yes.

TOM snickers.

Ella	I thought he was going to kill me.
Peter	Who?
Ella	Jeanine's father. He got outta jail and he was coming around. Then Tom sent me out to L.A., to get me away from him. Me and Jeanine took the bus. You remember that, Jeanine?

JEANINE doesn't answer.

Peter	Where is he now?
Ella	Gene?
Peter	Was that his name?
Ella	Yes. Gene. That's how come, "Jeanine."
Peter	I get it.
Ella	He's in prison, I think. Oh, he was such a handsome man, you know. I called him the dark prince. I was eighteen and he was twenty. But he was SO violent.
Tom	You never met ol' Gene?
Peter	No.
Ella	He was a poet, too, you know.
Peter	Never met him.
Ella	He wrote beautiful poetry. But he was SO violent.
Peter	*(Kindly)* Which shows do you like the best, Jeanine?
Jeanine	I like the products. You can see every kind of product on TV. And each one has a song, you know. I've got 'em all memorized in my head, all the products and all the songs. And, of course, each one has a little story, too. I know all the products, along with the stories and the songs. My head can do that by itself. My head remembers each story and song…it just won't stop singing.
Ella	My God, Jeanine. I don't know what you're talking about.
Tom	Hell you don't, Ella.
Jeanine	Sometimes they'll change the story and not the song, sometimes the song and not the story, sometimes the story AND the song. That's tough on my head. *(Laughs)*
Peter	You've got to learn to read, Jeanine.
Jeanine	If you know the products, you know it all.

TOM guffaws.

Tom	You hear that, Peter? She's more 'n half right, ain't she!
Jeanine	I also like the animal programs and the nature programs. I watch every one that's on the two channels. I wish we had PBS. There's more nature on PBS and more animals. But we'd have to have cable for that. Anyway, it's not so bad. I'm familiar with the animal kingdom and all nature, from the mountains to the sea, and from the icy world to the tropical forests.
Ella	She really likes that subject. She could have been a naturalist or a biology major. Something.
Jeanine	I can't believe all the different kinds of fish there are. And plants that bite, and birds that swim, and snakes that walk on water. *(Sings)* Time flies, and you are there, *et cetera.* *(Laughs shyly)*
Ella	You want a sandwich, Jeanine?
Jeanine	*(Going back to the TV)* Yes, Mom.
Peter	Please open the door now, Tom.
Tom	Have a sandwich, Peter.
Peter	I don't want a fucking sandwich, Tom.
Tom	Hell, man, then don't have a sandwich.
Peter	Should I feel frightened now, Tom, or just disgusted?
Tom	You can feel however 'n hell you want to, Peter. Shit, that's where it is, anyhow. It's where you get up in the morning and where you sleep in the night. Hell.
Peter	And you? Where are you, Tom?
Tom	I ain't where you are. I'm putting in my time. I'm here to make my mark. But I ain't where you are.
Ella	You see that, Peter? That's what he does. He does it constantly. There's a word for what he does. He's—

Peter	Condescending?
Ella	Yeah, condescending. I guess that's it.
Peter	Where do you get off, Tom? Who the fuck are you?
Tom	I'm the Father!
Peter	What the hell does that mean!?
Ella	Now look who's yelling, Peter.
Peter	I don't give a damn! Open the fucking door!
Tom	I'll open it when we've finished our business.
Peter	What business?
Tom	Won't take long. Sit down, Peter.

PETER *sits*.

Peter	What business?
Tom	Oh, come on, Peter. You supposed to be so smart-assed.
Peter	I don't know what you're talking about.
Tom	Hell, you don't.
Peter	*(Helplessly)* Ella?
Ella	I believe he wants to know where you been for thirteen years or whatever.
Peter	California.
Tom	Lots of folks we ran with are dead now. Bonnie's dead.
Ella	She died of leukemia, Peter.
Tom	She was poisoned to death by the air.
Ella	Tom always wanted to fuck her.
Tom	I don't deny that. Eric's dead.
Ella	Eric was killed by the police.
Tom	Paul is dead.
Ella	Paul OD'd.
Tom	Simon's dead.

Peter	Simon was murdered.
Ella	What happened?
Tom	Ella and Simon had a thing goin' once.
Peter	Did you?
Ella	It was nothing serious, Peter.

TOM snickers.

	Do you know what happened?
Peter	Only by hearsay. He was dealing coke in L.A. Large amounts. He tried to do a scam on some people.
Ella	And they shot him?
Peter	That's what I heard.
Ella	Poor Simon. He had a terrible crush on me.
Tom	How'd you hear?
Peter	I don't remember now, Tom.
Ella	Ain't life something, though.
Tom	We found a lyric of yours.
Peter	What lyric?
Tom	I put it to music. You want to hear it?
Peter	Oh, God.
Tom	I'll play it for ya. Where's my guitar?
Ella	Behind the sofa.
Tom	*(Getting it)* Jeanine! Jeanine, you want to be on the tambourine?

No answer. ELLA giggles.

	Jeanine!
Jeanine	Okay. If you want to.

Tom	I want to! Bring the tambo in here!
Jeanine	Okay.
Tom	Here it is.

TOM bangs on the guitar and screams the words as JEANINE beats on the tambourine. PETER covers his ears.

We murdered a man
You and me, you and me,
And we buried the body down
In the yard, in the yard—
We buried the man in the yard.
It's over and done
Ain't nothin' we can do,
For they know about the body
In the yard, in the yard—
We buried the man in the yard.
So give up your trouble,
You can throw away your life,
They will soon find the body
In the yard, in the yard—
We buried the man in the yard.
I'm sorry for it, friend,
I'm ashamed of what I did,
They are digging up the body
In the yard, in the yard,
We buried the man in the yard.
There he is, there he is,
He's a man like us,
They are bringing out the body

> *In the yard, in the yard,*
> *We buried the man in the yard.*
> *There he is, my friend,*
> *That we killed, you and I—*

Peter   *(Screaming)* ENOUGH!

Tom   *(Stops singing)* Thank you, Jeanine!

Jeanine   Okay. *(She goes back to the TV)*

Peter   That was awful, Tom.

Tom   You didn't like that?

Peter   That was an assault! *(Screaming)* FUCK YOU! FUCK YOU! FUCK YOU! YOU FUCKING PRICK! *(Pause)* How'd you like that? WHO THE HELL DO YOU THINK YOU ARE!

Tom   I'M THE FATHER!

Peter   YOU'RE AN ASSHOLE!

Ella   All right, that's enough. *(A pause)* Peter?

Peter   What?

Ella   Who was it? *(No reply)* Was it John?

Peter   John?

Ella   Our John. Who was with us in the days of trial.

Peter   The days of trial? John shot himself, Ella. *(Quietly)* The song was a dream.

Ella   Was it Luke?

Tom snorts.

Peter   I told you, Ella. It was a dream I had.

Ella   I don't believe Luke shot himself. I don't believe Luke could do that. I believe John shot him.

Peter   Oh, fuck this shit.

Tom   Hurts, eh, Peter?

Peter	No. I wrote a song based on a dream, that's all.
Ella	John killed him.
Peter	I don't know what happened, Ella.
Ella	And then John shot himself. Back of the cooling shed, on the farm in Pennsylvania. *(Sighs)*
Peter	I wasn't there.
Ella	You were his friend. You were friends with both of 'em.
Peter	I wasn't there.

TOM and ELLA exchange a long look.

Tom	They'd come to the end of their days, Ella Mae.
Ella	We heard the shots.
Tom	We thought it was a deer being kilt in the woods.
Peter	The song was a dream, like in the movie *Deliverance*.
Tom	Didn't see it.
Ella	We never go to the movies.
Tom	Part of the deepy, deep sleep.
Jeanine	Oh, Tom!
Tom	Jeanine'd live in a movie if she could.
Ella	Leave her alone.
Tom	I ain't botherin' no one.
Peter	They throw a body into the river, which gets dammed. So they think the body's gonna float up to the surface...body in the yard...starts to get funky...gonna dig it up.
Tom	Yeah...?
Peter	We killed something. Something alive. Buried it in the yard. It was a dream.
Ella	Are you okay?
Peter	No, I'm not. I'm not okay.

Ella	Would you like a cup of tea?
Peter	Are you kidding, or what?
Ella	No.
Peter	I don't want a cup of tea. Un-fucking-believable. Why'd I have to be walking into the Safeway at that moment? Why?
Tom	I knew you'd be coming along sooner or later.
Peter	Oh, horseshit.
Tom	Chickens gotta come home to roost. I knew you'd come along.
Peter	Yeah, you're the Father.
Ella	I felt that I'd see you again.
Peter	Are you the mother?
Ella	Well, I've given birth a couple of times.
Peter	No, I meant in the higher sense, like Tom here being the Father.
Ella	I don't know, to tell you the truth. Maybe I am, maybe all women are.
Peter	I guess that's right. That's right. You're the Mother, Tom's the Father.
Tom	The time hasn't improved you none.
Peter	Hasn't done shit for you neither, Tom.
Ella	*(Of PETER)* I don't think that's true. I think he's mellowed.
Peter	Yeah. Time for me to go, Tom.
Ella	He used to be SO angry.
Tom	His ears are still clogged up with his ego.
Peter	Oh, get off it. You're the biggest egomaniac on earth.
Tom	Is that a fact?
Peter	Yeah, the Father. I don't know what happened to you, man. When I met you, you were a sweet, mild-mannered, good-natured person.
Ella	That's the truth.

Peter	You sang your folk songs and drove around in your little Austin and peacefully smoked your dope. You were kind to Jeanine and good to Ella. At least, as far as I could see.
Tom	We took you into our home.
Peter	You took me into your apartment, which you were having trouble paying for. With me around, you got the rent paid and a steady supply of grass.
Ella	It was more than that, Peter, and you know it.
Peter	That was the bottom line. God, but we were fucked up. I was homeless and out on the street. I wasn't paying any attention to what was happening to me.
Ella	You were a poet.
Peter	What's a poet? Poets don't make a living! Nobody makes a living being a poet!
Ella	That's the trouble with this country.
Peter	No, it isn't! It has nothing to do with the country! That is the way it is.
Ella	I never thought I'd hear you say that, Peter.
Peter	Listen, I don't think this conversation is useful, Tom, Ella, and I'd like to go now.
Ella	Wait, Peter. You haven't told us what you do out there in California.
Peter	Yes, I did.
Ella	Tell us again.
Peter	*(Quickly)* I live a quiet, lonely life. I live in a cabin off a dirt path on the edge of a canyon. Through my windows I watch birds and squirrels and the neighborhood cats and dogs. At night there are raccoons and possums and an occasional coyote. I'm five minutes from downtown L.A. Eighty percent of the time I am alone in that cabin. The phone rings maybe

twice a week. I have no correspondents. I survive by teaching part-time at a small university. Once in a while I'll get a rewrite or a polish for the industry. I have a small following of readers and former students. Every day I fight the battle of accepting my lot and for the most part fail. I do not accept my lot. That's it. Open the door, Tom.

Tom   You don't think this is a useful conversation? I think it's useful. Jeanine!

Jeanine   Yeah?

Tom   Is this a useful conversation?

Jeanine   I liked the part about the raccoons and possums. That was very good.

Tom   *(Snickering)* See?

Ella   Do you have a garden?

Peter   A garden? Uh, no. That is, there's all kinds of stuff growing out there. I don't know what any of it is. Once a year I'll have it cleared. Then I'm always watching to see what's going to grow. Because it doesn't take long. Stuff starts coming up. Green. It's all foreign to me, looking at the green coming up...I'm a hermit, is what I am! I'm the solitary old coot in the canyon who throws rocks at dogs and kids.

Ella   I don't believe it.

Peter   I throw rocks at them. Busting into my solitude. Dogs and kids. Kids yelling, dogs shitting on the path. Nothing much worse than coming off the freeway and stepping in dog shit. Feels like life is trying to tell you something about your real worth as a person. If I owned a gun there'd be some dead dogs in the canyon. I'm the eccentric poet who lives by himself in the cabin off the path, the guy who never talks except to complain about the dog shit. Quiet. Comes and goes by himself. Drives a nine-year-old Toyota. Sounds of a clattering typewriter. Only human voices the ballgame on the radio. Two or three times a year a formal letter from him about the dog shit. Never has visitors, male or female. Empty vodka bottles in his trash. Right across the canyon lives a happy young couple with their little son. All day long I can hear and see the manifestations of their familial happiness. They have a happy dog. No doubt he shits on the path along with the other dogs. The woman is a luscious blonde. Once I watched her sunbathing in the nude. She saw me and hasn't done it since. I'm the horny, aging bachelor on the other side of the canyon. The man who chases the dog. "Got to keep the dog away from that guy, no telling what he might do!" One day they lost their kid. Lost in the canyon. It's like a jungle. First they're calling him softly: "Max! Max! Where are you, Max!" That's the kid's name. Then gradually it becomes hysterical. They've lost their child to the canyon. I'm listening to this and I too am frightened and filled with dread. To witness such a terrible tragedy. I finally go out into the yard. I'm looking for the kid along with the rest of the neighbors. The police are on their way. Everyone is running around frantically beating the bushes, everyone is included...but me. No one came to my door, no one approached me in the yard.

Ella	Did they find him?
Peter	Yes, thank God.
Ella	Where was he?
Peter	I don't know. Nobody thought of telling me, one way or the other.
Ella	I'm sure you're exaggerating, Peter.

Peter	I'm not. Those are the plain facts. I'm a recluse.
Tom	How do you account for that?
Peter	I can't.
Ella	You're not with anyone?
Peter	No. Why?
Ella	You don't have to be defensive, Peter.
Peter	I'm not being defensive.

TOM snickers.

What are you snickering about?

TOM smiles.

(To ELLA) Why do you ask?

Ella	I don't know. I wondered. It's a normal question to ask.
Tom	We heard you got married.
Peter	You heard wrong.
Tom	Okay.
Peter	I need a drink.
Tom	Alcohol?
Peter	Yeah, Tom.
Tom	Won't touch the stuff.
Peter	Let's go to the store.
Tom	Not since I left the Virginia hill country thirty-two years back.
Peter	I got to go anyway.
Tom	Haven't been near a bar since we played that joint on Avenue B.
Peter	Just as well. I'll go myself.
Tom	Hell of a thing, playing music for a bunch of drunks.
Peter	Time for me to move on.

Ella	You were never much of a drinker, were you, Peter?
Peter	I was. Always.
Ella	I don't remember you that way.
Peter	Can't be helped.
Ella	What?
Peter	How other people remember me. There's no accounting for it. Other people's dreams, opinions, delusions. Can't be helped. In fact, I've always been a heavy drinker.
Ella	You're just hard on yourself.
Peter	I'm an alcoholic. I'm just trying to get through the days and nights, one at a time, with the help of my friends. So if that's what you needed to hear, Tom, you can open the door now and let me be on my way.
Tom	Why would I want to hear that?
Peter	I don't know. People take solace from the sufferings and misfortunes of others. I thought you might qualify.
Ella	What a terrible thing to say!
Peter	Oh, come on, Ella. What's so terrible about it? See, now Tom the Father here can't feel quite so superior, having taken on the state, the economy, and the local police, because my life is as miserable as his.
Tom	*(Very loud)* I DON'T QUALIFY. I DON'T QUALIFY. I DO NOT QUALIFY. I AM NOT IN YOUR MISERABLE CANYON. I DON'T LIVE WHERE YOU LIVE. I DON'T THINK LIKE YOU THINK. I WALK OUT THERE AND I'M SINGING ME A SONG. I AM WALKING THE HIGH ROAD, FRIEND, AND I AM SINGING ME A TUNE. *(Laughs in PETER's face)*
Peter	Get away from me, Tom.
Ella	There's no need to shout.
Jeanine	No need to shout!

Tom	*(Shouting)* I AM THE FATHER. I SEE THEM, BUT THEY SEE ME NOT. THEY DO NOT SEE ME. THERE IS NOTHING THEY CAN DO TO ME FOR I WILL NOT ALLOW IT. I SQUAT DOWN WHERE I PLEASE. I AM A FREE MAN, THE FATHER. I AM SINGING. ALL THE TIME, ALL THE TIME I AM SINGING. ALL THE TIME.
Peter	I know what you are.
Tom	WHAT?
Peter	Don't yell.
Tom	TALK TO ME.
Peter	You see the ears. You see the teeth. You see the hair. You see crotches and assholes. You see the fear. You see the weaknesses and the egoism. You see the lust and the hate. You see the higher ape with his clothes on, with his face on. It's the acid. That's why you snicker.
Ella	That's very good, Peter.
Peter	Thank you. Open the door now, Tom.
Tom	No.
Peter	Why not?
Tom	I WANT TO HEAR WHAT ELSE YOUR FACE HAS TO SAY.
Peter	All right, Tom. It's the acid. Some people strive and work hard to become better, to mature; you just kept taking acid until you got to where you could feel permanently superior to everything around you. It was the acid.
Ella	You're blaming the drugs?
Peter	Yes.
Ella	What about what he has to say?
Tom	Ha!
Peter	What is it that he has to say?
Ella	Well, he's saying that you shouldn't participate.
Peter	I get it. Tune in, turn on, and drop out.

Ella	No, it's not that. That's old. He's gone beyond that.
Peter	Come on, he's going around calling himself the Father.
Ella	He doesn't do it very often.
Peter	What does he mean by it? What do you mean by it, Tom?
Tom	IT JUST CAME TO ME, DON'T YOU KNOW.
Peter	Please don't scream at me. I'm sitting two feet away from you. Why do you do that?
Tom	BECAUSE PEOPLE CAN'T HEAR.
Peter	I hear you.
Tom	THEY CAN'T HEAR. THEY'RE CONDITIONED TO IT. THEY'RE DEAF. THEY DON'T KNOW WHAT KINDA ANIMAL THEY ARE. THEY DON'T KNOW THEY'RE GONNA DIE.
Peter	And you know?
Tom	I know.
Peter	Is that how come you're the Father?
Tom	I told you. It come to me.
Peter	From where?
Tom	From above.
Peter	Okay.
Tom	I locked the door on ya to see if I can get ya to hear me.
Peter	I heard you.
Tom	You ain't heard shit.
Peter	Have it your way, Tom, and open the door.
Tom	See, I got no plan. I got no agenda. I take it as it comes, and here come Peter. I guess I got to go with it because I loved ya once and we communicated through the music.
Ella	You surely did, too.
Peter	A person doesn't just wander off into the Safeway and disappear. When they don't find me they'll have to call the police or the sheriff or somebody.

Tom	Well, if that's what's gonna happen, then that's what's gonna happen, and I'll deal with it when the time comes.
Peter	You don't care what happens?
Tom	'Course I care, but it's out of my hands. No reason to throw in the towel, heh, heh! I can roll with it. See, ain't nobody or nothin' can throw fear into Tom no more.
Peter	Congratulations.
Tom	Thank you. See, you're more 'n half-gone with fear and doubt and disappointment. That's because you had expectations, you had an agenda, you figure you turned out a failure. *(Barking)* RIGHT?

PETER winces but doesn't answer.

	You figure you ought to have a family and money in the bank and be one of them heavy hitters and you got none of it. RIGHT?
Ella	Ease off a bit, Tom.
Tom	*(To PETER)* And now you're starting to turn old. Heh, heh. Now me, I don't worry about any of that shit.
Peter	You don't.
Tom	No. I ain't got no agenda, and I got everything I need. Alls I got to do is make every moment of this life fresh and new, fresh and new, and make a response to my family when they need a response. And that's how come I'm the Father.
Peter	Can you do it without drugs?
Tom	I can do it with and I can do it without. But I PREFER being high, you HEAR ME. I don't see no sense in NOT BEING HIGH. *(Snickers)*
Ella	He's snickering again.

Tom	Now Ella, here, we been together past twenty years.
Ella	Ain't that a wonderment?
Tom	And she gets irritated with some of my habits, but she understands me now more often than she don't, and once in a while my kids do, and once in a while some of the youngsters who come around here to hear what I have to say.
Ella	He yells at them, too.
Tom	I tell 'em they don't have to act like trained dogs. I tell 'em to be peaceful. Take her as she comes. No competition in the damn marketplace.
Ella	And no meat.
Tom	It's hard for a carnivorous animal to stay peaceful, heh, heh.
Peter	What the hell happened, Tom?
Tom	Nothin' happened. One day just turns over into the next one. See, you can't hear. You're too full of what's in your own head. You're PATHETIC.
Peter	And you're prematurely senile, Tom. You go around like a crazy old man.
Ella	Don't start calling each other names.
Tom	You ever read the prophets?
Peter	Not lately.
Tom	They was crazy old men too, seems like. They're in the Bible.
Peter	Oh, come on Tom.
Tom	COME ON WHAT!
Peter	Look at all the aggression, Tom. Look at it. Listen to it. It's sheer aggression. All that talk about peaceful and nonviolent. You're the most violent man. I don't know what happened to you. I believe you snapped when—
Tom	WHEN?

Peter	I don't know. One too many acid trips. One too many bills to pay. I don't know. Isn't the screaming at people aggression? Tearing up the house? Keeping the kids out of school? Hassling the bureaucrats? Locking the fucking door, Tom?
Tom	*(Rises)* You're pathetic. *(To ELLA)* I'm going to the toilet. *(Passing JEANINE)* What are ya watching now, Jeanine?
Jeanine	Quiet, Dad.
Tom	QUIET? YOU'RE NOT EVEN LISTENING TO THE DAMN THING!
Jeanine	Because.
Tom	BECAUSE WHAT?
Jeanine	Just because.

TOM enters the john and slams the door.

Ella	I don't know why we heard you were married.
Peter	I was living with someone for a long time.
Ella	How long?
Peter	Seven years.
Ella	Well, that's a common law marriage, Peter.
Peter	Yeah, but we weren't married. Do you have a key to the door, Ella?
Ella	No, Tom's got the only key.
Peter	I'm sorry if I upset him, but he went and locked the door on me.
Ella	He's not upset.
Peter	It's going to cause trouble, Ella. Do you want trouble?
Ella	No.
Peter	Then do something. Ella?
Ella	What do you want me to do?
Peter	Ask him to turn me loose. Get the key from him.

Ella	I hope you get a chance to see Amy Lou.
Peter	Amy Lou?
Ella	She might show up. She's a piece of work, that one.
	(Shakes her head and sighs)
Peter	I can't believe this. Does she have a key?
Ella	I don't know. She might. I doubt it. What happened?
Peter	What happened?
Ella	Your relationship.
Peter	I don't know if I can explain it in a minute.
Ella	We got more than a minute. *(Smiles)*
Peter	She met someone else.
Ella	Uh-huh. I can feel it.
Peter	What?
Ella	That you've been alone.

PETER *jumps up and tries the door—it remains locked.*

Peter	Wait a minute—isn't there a window? There's got to be a window in the house.
Jeanine	There's one over here.
Peter	Okay.

He moves toward the window, up left, but just then TOM *comes out of the john, grabs a hammer, nails and some boards, heads* PETER *off and proceeds to nail the boards over the window.*

Tom! What the hell are you doing? For Christ's sake, Tom! Tom!

| Tom | *(Finishing the job)* No one gets in, no one gets out, heh, heh. |

Jeanine	Now you did it, Dad.
Tom	Now I done it.
Ella	How will we get any air?
Tom	We don't need more air.

ELLA giggles.

	I LOVE IT!
Peter	Tom!
Tom	I LOVE IT!
Peter	Please let me go, Tom.
Tom	We ain't finished yet.
Peter	Finished with what?
Tom	WE'RE GONNA DIG UP THE BODY, PETE.
Peter	What body?
Tom	THE BODY IN THE YARD. WE'RE GONNA DIG IT UP.
Peter	Oh, for God's sake, Tom!
Ella	Maybe Amy Lou will come home with some grass.
Tom	HELL, YES. WOULDN'T THAT BE NICE, PETE?
Peter	I don't smoke.
Tom	Oh, that's right. I forgot. You drink.
Peter	There's bound to be trouble, Tom.
Tom	You won't touch the natural weed, but you'll put that poisonous alcohol into ya. Don't make sense.
Peter	I said, THERE'S BOUND TO BE TROUBLE.
Tom	I heard ya. Put the kettle on, Ella. We'll have some tea while we're waiting for the trouble.

ELLA does so.

Tom	TAKE HER AS SHE COMES, PETE.
Peter	Tom, that song you found was a dream I had, thirteen, fourteen years ago.
Tom	I know it. By God, will ya look at what a piece of equipment a hammer is. Buy 'em in any hardware store. *(Cackles)*
Peter	That was a long time ago, Tom.
Tom	With a hammer and a saw, you can do just about any damn thing.
Peter	It was a dream, Tom.
Tom	I KNOW THAT.
Peter	There ain't no body in no yard.
Tom	I KNOW THAT, TOO. YOU THINK I'M STUPID?
Peter	I think you've blown your fuses, Tom.
Tom	Do ya?
Peter	Yeah, I do. And you're scaring me with that hammer.
Tom	*(Tucking it into his belt)* Oh, poor guy. Didn't mean to frighten you, son.
Ella	What are you doing to him, Tom?
Tom	HELL! NOTHING! WHAT ARE YOU DOING, WATCHING THE WATER BOIL?
Ella	I'm getting the tea.
Tom	WELL COME ON IN HERE AND SET.
Ella	Soon as it's ready.
Peter	Shit! Open the door or I'm gonna start to scream!
Tom	No.
Peter	*(Screaming)* OPEN THE DOOR! OPEN THE DOOR! YOU FUCKING ASSHOLE!
Jeanine	Dad!
Ella	*(Sweetly)* Peter, can you wait just a little while?
Peter	FOR WHAT?

Ella	He'll let you go. It would be nice to have tea together.
Tom	Yeah, we'll have a cup of tea.
Ella	Alright?

PETER *doesn't answer.*

	I'll bring it right in.
Tom	Ain't they something? Women? I live in a house with three of 'em. And they gots to have their attention, heh, heh. They got to have that love and attention or they can't live.
Peter	So?
Tom	*(Mocking him)* So?
Peter	Are you above that?
Tom	Yup. I'm the Father.
Peter	You're a bum. You're an aging acid-freak welfare bum.
Tom	He's starting in to call me names now, Ella.
Ella	Well, sticks and stones.
Peter	All these years, you've just been avoiding having to work for a living, Tom. You were doing it when I met you, and you're still doing it. You don't want to work to take care of your family. You think you're too good to work for a living. You think you're better than all the working stiffs out there. You think you should be taken care of by the state.
Tom	Why not?
Peter	Because nobody owes you, that's why. Get a job, man. Nobody owes you shit.
Tom	Somebody's got to say NO, Pete. And that man is me. I SAY NO!
Peter	Get a job.
Tom	I SAY NO! There's a PINK SLIME in the ocean, Pete, a blotch, they can see it from outer space, it glows like NEON!

Peter	Get a job—
Tom	It's a TOXIC MASS, it's fucking PINK, it's so fucking big and bright you can see it from the MOON!
Peter	Get a job.
Tom	What's a VIRUS, Pete?
Peter	Get a job.
Tom	NOBODY KNOWS! IT'S A MATHEMATICAL INFECTION!
Peter	Get a job.
Ella	Tell him about vaccination, Tom.
Tom	You tell him, Ella!
Ella	They cut a cow and then they infect the wound, Peter, so the cow will grow the antibodies, and then they take those and freeze-dry them.
Tom	TO VACCINATE THE BABIES WITH.
Peter	GET A JOB.
Ella	Climate's changing. The temperature is going up. Too many people and not enough trees.
Tom	Nature is not nature! It's not nature anymore! Forever! It's befouled forever! With us! People! With dumps and plastic and pipes and dirty needles and poison—toxic waste! In the air and the water and the land! Because people have got to have their cars and comforts and egos and shit! Forever! Forever, Pete! We are not taking care of it! It's not working! And you want to talk about getting a fucking job? *(Scoffs)* I won't do it! I won't participate!
Peter	Get a job.
Jeanine	Dad!
Tom	WHAT?
Jeanine	You're making me miss an important part of the story!
Tom	HOW'D I DO THAT?

Jeanine	With all the yelling, Dad!
Tom	WELL YOU GOT THE SOUND OFF ANYWAY.
Jeanine	It's a distraction on my head, Dad!
Tom	DON'T CALL ME DAD. CALL ME TOM!
Jeanine	Tom!
Tom	That's my name. It ain't Dad. *(To PETER)* I hate it when they call me Dad. I forbid it from Amy Lou as much as from Jeanine.
Peter	I thought you were the Father.
Tom	That ain't Dad.
Ella	*(Bringing the tea)* No more fighting now. We're having tea. You take milk and sugar, don't you, Peter?
Peter	No.
Ella	Oh. I remember you taking milk and one sugar.
Peter	Not anymore. Just straight is fine.
Ella	Okay. *(Pause)* I didn't mean to make you feel bad.
Peter	You didn't?
Ella	'Course not. I just feel sorry about it all.
Peter	So do I.
Tom	This here is some weak tea, Ella.
Ella	I'm sorry, but I'm saving some for Amy Lou and some for the morning. Is it too weak for you, Peter? I suppose I could add more and let it steep if you want.
Peter	It's fine.
Ella	It's no trouble.

TOM snickers.

	Company comes first.
Peter	No, thanks. This'll do.

Tom	She wants everything to be nice.
Ella	I do wish we had a joint around.
Peter	*(To himself)* God.
Ella	Good chance Amy Lou will bring some home with her.
Peter	I told you I don't smoke, Ella. I haven't for years.
Tom	He drinks.
Ella	I was thinking for myself. But you shouldn't drink, Peter. It's not good for you.
Peter	Right.
Ella	You need someone to take care of you.
Peter	Yes.
Ella	It's no good being by yourself.
Peter	True.
Tom	Hell, the bachelor's life ain't bad.
Ella	You wouldn't know.
Tom	I was single before I met you.
Ella	Yeah, and it's been downhill ever since.

TOM *laughs.*

But I wouldn't trade a minute of it.

JEANINE *laughs.*

I don't know what she's laughing at.

Tom	It's the story in her head.
Jeanine	No it's not, Dad!
Ella	I hope you'll get to see Amy Lou, Peter.
Peter	Yeah.
Ella	She's really a knockout, Peter, but she's oh-so-wild.

Tom	Untamed.
Ella	*(With a touch of envy)* Does anything she wants. No restraining her at all. *(Sigh)* Tom spoiled her.
Tom	No point in passing blame around, Ella. She's free as the wind is all.
Peter	Well, I hope she makes out okay, considering she can't read. *(Rising)* Thanks for the tea, Ella.
Tom	*(Ominously)* Where you going?
Ella	Oh! Wait and I'll show you some photographs of Amy Lou, Pete? Okay?
Peter	Okay. Yeah, sure.
Ella	I'll find them for you!
Peter	I'll look at the pictures and then you'll open the door, Tom, and we'll call it a night.

TOM doesn't answer, but takes the hammer out and plays with it.

Ella	*(Searching)* Jeanine, where'd I put the album?
Jeanine	What album?
Ella	The notebook with the pictures in it, Jeanine!
Jeanine	I don't know, Ella.
Ella	I wish you'd take more notice of the world around you, Jeanine.
Jeanine	I never had nothing to do with that notebook.
Ella	You have nothing to do with nothing, Jeanine.
Jeanine	You put it somewhere when you was stoned.
Ella	*(Exploding)* Don't you dare talk to your mother like that! *(Throwing something at her)* DON'T YOU DO IT!

JEANINE withdraws and falls silent. TOM snickers.

Ella	I'm sorry, Peter. Please excuse me. Well, here's some pictures of Jeanine. *(Sits close to PETER to show him the photos. Off, the* SOUND *of sirens.*
Tom	The wild dogs are out again, keeping the wolves back.
Ella	Oh, don't listen to it, Tom. Look, Peter, here's Jeanine.
Tom	You're sure acting the proud parent, Ella.
Peter	Well, she is definitely good-looking.

JEANINE chuckles.

Ella	See how much she looks like Tom?
Tom	Hell she does.
Ella	How old was she when you last saw her, Peter?
Peter	Uh, three? I don't really remember.
Ella	It was winter.
Peter	Yeah.
Ella	And she was almost three.
Peter	Oh, yeah. It was up at the farm. There was snow on the ground. The lake was frozen. You went ice skating.
Ella	Yes!
Peter	You looked like a young girl, all fresh and new, gliding around on the lake.
Ella	I was pregnant with Amy Lou.
Peter	Jeanine was bundled up for the cold. The sun was bright. I remember that. I miss that.
Ella	Do you?
Peter	Yeah, I miss the cold, clean air, the bite. I miss those sunny, winter days, Ella.

Ella	*(Suggestively)* We had some good times, didn't we, Peter?
Peter	*(Looks at ELLA, amazed)* What are you talking about?
Ella	Well, I'm saying we had some good times, that's all.
Peter	I don't want to get into this shit.
Ella	Why are you so upset?
Peter	Are you kidding, or what?
Ella	No...I...
Peter	YOUR HUSBAND LOCKED THE DOOR ON ME AND I CAN'T GET OUT.
Ella	I know that. Let's make the best of it.
Tom	No sense in calling up bygone days, Ella.
Peter	Then why did you lock the door?
Tom	I'm talking to Ella.
Peter	If you didn't want to call up bygone days, why did you lock the door?
Ella	He just wants you to stay, Peter.
Peter	What?
Ella	Stay.
Peter	My God.
Ella	You said you were lonely.
Peter	I live in California! I'm going back in three days!
Tom	What for?
Peter	I like my life. I don't have any complaints. It's quiet. It's simple. It's my life.
Ella	No one should live by themselves.
Peter	Says who?
Ella	Says me.
Peter	Who are you?
Ella	What do you mean?
Peter	I mean, who are you? Who are you to decide? Who are you to make pronouncements?

Ella	I'm me.
Peter	Yeah. And you know.
Ella	What?
Peter	How people should live.
Ella	*(Defensive)* Yeah, in general. I'm not saying everybody is the same, but definitely most people shouldn't live alone.

Tom snickers.

	Stop it, Tom.
Tom	Hell, you die alone, Ella.
Ella	All the more reason not to live alone.
Tom	*(Laughing, to PETER)* She's got me there.
Peter	Oh, for Christ's sake.
Ella	What?
Peter	More fourth-rate pithy homilies, Ella.
Ella	I don't care what you call it. I still think it's true.
Peter	Okay.
Ella	A man needs the love of a woman.
Peter	There's another one.
Ella	I don't care.

Tom chuckles.

Peter	What are you laughing at, Tom?

Tom laughs.

It's not funny.

Tom laughs.

What are you doing with the fucking hammer?

Tom laughs.

What's the matter with you? Are you bored? Did you lock me in here so you could watch a scene between me and your wife?

Tom	I told you, son, I play it all by ear.
Peter	I'm not your fucking son!
Tom	You want the key, then come ahead and take it.
Peter	I don't want to fight with you, Tom.
Ella	There'll be no violence in this house!
Tom	Come on ahead.
Peter	I won't fight. Just open the door.
Tom	I'll open it when I get ready.
Peter	Tell you what, you let me go and I won't do anything. But you let me go now.
Tom	Do? What are ya gonna do?
Peter	I'll go to the police and I'll swear out charges against you.
Tom	For what?
Peter	Imprisonment. Kidnapping. Assault with a hammer.
Tom	Oh, hell, who cares? *(Laughs)*
Peter	I promise you I will, Tom, unless you let me go now.
Ella	Would you do that?
Peter	Yes.
Ella	You wouldn't. I don't believe you would. I don't believe you'd do that, Peter.
Peter	Why not?

Ella	Because I know you don't hold with the police.
	You, of all people.
Peter	You got that wrong, Ella.
Ella	Then you have changed.
Peter	Damn right.
Ella	A lot.
Peter	I sure hope so.
Tom	Hell, I told ya, you can go to the cops, you can sic the sheriff on me, you can call out the National Guard if you want to. It don't mean anything at all to me. More hair of the dog.
Peter	I don't know what that means. Do you want trouble?
Tom	Trouble? What's trouble? There ain't no trouble. It's all trouble, or it's all happenings, scenes, one after the other. And that's it. Go on and bring the trouble.
Peter	Open the door and I will.
Ella	No, you won't.
Tom	See, I don't believe in crime, and I don't believe in criminals. There's no crime, and there's no justice, either.
Peter	Is that so?
Ella	It's society that commits the crime, and it's people that pay for it. More lives down the river.
Peter	Oh, horseshit.
Tom	There's no crime and there's no justice, Pete. There's just a bunch of humans doing shit to get by, and another bunch wearing uniforms and guns, roaming around in their power trips. Guard dogs, I call 'em.
Peter	If you say so, Tom.
Tom	I SAY SO.
Peter	Good. I don't want to argue. I want to go.

Ella	Come on, Peter, say what you have to say.
Peter	What for?
Ella	Because otherwise it's not fair.
Peter	Why?
Ella	It's not fair to say something and not say it.
Peter	Did you just hear yourself?
Ella	You know what I mean.
Peter	It's useless. You're both out of your minds. There's no connection to the real world.

TOM scoffs.

There are people out there who deserve to be drawn and quartered.

TOM scoffs.

Criminal psychopaths.

TOM scoffs.

	You should count your blessings, Tom.
Tom	I COUNT 'EM, PETE.
Peter	That you were born in a country where they let you live.
Tom	DAMN RIGHT. I'M AN AMERICAN.
Peter	Where you are protected by law and order.
Tom	I'M AN AMERICAN.
Peter	And supported by the state.
Tom	AN AMERICAN.
Peter	Like a parasite.

Ella	That was a hurtful thing to say, Peter.
Peter	I didn't intend it as a compliment.
Tom	Now we're getting to it, heh, heh.

A sigh from JEANINE.

Ella	Jeanine?
Jeanine	What?
Ella	What are you watching?
Jeanine	That was a good story, Mom. It was new, but the products were the same, but it was a new story, all about lawyers.
Tom	*(Cackling)* Lawyers!
Jeanine	But I don't know if I liked the characters, but I liked the story, but it was interesting to see, about lawyers.
Ella	"But, but, but," what is this but everything all of a sudden?
Jeanine	*L.A. Law.* Is that California?
Ella	Jeanine, you've watched enough for one day.
Jeanine	Yeah, that's California.
Ella	Did you hear what I said, Jeanine?
Jeanine	But I'm watching another new one now.
Ella	No BUTS! Go to bed!
Jeanine	It's the new fall season on NBC!
Tom	Leave her be, Ella. She'll conk out pretty soon.
Ella	*(To PETER)* See, he spoils her. And he spoiled Amy Lou. Spoiled brats. I can't do nothing with either of 'em. That's all she does. Day in and day out. Once in a while she'll go for a ride. She'll do the dishes. She'll sweep. Then it's the television, day and night. I hope the damn thing breaks, Jeanine!
Tom	She'd just stare at it, anyway, heh, heh.

Ella	It's not a joke, Tom!
Tom	Got enough stories in her head to last her a lifetime.
Ella	I've got to go someplace. I've got to do something. I've got a teenage daughter has a better time than I do. Amy Lou. She's out there now, enjoying herself. I never get out. I never meet people. No excitement. I've got to have some excitement sometimes. He takes me for rides. Rides in the country. When the Buick feels up to it. When there's gas in the car. Mostly it's the same same-old, same-old. And then you come walking in the door, Peter, and I thought…*(Bursts into tears)*
Peter	Oh, for God's sake, Ella.
Ella	*(Recovering)* I don't know what I was thinking. We haven't seen you in fifteen years. Can you imagine? Fifteen years! What a shock!
Peter	It was a shock for me, too, believe me.
Tom	Trouble is, now he don't like the company, Ella. He's all fired up to be someplace else.
Ella	I know he is.
Tom	Says we've blown our fuses.
Ella	He didn't mean it.
Tom	Called me a parasite.
Ella	*(Tapping him on the knee)* What a horrible thing to say, Peter.
Peter	*(Moving away)* I meant it.
Tom	Time was, he couldn't avoid sniffing up that tail of yours.
Ella	Yeah.
Tom	Followed it everywhere. Ain't that right?
Ella	That's right.

PETER *stands as though preparing to run.*

Tom	Wasn't getting any on his own.
Peter	That ain't the truth, Tom.
Tom	Had to have a piece of mine.
Peter	It didn't go down that way, Tom.
Tom	Look at him squirm, Ella. He walks in here chock full of himself, and now he's on the squirm. *(Cackles)*
Ella	Jeanine, are you listening to any of this? *(No answer)*
Tom	She knows all about it, Ella. She was there.
Ella	She was just a baby, Tom.
Tom	Don't matter. She was around, and she knows what happened.
Ella	It's none of her damn business!
Tom	Alright, Ella.
Ella	Don't "alright" me, Tom! *(Pause)* At least close the curtain!
Tom	I'll do that for ya, Ella. *(Draws the curtain, which cuts off TV area)*
Ella	Thank you. *(To PETER)* She doesn't pay any attention to me anyhow. No one does. But that don't mean she don't listen to what she wants to hear.
Tom	I give ya the attention, Ella.
Ella	*(To PETER)* Yeah. He acts. He knows he's got to give me a measure of attention or I'll start to scream.
Tom	That's no lie. He's HEARD that, Ella.
Ella	*(To PETER)* So every day he picks an hour or two where he sweet-talks me and attends to me. He's acting.

TOM *smiles at* PETER.

I don't care. When the time comes for me to scream, I'm gonna scream. I'll raise hell and then it'll pass and I'll go along for a while. There's no hope on this plane of existence.

Tom	You got that right.
Ella	No hope. No hope in shit and piss and going to the store and putting gas in the car. Nobody's going anywhere but the grave. The only hope is in God, the Father, because He is on another plane of existence. And I'm ready. I'm ready. I'm ready for the end, the End of Days. *(Sighs)*
Tom	What is that, Pete? What is that called?
Peter	What?
Tom	What she's talking.
Peter	I don't know. The Second Coming?
Ella	All the dead bodies going into the ground, and Mother Earth receives them, and turns them over. Everything alive goes back into earth, where she turns them over.
Tom	No, there's a word, Pete. Come on, you're the word-man, you're the poet. What's the word I'm looking for?
Peter	Apocalypse.
Tom	That's it! That's the word! Apocalypse! Heh, heh.
Ella	And then the Early Ones will rise.
Peter	*(Softly)* Who are they, Ella?
Ella	*(In the eerie tones of a prophetess)* The First People, the Human Beings, who could obey Nature, and hear the electrical music of the stars.
Tom	*(Banging the hammer)* Hey, HEY!
Peter	Ella?
Ella	Yes?
Peter	Tell him to let me go, Ella.
Ella	Not yet.
Peter	What do you want?
Ella	*(Giggling)* I want to be in Paradise, or life's not worth the trouble. Can you do that?

Peter	No.
Ella	I've had my moments. I remember one time, it was over in Rhode Island, we were visiting friends of yours, Peter, I was pregnant with Amy Lou, and you were standing with me in front of the house, and Tom was walking in a field with Jeanine. A beautiful fall day. Oh, it was just a golden day, and I took your hand, and you said, "Tom looks just like a prince out of a fairy tale." Do you remember that?
Peter	We were stoned.
Ella	So what? My sweet prince. He never raised his voice in those days, ever.
Peter	No, he didn't.
Tom	Heh, heh.
Ella	It starts out with the best thing there is—making love—and then you get wore down with bills and the kids.
Tom	It's been tough on Ella.
Ella	I remember another time, it was on the farm in Pennsylvania, we had built a big bonfire, and Tom was playing and singing for everyone and I was watching you and you looked SO handsome I went up to you and kissed you. Remember?
Peter	I remember. We were probably stoned then, too.
Tom	Don't be taking it all back now, Pete.
Peter	I'm not trying to.
Tom	The hell you ain't.
Ella	I remember one time in the city we were loaded. You went and got us some very good acid and the three of us got high. I had a very good head on that day. Tom was in the other room. You were lying on the couch with an arm over your eyes. I was ready for anything that day. I came

and sat near you, and I said, "Are you afraid to look at me, Peter?" And you said, "Yes." I got you to come inside with Tom and me. You were SO shy. Then I asked you to take off your shirt, and you started to, and then there was a knock on the door. I couldn't believe it. It was that girl Rifka, and her boyfriend, remember?

Peter Yeah.

Ella So we started entertaining the company. You and Tom played. Tom was flirting with Rifka. He'd always wanted to fuck her. We ate some watermelon and it was weird. That was the sexiest watermelon I ever ate. Along in there our feet touched, and it was thrilling. I said, "Was that you, Peter?" Finally, they left, but my head was gone by then, and you ran away.

Peter That was the night you called me a sonofabitch and a bad person.

Ella Did I?

Tom You remember what happened before that, Pete?

Peter Yeah, you and me had a conversation on the stoop.

Tom You were throwing up into the gutter.

Peter WHAT DO YOU WANT? WHAT IS IT THAT YOU WANT? WHY ARE YOU DOING THIS? WHY BRING IT UP AGAIN? THE DISTRESS AND THE TORMENT AND THE SICK LUST AND THE SHAME AND THE GUILT? *(He pauses for breath—to ELLA)* Your head—your head is a maze—a labyrinth—of fantasies and dreams—It was that way then and it's that way now.

Ella *(Stunned)* What?

Peter It's a fucking dream-world. Look at it—you live in squalor and poverty and you don't do anything—you don't know how to do anything but pretend to be a housewife and a

	mother, and you cover it all up with grass and justify it with a crackpot religious belief.
Ella	Crackpot?
Peter	Crackpot! When all that shit was going down—Jesus Christ, what was it? You were this pretty, sex-obsessed, petit-bourgeois neurotic with a little kid on your hands, in over your head, married to a hillbilly folk singer who wouldn't get a job! The fairy-tale white prince! The golden-haired boy with the guitar! This prince of yours was lighting up his kingdom with grass and acid, which he had to do, since he was never going to make any fucking money! And then I come along! I walk right into it!
Tom	*(Hoarsely)* Poor Peter. *(At first lightly, he begins tapping with his hammer, a slow, steady beat)*
Peter	At least I had a job! I had a job and the fucking reefer, eh, Tom?
Ella	*(Rubbing her head)* Oh, my head...my head is gone...I...
Tom	Yeah, Pete, you had the job and the reefer, Pete. But I had the family, and I had the music, and I had the friendliness what took you in, Pete. I'M THE FATHER, PETE.
Jeanine	Dad...?
Ella	Shut up, Jeanine.
Tom	Fuck this shit. You try to keep everything fresh and pure and you end up decrepit anyway. Fuck it. People are animals and worse than animals. Playing with the fucking machinery. Heh, heh. You spend your life working for the Man and then they stick you in the ground and say you done good. Head down and paying the bills and grief and sorrow and then it's over. Fuck that shit. YOU DIDN'T EXPECT ME TO BE ONE OF THEM, DID YOU, PETE?

206

Peter	One of who?
Tom	ONE OF THE SLAVES, PETE. Heh, heh. There's a bunch of pricks right now I'll bet sitting up in the wide offices of the tall towers of the cities, they forgot that shit comes out of their assholes and lies come out of their mouths, they are planning to get a jump on the Chinese and the Japs, don't you know, because they've figured out what's happening, see, in this dump we live on, let's blast the fuckin' thing and end up the rulers and get the population back down, especially the Asians and the blacks, let's blow the fuckin' thing, am I right, Ella?
Ella	That's right, Tom.
Tom	Yeah, and I'm an APPALACHIAN, PETE, I am THE REAL THING, a Scotch-Irish AMERICAN from the real HEARTLAND of this country, who has stood up and said NO! I am a sweet low-lander son of my daddy, HE COULD TELL A FOLK TALE, PETE, the peoples would come from all over to hear the man, he died of coal dust in his lungs, HE WAS THE AGE OF FORTY-FOUR YEARS, PETE.
Ella	You killed him, Peter.
Peter	What? Who did I kill?
Ella	Tom.
Tom	Oh, he could speak, he was a SPEAKER, my daddy was, he had the music in him from the old folks, from the home country, HE was a POET, natural-born!
Peter	Ella, listen up. Please. That song I wrote, it was about something—a body—that Tom and I buried together. It wasn't Tom.
Ella	No?
Peter	No, it was—
Tom	You got him on the squirm again, Ella.

Peter	I guess it was the friendship that we buried, and there was nothing to be done.
Ella	That's what killed him. That's when he changed. Before that happened, he never raised his voice, he never screamed at people how wrong they were, he never banged on his guitar, he never...*(Bursts into tears again)*
Jeanine	Mom! Mom!
Ella	What is it, Jeanine?
Jeanine	It's the story, Mom!
Ella	Change the channel, Jeanine!

TOM *snickers, still tapping out a beat with his hammer.*

Peter	The day you called me a sonofabitch, I was down on the street with Tom, I was throwing up, I was high and I was in a terrible state, I told him I couldn't take it anymore.
Ella	You told him I was coming on to you.
Peter	I told him something had to give!
Ella	It was only natural. We lived together, we were attracted to each other, drawn to each other.
Peter	I didn't want a scene. I wasn't ready for a scene, I couldn't have handled a scene. I couldn't share you. I had to have you, but I couldn't share you with him.
Tom	YOU FUCKING EGOTISTICAL BASTARD! He thinks he's important! That's not important! You're not important! Listen to him! He couldn't share! Who is he? Who the fuck is he?
Ella	A betrayer.
Tom	He couldn't share!
Jeanine	Dad! Dad!

Tom	JEANINE, TURN THE DAMN THING OFF AND GO TO BED. AND DON'T CALL ME DAD!

A pause, then JEANINE *opens the curtain and comes part way into the room.*

Jeanine	Tom? Why are you hitting with the hammer, Tom?
Tom	I'm making me a song, Jeanine. I'm singing a song, and this here is the beat.
Jeanine	Don't sing it, Tom.
Tom	Why not?
Jeanine	It's hurting my head. I can't listen to the story.
Ella	The sound is OFF, Jeanine.
Peter	My God.
Ella	Stop hammering, Tom, it's giving us all a headache.
Tom	Well alright, then, I believe I will stop, no problem there, I'm done. *(Stops)*
Ella	You hurt his feelings, Jeanine.
Jeanine	Stop crying, Ella.
Ella	Go back to your story, Jeanine.
Jeanine	Thank you, Tom. *(Returns to her spot in front of the TV)*
Peter	You called me to you, Ella. You remember that? You called me, up there at the farm, on that foggy night, you called to me.
Ella	Did I?
Peter	Yes, you did. I knew something was going to happen. Years of flirting and touching and feeling and looking and smiling. I knew it was all coming down that night at the farm. I'm standing there by the lake smoking a joint and watching the mist on the water, my heart is pounding—

this is it, this is it, I'm finally gonna fuck her and screw
Tom, and fuck everybody, this is it—and then I hear you
calling my name, you're up the hill by the house, in the
light from the kitchen window, I can see you swaying there
in the fog, the way you used to shift your weight from leg
to leg, that nervous, sexy way of moving, and I said, "I'm
down here," and I went up to you like a dog. The poet!
What was I doing? What was I planning? A life of crime?
Then fifteen years go by and I'm living alone in a cabin in
Los Angeles, a fucking recluse! Then I walk into a Safeway
in Woodstock, New York, to buy a deck of cards and I
hear a voice and it's you! And I'm here and you lock the
fucking door! You're crazy as a fucking loon, Tom! And
so am I! We're in the same boat! We're both the dregs,
Tom, in the bottom of the barrel! The FATHER and the POET!
Oh, but it was sweet there for a minute, eh, Ella? For five
minutes? For an hour? I can't help but agree with you
there. You were sitting on the bench overlooking the lake
and I leaned over you and blew reefer smoke into your
mouth. "That's a sweet trick," you said. We went for a
walk, but we both knew we were going to my room in that
ramshackle, rotting bungalow that was leaning part way
into the lake. We were so anxious, we stayed downstairs
necking and grinding at each other for a long time, and
then we went up to my room at last. Moonlight was
shining on the water, just like in the fairy tales. And then we
heard a baby crying. It was Jeanine, and you ran off to her.

Tom   Poor Peter. He comes up to me one day down in the city,
I was playing a benefit for one of them street kitchens,
and he says, "Tom, I met a woman," as if I gave a fuck,

as if it was VERY IMPORTANT to somebody—he says, "I met a woman, and I'm going for it, maybe you could pass that on to Ella, Tom!" *(Cackles)*

Ella   That was the second one.

Peter   The second?

Ella   Betrayal.

Tom   I laughed into his face. I said, "WHO GIVES A SHIT? I KNOW YOU SCREWED ELLA. WHAT DOES THAT MAKE YOU? You slip it to my old lady in the dark and you think you got to apologize to me for dickin' some other broad?"

Peter   I don't remember that, Tom.

Tom   Yeah. Ella and me got nothing hid from each other. We're on the same path. Like it or not, we're on the same path. We know all about that back alley shit and it means nothing to us, nothing at all.

Ella   Amen to that.

Peter   You should've stayed in Virginia, Tom. You're a country boy.

Tom   Fuck you, Pete! You should of stayed in your cabin in Los Angeles!

Peter   *(Hard)* Yeah, well, we'll play it out, Tom.

Tom   You bet we will, Pete. You bet.

Ella   *(Listening)* Tom?

Off, SQUEALING of an approaching auto careening to a stop at the side of the house. Car door SLAMS.

Who's that, Tom?

SOUND of FOOTSTEPS racing to the house and then a CRASH at the door.

Amy Lou	*(Off)* Open the damn door!
Ella	It's Amy Lou!

Tom opens the door. Peter takes a step backward. Amy Lou rushes in and Tom closes the door, but doesn't lock it. They look at Amy Lou—she is disheveled, hysterical. A bloody red blotch shows through her white bandana. She and Peter take each other in, stunned.

	What happened to you?
Tom	What did you do, girl?
Amy Lou	Goddamn it!
Ella	You're bleeding!
Tom	Fetch a towel, Ella Mae, and that peroxide, and some bandages!
Ella	What happened?
Amy Lou	I hit my head, damn it!
Ella	How?
Amy Lou	*(From sheer frustration)* AAAAAAAAAHHHHHHHHHH!
Tom	Go on, Ella!
Ella	*(Frightened)* We don't have any bandages, Tom!
Tom	Get what there is, then, Ella!

Ella goes. Jeanine holds her head and whimpers.

Amy Lou	SHUT UP, JEANINE!
Peter	Tom, she needs a doctor.
Amy Lou	WHO THE FUCK IS THIS?
Peter	Let's get a doctor, Tom.
Amy Lou	WHO IS HE?

Tom	This here is Peter.
Amy Lou	PETER THE POET?
Tom	Yeah.
Amy Lou	WHAT'S HE DOING HERE?
Tom	I ran into him.
Amy Lou	FUCK THAT SHIT!
Tom	Simmer down, Amy Lou.
Amy Lou	I SAY FUCK THAT SHIT.
Tom	And I brought him home.
Amy Lou	WHAT THE FUCK FOR?
Peter	I had no idea—
Amy Lou	I SAY YOU'RE TOO DAMN LATE!
Peter	No idea you were here.
Amy Lou	I'M THE POET.
Peter	Okay.
Amy Lou	I SAY MY POETRY.
Peter	I write mine.
Amy Lou	THAT AIN'T NOTHIN'! THAT'S SOME OLD SHIT!
Peter	I'm glad to see you.
Amy Lou	I SAY YOU'RE FUCKIN' LATE!
Peter	Let's go to the hospital.
Amy Lou	I CAN'T BELIEVE IT! I CAN'T FUCKIN' BELIEVE IT!
Ella	*(Returning with a towel and a bottle of hydrogen peroxide)* Here. Here, Amy Lou.
Tom	What happened, girl?
Amy Lou	EVERYTHING HAPPENED! THAT'S IT! IT'S ALL FUCKIN' OVER!
Peter	Where's the hospital at, Tom?
Amy Lou	NO! I DON'T WANT NO DOCTOR!
Jeanine	You hurt yourself?
Amy Lou	*(With fierce sarcasm)* YEAH, I HURT MYSELF, JEANINE!

Peter	It looks pretty bad, Tom.
Amy Lou	Oh, fuck you!
Peter	Let's run her over in the Buick. Come on.
Amy Lou	No, Tom! Don't do it!
Peter	Amy Lou, I'm a friend.
Amy Lou	YOU AIN'T NO FRIEND!
Peter	Listen to me! You're coming with me!
Amy Lou	I'm not going anywhere with you!
Peter	Why not?
Amy Lou	Don't let him take me, Tom!
Tom	Sit down, girl, and let your mother help you.
Amy Lou	*(Collapsing onto the couch)* Oh, God! Oh, shit! *(Bursting into tears)* It hurts!
Ella	*(Dabbing at the wound with the towel and peroxide)* Oh, my poor baby. Oh, my poor baby.
Amy Lou	Oh, stop with the 'poor baby,' Ella!
Tom	How is it, Ella?
Ella	I think it looks worse than it is. At least I hope so, Tom.
Tom	*(To AMY LOU)* Let it rest now, darlin'.

AMY LOU falls into her mother's arms.

Peter	Tom? Listen to me. She doesn't know what she's doing.
Tom	*(Holding AMY LOU)* Hang on, honey. Hang on, baby. *(To ELLA)* The bleeding?
Ella	*(Removing the towel)* It looks better, Tom. Oh, it looks better.
Tom	Hold that towel tight to the wound, Ella.
Ella	That's what I'm doing, Tom! Oh, Amy Lou, what did you do to yourself?

Jeanine cries.

Amy Lou	SHUT UP, JEANINE!
Tom	We might have to go and get you stitched, Amy Lou.
Amy Lou	Oh, it don't matter. It don't matter no more. Willie is dead on the floor. The sonsabitches shot us.
Peter	What?
Tom	They shot you?
Amy Lou	They're coming for me, Tom.
Ella	Where, Amy Lou?

Amy Lou sobs.

Where was this?

Jeanine	Is she bleeding, Ma? Still?
Ella	I don't think so, Jeanine.
Amy Lou	*(Hysterically)* Christ, Jeanine, you're such a freak! I don't know why I came back here. Why'd I come here? I just drove Willie's Toyota truck straight up the road and I end up here in this fuckin' place. Where else was I gonna go? Without Willie Lefferts? The owners shot his brains out!
Ella	What owners, Amy Lou? Amy Lou?
Amy Lou	THE OWNERS! THE OWNERS AT THE FOUR CORNERS! THE OWNERS OF THE ALL-NIGHT JOINT AT THE FOUR CORNERS WHAT TAKES YOUR MONEY FOR EVERY GODDAMNED THING! THE SONSABITCHES! WE WENT IN THERE TO TAKE SOME MONEY BACK! ME AND WILLIE!
Peter	You did what?
Amy Lou	AAAAHHHH!
Tom	Easy now. Easy, girl.

Ella	WHAT POSSESSED YOU TO WALK INTO A LIQUOR STORE WITH A GUN, AMY LOU?
Tom	None of that, Ella.
Ella	STUPID! STUPID!
Amy Lou	We're outlaws. And we see ourselves as such.
Peter	Outlaws?
Amy Lou	Outlaws, for sure. We didn't mean for no one to get shot. But we're outlaws anyway. That's how we're treated, always, Willie bein' a breed, and me the nigger trash with him. *(To ELLA)* WHAT THE FUCK DIFFERENCE DOES IT MAKE? WALK IN WITH A GUN, WALK IN WITHOUT A GUN? EVERYBODY JUST RUNNIN' AROUND BUYIN' SHIT!

TOM cackles.

Ella	A GUN'LL GET YOU SHOT, AMY LOU!
Amy Lou	Yeah, you got that right, Ella.
Ella	Jesus God!
Tom	Lemme see your head, girl. *(Looking at the wound)* Bleeding's a lot better. ...
Ella	Thank God for that.
Tom	I think it's a nick is all. Pellet from a shotgun.
Peter	Can I see it?
Amy Lou	No! Stay away!
Tom	Does it hurt ya bad?
Amy Lou	YEAH IT HURTS! *(To PETER)* What are you lookin' at?
Peter	I'm looking at you.
Amy Lou	I won't go with them, Tom.
Peter	Tom, she doesn't know what she's saying.
Amy Lou	I won't go.

Tom	I know you won't, girl.
Amy Lou	Good, then. That's good. *(Heaving a sigh)* Good. Ain't nothin' there no more, no more.
Jeanine	Where?
Amy Lou	IN THE WORLD, JEANINE. But it don't make no difference to ya, does it, seein' as you never went out anyway. JEEZ, DIDN'T YA EVER WANNA GET LAID AT LEAST?
Ella	Watch your tongue, Amy Lou.
Amy Lou	OH ELLA, YOU'RE THE HORNIEST WOMAN I EVER MET IN MY ENTIRE LIFE. AND JEALOUS, TOO.
Ella	Jealous?
Amy Lou	Of Willie and me. My sweet boy. *(Sobbing)* We figured we'd get us a little money and hop onto the thruway an' disappear...but them owners...
Ella	Jeanine, stop standing there and fetch a clean towel.

JEANINE is in a trance.

JEANINE!

JEANINE shudders and goes.

Amy Lou	Tired of it.
Ella	We all are.
Amy Lou	Real tired.
Peter	You're just a kid, a baby—YOU DON'T WANT TO DIE.
Amy Lou	Tired of all the dummies out there eatin' an' shittin' an' talkin' an' buyin' and lyin' and spoilin' nature with their selfish ways.
Peter	DID YOU HEAR ME?

Jeanine brings a new towel.

Ella	Here, honey. Here's a fresh towel.
Amy Lou	Don't call me "honey." You never call me "honey."
Ella	Relax your hand, Amy Lou, let go.

Amy Lou lets go, Ella replaces the towel.

	There. Good. Bleeding's stopped. Thank the Lord.
Peter	Let me see. Can I see it?
Amy Lou	No!

Peter steps back.

God, it hurts, though. Stop looking at me, Jeanine! I got shot in the head, Jeanine! You're a piece of work, Jeanine! Why don't you go to Australia, Jeanine, and start over? That's what I'd do, I'd go to Australia if I was you. You could be with all the animals there, roaming the plains... (*Trails off*)

Sound of sirens, off.

Jeanine	I might do that one day.
Amy Lou	Yeah, sure. When?
Ella	(*As though realizing the truth for the first time*) Oh, Tom! Peter! Do you know what she's done? Oh, my god. Oh, my head.
Amy Lou	Your head? Listen to her! Shit, why did I come back here? Why didn't I just drive and drive and drive away?

Ella	YOU LITTLE SLUT. YOU SHUT YOUR DIRTY MOUTH. YOU SHOULD THANK GOD YOU HAVE A PLACE TO COME BACK TO.
Amy Lou	Yeah, sure.
Ella	THAT'S RIGHT. TOM? WHAT ARE WE GONNA DO, TOM?
Amy Lou	We went in there to the Four Corners to take the money. Them owners said no. They weren't to give us a dime. Even a piece of candy was too good for us trash. Then Willie lost his temper and shot one of them with his rifle. It's just one of them single-shot-22 squirrel guns but Willie shot that man through the neck with it. Then the other owner pulls out a sawed-off shotgun and blew Willie away, blew his brains all over the fucking crap they sell in there, the Fritos, and the popcorn and potato chips and shit, OH IT WAS SOME REAL SHIT, JEANINE, I couldn't fucking believe it, it took about a second's worth a time, an' Willie's on the floor an' I'm screaming at that owner, YOU SONOFABITCH YOU SONOFABITCHIN SCUMBAG COCKSUCKER, AND THEN HE HIT ME!
Peter	What ARE you gonna do, Tom?
Tom	I'M GONNA DEAL WITH THE TROUBLE, PETE.
Peter	How?
Tom	HEAD ON, PETE! I'M GONNA CRASH THEM FUCKERS HEAD ON!
Peter	Head on?
Tom	We're gonna ride, we're gonna ride, eh, Pete? WE'RE GONNA SING US A SONG LIKE IN THE DAYS OF OLD.
Ella	ALL RIGHT!
Peter	No. Let me take her, Tom. *(He circles* AMY LOU, *who avoids him)*
Amy Lou	GET HIM OFF ME, TOM!

Tom	*(To* PETER*)* Listen, you prick, sit down and behave yourself or I'll crack your face with this hammer and saw your fucking head off with that saw there.

PETER stops.

	I'm glad we got this prick here with us, Amy Lou, though I know you don't like him real well, he will come in right handy to us, heh, heh, pitiful as he is.
Amy Lou	I LOVE IT!
Jeanine	Tom?
Tom	I'm talking about carpentry, Jeanine.

AMY LOU giggles.

	You like that one, girl?
Amy Lou	You're a trip, Tom.

PETER lunges at TOM *and slugs him twice, knocking him to the floor. The hammer goes flying. A shocked pause.*

Tom	Motherfucker.

ELLA and JEANINE *rush to* TOM'S *aid.*

	Damned if he didn't hit me.
Amy Lou	PUNCH HIM BACK, TOM.
Ella	OH, LORD.
Tom	Get away, Ella. Jeanine. No harm done. Fucker showed his true self.

Peter	Now. Listen to me. Shut your mouths and listen to me. I have rights.
Tom	RIGHTS? I SAY THE HELL YA DO. YOU GOT NO RIGHTS.
Peter	Let's go, Amy Lou. You're coming with me.
Amy Lou	What the hell for?
Peter	I want to know you. I want to have the chance to get to know you.
Amy Lou	What are you?
Peter	*(Stammering)* I'm...I'm...I'm your father.
Amy Lou	You're another fuckin' idiot is what you are.

Sound of SIRENS approaching.

	Here they come. The fucking guard dogs are coming for me, Tom. Fuck it.
Tom	You ready, Ella?
Ella	I'm ready.
Amy Lou	Trash it!
Peter	Why?
Amy Lou	Fuck off!
Peter	Why don't you hear me?
Amy Lou	I AIN'T NEVER HEARD A WORD FROM YOU BEFORE!
Peter	I'm sorry. I didn't know.
Amy Lou	Fuck you. You're gone. You're nothing.
Peter	Fuck you, too. You're less than nothing. Nothing but a whacked-out roll in the sack.
Amy Lou	WHAT ARE YOU, THEN?
Ella	I'll tell you what he is.
Peter	SHUT UP. *(To AMY LOU)* I love you.
Amy Lou	Horseshit! You don't know me!

Peter   I love you. I'm...your father...

Sound of SIRENS, *closer.*

Jeanine   Are they coming, Tom?

Amy Lou   Christ, Jeanine. *(Weaker)* Are you watching a movie
              now, Jeanine? You're watching a movie, aintcha?
              And I'm the star in it, huh, Jeanine?

Jeanine   You're the pretty one, Amy Lou. You're the
              pretty one.

Amy Lou   *(With profound frustration)* AAAAAHHHH! GO WATCH
              TV, JEANINE!

Jeanine   NO I WON'T! AND DON'T YOU BOSS ME!

Amy Lou   I can't believe this. We got my fat white sister's
              total attention!

Peter   Please, listen to me, Amy Lou. We'll get you
              fixed up, we'll start over, we'll make a life with
              our own—

Amy Lou   I LOST MY OWN. I LOST MY WILLIE. IT'S OVER.

Ella   It's all coming down now, Tom. Our daughter has
              brought it to us. Our beautiful, foul-mouthed,
              illiterate, untamed bitch of a daughter has brought
              it to us! And Peter, too! Peter's here, too! And just
              in time!

Jeanine   What's going to happen, Ella?

Ella   The end, Jeanine! The end is going to happen!

Sound of SIRENS, *closer.*

Amy Lou   Here they come.

Tom	OH HELL, GIRL, THERE'LL BE NO ARRESTS AND THERE'LL BE NO ENTRY. I'M THE FATHER!

Sound of more SIRENS.

Amy Lou	LET'S STAY RIGHT HERE, TOM!
Tom	That's just what we're doin', girl!
Peter	TOM? TOM? YOU'RE IN DEEP SHIT, TOM.
Tom	So are you, pal.
Ella	*(Ominously)* So are you.

TOM just looks at ELLA and smiles. She smiles back and hisses at PETER.

	You've done it again, Peter. You've betrayed us again. I think it's sad.
Peter	Bullshit!
Ella	But that's what you are. *(Hisses)* A betrayer.
Peter	It ain't over, Amy Lou. We go on from here.
Amy Lou	I SAY IT'S OVER.
Ella	Amen. It'll be the Lord that does the finishing now.
Peter	The Lord? What are you talking about? *(To TOM)* YOU'RE GONNA SPEND THE REST OF YOUR LIFE IN THE STATE PEN.
Tom	HELL I WILL. I'LL BURN THIS HOUSE DOWN WITH EVERY-BODY IN IT 'FORE I TAKE ONE STEP WITH A GUARD DOG.
Ella	HEY!
Peter	THAT'S GREAT, TOM. THAT'S REASONABLE. YOU FUCKIN' BRAIN-DAMAGED ASSHOLE.
Tom	*(To ELLA)* Wonder who'll be with 'em.

Ella	Bill Fraley will be there.
Tom	Yeah. And Frank? Frank Stratton?
Ella	He's the only other cop.
Amy Lou	He's the one asked me to give him head once.
Ella	Damned filthy guard dog. He tried to get friendly with your father, time we had that trouble with the marshals.
Tom	I wanted to see if he could stand reason. *(Cackling)* He couldn't.
Peter	Reason? Reason?

Sound of more SIRENS.

Tom	An' a small army of state troopers. The dogs must have their day. Ella?
Ella	I feel right. I feel right, Tom.
Tom	ALL RIGHT.
Jeanine	Ella? What are you all doing?
Ella	*(In that strange prophesizing tone of voice)* We're on the line, Jeanine, that's all.
Peter	The line?
Ella	Between the dogs and the family—
Tom	I'M THE FATHER.
Ella	Between the dogs and the old race, the People, the Human Beings.
Tom	What hears the electricity of the stars.
Ella	You got to sacrifice, and go straight up. You got to go straight up, or get dragged down by the dogs. The time is come. The time is ripe. She doesn't know what she's done, but it's done. It's done, and now we're on the line. Now we have the chance to declare ourselves.

Tom	AMEN.
Amy Lou	*(Laboring)* The weirdest thing is how fast it happens... like lightning...the world's changed...you're looking out...and you're not you...and the world's not the world...it's new...forever...in a second...

Sound of SIRENS closer.

Ella?...Ella's getting ready to go to Heaven...*(To PETER)* Who are you? Why are you standing there watching me? GET AWAY FROM ME! YOU'VE KILLED MY SWEET BOY AND THE WHOLE WORLD'S DEAD!

PETER goes to AMY LOU and succeeds in holding her in his arms. She gives up fighting him and subsides.

Peter	*(Gently)* She's quiet now, Ella.

ELLA makes a strange keening sound, picks up the tambourine, and starts shaking it.

She's gone.

JEANINE runs out of the house.

Tom	Better jump now 'fore the precipice looms up, Pete.
Peter	No. I'm staying for the trouble, Tom.
Tom	Well, well, look at what's still here, Ella.
Ella	Let's go, Tom.

*ELLA shakes the tambourine and hums a spiritual as TOM
starts nailing boards up over the door.*

Tom FRANK STRATTON, I KNOW YOU'RE OUT THERE! I TAKE IT TO
YA! FRALEY, I KNOW YOU'RE OUT THERE! I TAKE IT TO YA!
WHAT I AM! THE FATHER! THE FATHER! NOBODY GETS IN
HERE! I'LL CUT OFF HEADS! I'LL BURN THIS HOUSE DOWN!

BLACKOUT.

*

Epilogue

*HARSH LIGHTS DIM UP on the apron and the HOUSE LIGHTS
rise to half. JEANINE steps forward, shielding her eyes from
the glare. She speaks to whomever will listen:*

Jeanine Don't hurt them. They're not bad. They're disappointed, is
all. The story didn't come out right and they're disappointed.
Tom acts hard, but he don't mean nothing by it. If you'd
just leave them be, it'll turn all out right in the morning. I
know it will. We can all go away now. They like to get high,
but it doesn't last. It won't last till morning. The story's over
and then something else happens. That's the story of those
two, and my sister, Amy Lou. She went where she shouldn't
go, and it happened, and now it's over. She's sorry for it.
We all know that. She likes to soar, like Tom and Ella, she
likes to fly. And I, too—I love it. Don't we all want to fly

226

and fly and fly? So you don't need to go in there, because that's what they're doing now—they're flying.

BLACKOUT.

The End

Skinwalkers

by Murray Mednick

Skinwalkers *had its world premiere at 7 Stages Theatre, Atlanta, Georgia, on January 29, 2005.*

Directed by Del Hamilton

With the following cast:
Myra: Maia Knispel
Don José : Normando Ismay
Aurora: Rachel Mewbron
Kathrine: Sandra Leigh Hughes
Tom: Daniel Pettrow
Sidney: Pierre Brulatour
Hartley: Michael Hickey
Frank: Isma'il ibn Conner

Stage Manager: Heidi Blackwell
Assistant Stage Manager: Jennifer Brown
Set Designer: Rochelle Barker
Props Design: Elizabeth Cooper & Justin Welborn
Mask Design: Michael Hickey
Costume Design: Johanna Schmink
Light Design: Jessica Coale
Sound Design: Brian Ginn
Technical Director: Mack Headrick
Production Assistant: Morgan Irwin Whyat

Characters

Myra

Aurora *(13 years old)*

Kathrine

Tom

Sidney

Don José

Hartley

Frank *(Blind)*

Alberto *(O.S.)*

Voice Off

Scene

On SIDNEY and KATHRINE'S ranch near Lamy, New Mexico; MYRA and TOM'S cabin; DON JOSÉ 'S parlor; a saloon in Lamy. Sets and props are minimal.

In the distance: SOUNDS of coyotes, dogs. As though from the past: a CAR CRASH.

LIGHTS. MYRA, TOM, KATHRINE, and SIDNEY.

Sidney Judge Bixby was driving home from Farmington. He was driving down a dark and desolate road. A dog ran out in front of him and Bixby stopped. The dog had a human face. "You're coming with me," the dog said. "No, I'm not!" shouted the Judge, "I got a wife and grandchildren and I'm the Santa Fe Judge!" And he slammed on the gas pedal and took off. It was the shock of his life, and he soon retired. His wife will swear to it. Two weeks later an Indian woman and a child were hitchhiking on the same road. Anglo couple picks them up and they all crashed— right there on the same spot as Bixby had his encounter with the dog.

Myra Good ghost story, Dad.

Sidney Well, you can all make up your own mind, whether you think it might be true. Bixby is an outstanding member of the community, and his wife has never been known to lie.

Myra Dad? *(OUT)*

LIGHTS UP on TOM sitting with DON JOSÉ .

Don José	How do you know Sidney Manning?
Tom	He's my father-in-law.
Don José	Health problems?
Tom	Him?
Don José	No. You.
Tom	I'm fine.
Don José	I know your wife.
Tom	Myra.
Don José	Sensitive woman.
Tom	Yes. She is.
Don José	Do you feel that women have understanding?
Tom	What?
Don José	Women.
Tom	Is that a trick question? Ha, ha.
Don José	Do you feel trapped?
Tom	Trapped?
Don José	In the body.
Tom	In the body? No.
Don José	What do you want?
Tom	Would you mind being interviewed?
Don José	For what?
Tom	For the radio. KPFK. In San Francisco. *(OUT)*

LIGHTS UP on MYRA and SIDNEY.

Sidney	Cattle equals grass, which equals rain. We've had good rain. Grass is up, everything green, cattle sleek. I'm gonna leave this place alone. Let the grass come back. You can see the seed sometimes, blowing across the fields in a cloud.

Myra	Dad?
Sidney	People talk about species dying out. One day, people will die out. Nothing stays the same, you can't keep everything the same. No point in trying to save species, though there'll always be those worried about that. Can't be helped. *(Out)*

LIGHTS UP on TOM and DON JOSÉ.

Tom	You have a reputation.
Don José	Ha, ha. *A brujo.*
Tom	Well, okay. A man of knowledge.
Don José	A sorcerer. Means I can turn myself into animals.
Tom	Oh. Is that real? *(Pause)*
Don José	I'm honored. I'm flattered.
Tom	I don't know much about these things.
Don José	You don't?
Tom	No.
Don José	Would you say you were a humble person?
Tom	No.
Don José	Would you say you were a spoiled person?
Tom	No.
Don José	A vain person?
Tom	Yes.
Don José	A special person?
Tom	Uh, no.
Don José	Marriage. There's the cure. But you got to work it. Big payoff and reward, then. Bearing the mate. Let the Wolf lie down with the Lamb.
Tom	I'm sorry…?

Don José	Two sides of a man.
Tom	You mean…?
Don José	Like an alternating current. Two natures. *¿Entiende usted?*
Tom	Would you mind if we recorded this?
Don José	Not really.
Tom	It'll be on the air.
Don José	On the air?
Tom	Around Christmas maybe.
Don José	On the air. Fantastic. *(OUT)*

LIGHTS UP on MYRA and SIDNEY.

Myra	Something happened.
Sidney	It's a gamble on the weather. Rain. You've got good years and bad.
Myra	I think Tom…uh…Tom and I…
Sidney	Weather changes. Market goes up and down. Had a late freeze this year, altered the food chain. Bears coming down out of the mountains for something to eat.
Myra	I think we hit someone on the road.
Sidney	But a man's character won't change a hell of a lot. It'll stay more or less the same. Throughout his life, it'll be the same. I'm sorry, honey—what did you say? *(OUT)*

LIGHTS UP on TOM and DON JOSÉ .

Don José	You see, there's Body and there's Mind.
Tom	Okay.
Don José	Go ahead. Turn that thing on.
Tom	Okay. *(Turns on recorder)*

Don José	You believe your thoughts.
Tom	Do I?
Don José	Yes. Big mistake.
Tom	Why?
Don José	You think about yourself.
Tom	Oh.
Don José	I'm not saying you're stupid.
Tom	You mean like a commentary?
Don José	Yes. That's it.
Tom	It's a story, really.
Don José	Yes.
Tom	The story of my life.
Don José	That's right.
Tom	Why we're interested in local traditions.
Don José	Why?
Tom	Something real.
Don José	Go ahead. Ask me something.
Tom	Is there a true indigenous religion?
Don José	'Course there is. We got our own here. Santos. Could be Jews, for all we know. Ha, ha. The hidden ones. Marranos, *conversos*, exiles. Sixteenth century. Ended up in Pueblo land. Took to cattle. Indians were astounded. We have *remedios*. Would you like one?
Tom	What are they, exactly?
Don José	Herbs.
Tom	Could you say more?
Don José	Plants. They push up out of the ground toward the sun.
Tom	Local?
Don José	Grown here and in old Mexico.
Tom	How did you learn your knowledge, Don José ?

Don José	From my father. My father learned from his father. The aim is wholeness, or unity.
Tom	I see.
Don José	Do you read? I recommend Spinoza. He was one of us. *(OUT)*

LIGHTS UP on MYRA and SIDNEY.

Myra	It was pitch black. We were coming down into the basin over the narrow overpass near Lamy.
Sidney	Dangerous intersection there.
Myra	And we hit something.
Sidney	What?
Myra	I don't know, Dad.
Sidney	Did you get out and look?
Myra	Yes.
Sidney	Did you see anything?
Myra	No. But it was so dark.
Sidney	Bear or coyote?
Myra	No, Dad.
Sidney	Another animal?
Myra	We didn't see one.
Sidney	Any sign of blood?
Myra	No.
Sidney	You find a dent? On your car?
Myra	No.
Sidney	That's all right, then. *(OUT)*

LIGHTS UP on TOM and MYRA.

| Tom | I didn't see anyone. |

Myra	I did.
Tom	How? You couldn't see. You couldn't see a thing. I didn't see anything. What did you see?
Myra	I saw a face.
Tom	You saw a face?
Myra	Didn't you?
Tom	I don't think so.
Myra	What did you see?
Tom	I didn't see nothing.
Myra	We hit something.
Tom	I didn't see a face.
Myra	Something hard.
Tom	What face? Whose face?
Myra	I don't know. Like a mask, or a grin.
Tom	A mask? A grin?
Myra	Teeth.
Tom	Teeth?
Myra	Eyes.
Tom	Eyes?
Myra	Just for an instant.
Tom	A dog?
Myra	You didn't hear it? You didn't feel it?
Tom	I heard something. I did hear something.
Myra	What did you hear?
Tom	You know, like an animal.
Myra	Like a bear?
Tom	No, no.
Myra	You didn't hear a scream?
Tom	I wouldn't call it a scream.
Myra	What would you call it?

Tom	Like a whine, like an engine, a motor.
Myra	It was a voice. I heard a voice.
Tom	A human voice?
Myra	You're in denial, Tom.
Tom	There was nothing out there.
Myra	Okay. That's not what you said.
Tom	What did I say?
Myra	You said a whine, or an engine. Or an animal. Okay?
Tom	Nothing, Myra.
Myra	Okay. I heard the darkness. Okay? *(OUT)*

LIGHTS UP on MYRA and AURORA.

Aurora	Skinwalkers. You gots to check it out. Could be a hex or a spell. A curse or an implant. We check you out. Entry could be made at birth.
Myra	Who are they?
Aurora	Could be a consciousness left its body through death and is now an invisible entity. Earthbound.
Myra	Why?
Aurora	They don't want to leave. They are emotionally attached to their former habits.
Myra	Oh, my goodness!
Aurora	They jump into a living person so they can enjoy their habits vicariously.
Myra	Oh. How?
Aurora	Sometimes it's an accident. Then they find themselves locked in there and they can't get out.
Myra	Locked in where?
Aurora	In the living body. They get in through a crack in the aura.

	They can be inside the aura, or attached to it outside, which is when they have the least influence.
Myra	Oh, my goodness!
Aurora	*(Laughing)* AuraCleanse.
Myra	What's that?
Aurora	My new company. I'm serious. There are also some who hang around due to fear of hell and eternal damnation. Sometimes a part of your shell is left over from a former life. It is still animated and magnetically attracted to the body and hard to get rid of. Most common entry is made through mind-expanding drugs and alcohol. But they can also come in when a person is anesthetized.
Myra	Or emotionally—?
Aurora	Or momentarily unconscious from a blow to the head or a fall.
Myra	Strong emotions?
Aurora	Strong emotions—strong emotional outbursts like anger attracts them. You are beside yourself or out of your mind.
Myra	What can one do?
Aurora	I urge you to practice control of thoughts and feelings. Takes time. Lots of time. These things been around long, with established habits and patterns. Gots to reprogram.
Myra	I see. *(Pause)*
Aurora	Forgive. *(Out)*

Lights up on Tom and Frank.

Frank	It's hard. You work your ass off, raise a family, have a decent old age. It's hard, *amigo. Duro.* Why people are irritated.

Tom	There's tension.
Frank	*Eso es.* The good life's scarce. You got these three different ethnic groups, *¿verdad?*
Tom	The Spanish, the Anglo, the Indian.
Frank	No love lost there, I can tell you. Are you taping?
Tom	Yes.
Frank	They turn to alcohol and drugs. What the fuck, right? Relief. We ain't seen the bottom of it yet.
Tom	Go on.
Frank	Everything turning to shit. Taco Bell. No way out. So.
Tom	Santa Fe has the highest crime rate in the country.
Frank	I can hear that.
Tom	New Mexico: highest suicide, highest incest.
Frank	Yeah. Guys beat their wives and fuck their daughters. It's traditional, some of these families here. *Ai.*
Tom	Tailgating is the worst I've ever seen.
Frank	What's that?
Tom	These pickup trucks cruise up behind you with their high beams on.
Frank	*Ai.*
Tom	Won't let you pull over. *(Looks around)*
Frank	What are you looking for?
Tom	Me?
Frank	Just now.
Tom	You could tell?
Frank	I'm blind, but I can hear. I can sense. *Ayudame.*
Tom	I'm sorry?
Frank	Listen up. You watching for someone?
Tom	There's a face. I'm looking for a face.
Frank	Whose face?

Tom	Just a minute. Too much noise. People in bars. Quack, quack. You know? Just a minute. *(OUT)*

LIGHTS UP on MYRA and KATHRINE.

Myra	We may have hit someone. On the road.
Kathrine	When?
Myra	The other night.
Kathrine	Where?
Myra	We came over the hill and across the bridge—at the turnoff to Lamy, near the railroad tracks—
Kathrine	Oh, that's a dangerous spot.
Myra	We didn't see anyone—
Kathrine	Well, you're imagining things.
Myra	And it was so dark!
Kathrine	You would know it if you hit somebody.
Myra	I don't know it!
Kathrine	We would all know it by now. What about Tom?
Myra	He doesn't think so.
Kathrine	Well, there you are.
Myra	But he doesn't know.
Kathrine	Doesn't help to imagine things.
Myra	He's asking around. Down at the depot. Down at the railroad tracks. At the hotel there. There's a restaurant and an antique bar.
Kathrine	Oh, yes. Antique.
Myra	The "Legal Tender." *(OUT)*

LIGHTS UP on TOM and FRANK.

Tom	This is great.
Frank	Oh, yeah, this is terrific.
Tom	Great bar.
Frank	This is my home, right here.
Tom	I started drinking when I was fifteen. Before that, I was always looking. Milkshakes, whatever. Anything to distract the pain. Medicate. We used to go to this roadside pizza joint and drink the hard stuff: rum, vodka, Seven-and-Sevens were popular then. No questions asked.
Frank	*Eso es.*
Tom	It's a miracle more of us weren't killed on the roads.
Frank	Many are.
Tom	Reminds me of a friend of mine. He was a cowboy type. Richard. He'd like this place. He liked to go to bars. It's the American Way. Guys communicate to guys in bars. You just turn yourself into a stupid shit. Play games. He liked to go to bars and shoot pool. Gets to be all about winning, and acting tough. Shuffleboard. Darts. Play the juke. Got American songs on there, full of alcoholic sentiment.
Frank	What happened to him?
Voice Off	Things are slipping away, Tom!
Tom	Someone call to you?
Frank	No, I don't think so.
Tom	I heard something.
Frank	On my beeper? I would hear that. I don't miss much. Your friend?
Tom	Killed in a crash. Drunk. Up in Michigan. In the dead of winter, in the dead of night, an icy night, shining white. We were in separate cars. We see his Ford smashed up against a tree and we scrape him off the road and bring

him in. No head. Cops out looking for the head. He must have screamed, crashing through. The strange thing is: the sky went dark. I can't get over that: the sky went dark the moment he died. *(OUT)*

LIGHTS UP on MYRA and AURORA.

Myra   Tom was at the wheel.

Aurora   Drunk?

Myra   Yeah.

Aurora   You, too, eh?

Myra   We were drunk. It was so dark you couldn't see a thing. Hairpin turn beneath a dangerous hill. Narrow bridge. Dark and misty. Something appeared in the road. Like a light.

Aurora   Eyes?

Myra   We hit him and we ran.

Aurora   Did you a see a look?

Myra   A look?

Aurora   Was there a look?

Myra   A face.

Aurora   He saw you.

Myra   Yes. I felt seen. It was unreal.

Aurora   No. In the real world, there is a light, there is a look. …*(OUT)*

LIGHTS UP on TOM taping DON JOSÉ .

Don José   People are blind. I say to a person, look, you have a tendency, an attitude, a predisposition, it colors everything in your life. And they look at me and nod and say—"Yes, I

	see that, I understand, I see what you're saying, of course
	it's true—" And they go on as before. How can they help it?
Tom	How can they—uh—help it?
Don José	There is another reality. It has neither shape nor form, but
	it can appear to man, or it can come down through the
	top of his head like a thunderbolt. There is a door there.
Tom	What?
Don José	The thunderbolt.

DON JOSÉ turns to face TOM: His face—a mask—is the face of an ancient Tewa petroglyph. TOM jumps.

Tom	Don José ?
Don José	The thunderbolt can transform a man through the door on the top of his head. *(OUT)*

LIGHTS UP on MYRA and AURORA.

Aurora	I'll need time on this.
Myra	Yes?
Aurora	See if I can clear it for you.
Myra	Oh. Can you? Clear it?

Enter KATHRINE. AURORA slips away.

Kathrine	Oh. Is that the girl...?
Myra	Yes, she works for the Saunders. Aurora.
Kathrine	That's right.
Myra	She takes care of their kids.
Kathrine	Is she Indian?

Myra	I don't know. I don't think so. Maybe half?
Kathrine	Yes, you can't tell, can you?
Myra	Mom?
Kathrine	How's your project going?
Myra	We're meeting with people. Gathering material. I'd like to look at archives. Talk to the hands. Do some more interviews.
Kathrine	You should talk to Hartley. He knows a lot.
Myra	He's on my list.
Kathrine	He's a real cowboy, that one.
Myra	And I'm really interested in the archaeology.
Kathrine	Oh, yes. That's the main thing.
Myra	I thought I was pregnant.
Kathrine	Did you?
Myra	Yes. I'm not. It was false.
Kathrine	I'm sorry, dear.
Myra	I miscarried.
Kathrine	I'm sorry.
Myra	Are you?
Kathrine	Well, yes, dear.
Myra	I'm not. *(OUT)*

LIGHTS UP on TOM and SIDNEY.

Tom	Can you make a profit?
Sidney	Well, you can. Depends greatly on the rain. Price of cattle dipped ten points awhile ago. Nobody knows why. Could've been speculators, buying futures. Nobody knows. There's foreign competition as well. 'Course, it's also real estate.
Tom	I saw where they're widening the road out by the gate.
Sidney	Yes.

Tom	Myra went out there, saw they got a dig going.
Sidney	That's right. Many's the skeletons they're digging out of there. It's the law of the state. If you're gonna lower the grade of the roadbed, and it's on an archaeological site, as this one is, then you got to let in the archaeologists first. And then they set up a dig before the road can proceed. It's state law.
Tom	Myra says they're taking out whole skulls and femurs—
Sidney	That's right.
Tom	Old Tewa people buried in trash. That is, they're buried in these pit houses with the trash.
Sidney	That's right, buried with the garbage.
Tom	Myra says the archaeologist—
Sidney	That's Wayne Early. Fine man.
Tom	He says the Indians then had a different idea of trash than we do.
Sidney	How different?
Tom	Well. I don't know how. Like it was sacred trash, or the trash was sacred, or something.
Sidney	There's trash people and there's "made" people. Trash people are throwaways, no accounts. "Made" people are a higher class of people.
Tom	I see that.
Sidney	Wayne says that whole other side of the road there's a pueblo. The petroglyphs themselves are up higher, in the rocks.
Tom	I know. Myra was telling me—
Sidney	Wait here a second, will you? *(Exits)*
Tom	*(Aside)* Sidney is a "made" person.
Voice Off	You're a fucking worm, pal. You're a piece of shit. You are trash. You got no reason to live at all.

TOM stands, looks, sits. SIDNEY re-enters with a map.

Sidney   See, you look at a map, and you see where the land's all cut up, those are homesteaders. Then you see these open areas, those are either state land or they're old land grants from the Spanish days. Most of the land is owned by the state.

Tom   It's amazing.

Sidney   Sure. So you look at this map, and right here is the ranch. You can see—there's hardly a mark on it, it's almost exactly the original land grant from the King of Spain.

Tom   Amazing.

Sidney   See, the United States came in, and they said—all the original deeds, we'll respect those, everybody's got title, they'll keep their title.

Tom   Are there problems with that?

Sidney   Well, you'd best have title insurance, but the U.S. made a deal with New Mexico, they said all's clear and all's safe. So it's usually all right. Now, you look at the map, and there's the old pueblos spread out over the ranch. And here's the rock art, and so on, and so on.

Tom   I'll be darned. So you got three or four levels of history right here on this map.

Sidney   You bet we do. And here's the road, goes right through the one here, and here's the dig.

Tom   I see.

They stare at the map.

That's really something.

They stare.

Tom   Yeah. *(Sits)*

Sidney   And here's the house. Same as it was. *(Looking around)* We had all this rain, hands afraid I'll raise hell, they watered on top of the rain. Now, you see those ash, the young ones there? I put those in in '87. ...*(Out)*

LIGHTS UP on TOM and MYRA.

Myra   You know why they got a dig out there?

Tom   Because they're widening the road.

Myra   You know why they're widening the road?

Tom   For the trucks heading down for I-40.

Myra   No, for WIPP. You know what WIPP is?

Tom   We ain't been here that long.

Myra   Waste Isolation Pilot Plant.

Tom   What's that?

Myra   To do with the nuclear waste, coming down from the north. They're widening the road to minimize the chance for accidents. Avoid poisoning the whole countryside. Man, beast, and bones of the old dead people.

Tom   Bones, too.

Myra   Everything.

Tom   You have an appointment with José Ortiz?

Myra   Yes.

Tom   Why?

Myra   I know the man. He sells *remedios*. Did he do anything weird?

Tom   I don't know.

Myra   What did he do?

Tom	At one point he put on a mask.
Myra	He has masks.
Tom	You don't think it's weird?
Myra	I think he's for real.
Tom	He likes you.
Myra	Oh?
Tom	He scared me with that mask. I don't know why he did that. *(OUT)*

LIGHTS UP on SIDNEY and KATHRINE.

Sidney	There'll be scarcity and a husbanding. It's a natural law. The strong will eat the weak. I say eat.
Kathrine	What'd you say, dear?
Sidney	Resources. I like this guy, Rainwater. I like his name. Rainwater.
Kathrine	Oh. Is he the one...?
Sidney	Yeah, he's got a billion. Microsoft, oil and gas, etcetera.
Kathrine	Oh, yes.
Sidney	And land. Land's a commodity resource.
Kathrine	That's what you always say, dear.
Sidney	That's why I like him. He agrees with me.

Both laugh.

	Knows how a fortune's built. Stick with one or two things. Systemic change. Things change and open up. Get in on it early, and stick with it.
Kathrine	That's right, dear.
Sidney	Understands capitalism, does Mr. Rainwater. And this is

the place to be. Right here in America. We understand it
here. We have the data here.

Kathrine   Well, definitely. *(Pause)* Now, Tom...?

Sidney   Tom? Yeah? What about Tom?

Kathrine   Well, I don't know. Does he have a plan? Do you think he
has a plan? *(Pause)* I'm worried about those two.

LIGHTS UP on MYRA and DON JOSÉ .

Don José   See there's a force on the land, all over, on the surface of
the land, in the holes, the crevices, the hot lava of the
earth, and in the air—it's the force that's built up from the
slaughtered beasts. It's starting in to fill up the atmosphere. You get to saturation, it causes drought and disease
and body formation. Let the blind see, and the deaf hear.

Myra   Body formation? Like ghosts?

Don José   No, like bodies.

Myra   Like...?

Don José   Karma. You understand karma? Means my actions in this
world have a consequence in the spirit world. Cause and
effect. In fact, it's what I am. *(Silence)* Yes?

Myra   I think so.

Don José   The animals are slaughtered, by the millions, the tens of
millions, without thought, without respect, without pay-
ment, and after much suffering. This leaves a residue on
the land, and a cry in the spirit world. Poisons are formed
on the earth, and bodies are made in the spirit world.

Myra   Like the Skinwalker?

Don José   Some people say the Skinwalker, some say it's Coyote,
some say it's the guardians.

Myra	The guardians?
Don José	Yes, everything in nature has a guardian, an ally, in the spirit world. The trees, the insects, the mountains, the water, all things. Some people say. You see all these herbs? Herbs are interesting. They are there for man. Nature has prepared them as help for man. They are the little healers, from nature to man. If man will take care of nature, then nature will provide for man.
Myra	Have you seen the petroglyphs on my father's ranch?
Don José	Yes.
Myra	How do you see them?
Don José	There are certain places where the spirit world and this world meet. There are some of those places on your father's land.
Myra	I feel that.
Don José	Yes. Two worlds. *Así es.*
Myra	The petroglyphs?
Don José	*Así es.*
Myra	Thank you.
Don José	You have a path. You have work to do.
Myra	Thank you.
Don José	*De nada.*
Myra	And my husband? Tom?
Don José	*Tiene vergüenza.*
Myra	Pardon?
Don José	He has shame.
Myra	Yes. He...
Don José	*Y miedo.*
Myra	I'm sorry?
Don José	Fear. He has work to do. *Tiene trabajo.*
Myra	What should he do?

Don José	*Entrada es subida.* Yes?
Myra	What does that mean?
Don José	The way in is the way up. Your father, got to give the man credit. What he's achieved. No room for the ego, or petty fears. Takes nerve, courage, character. You must appreciate a man like that.
Myra	Thank you. I do. And my husband, Tom?
Don José	Tell him to give himself up. Tell him to get down on his knees and surrender. *Es paria. Orgullo. (Laughs)*
Myra	I'm sorry?
Don José	Write it down.
Myra	And my work...?
Don José	Stop. Think. Think it through. People don't think. At night, before you go to bed, you think about the next day, what you have to do, how you will do it, in what order, with what aim.
Myra	Sometimes I do, but—
Don José	That's what we're here for, to take care. *(OUT)*

LIGHTS UP on TOM, recording.

Tom	I saw a man in a tree. When the wind blew, he talked sound- lessly and made faces at me. He jabbered in the language of trees and old gods. He wore an ancient headdress and had arms like wings. Disdainfully, he mocked me for an idiot, and warned of sufferings yet to come. *(Exits)*

Enter MYRA.

Myra	Tom? *(Out)*

254

LIGHTS UP on TOM and HARTLEY.

Hartley	I have a total of 726 arrowheads.
Tom	Wow, Hartley.
Hartley	Every kind of point. All sizes. Some ancient, some recent.
Tom	Where'd you find 'em all?
Hartley	Some over in West Texas. But mainly right here. They're all over the place. You just have to have an eye. Especially in the winter, I got time to wander. I'm out there, walking the land.
Tom	You ever seen a spaceship?
Hartley	Hell, no.
Tom	Myra read of one, is all. She believes it was a sighting.
Hartley	When was this?
Tom	Late eighteen hundreds?
Hartley	I'll be darned. *(Silence)* You're welcome to see my collection any time, Tom. More than welcome.
Tom	Thank you.
Hartley	Been offered tons of money for it. But I won't sell.
Tom	I'd like that.
Hartley	And I'll take you hunting for arrowheads, if you want to go.
Tom	Sure. Are there many accidents out there, Hartley?
Hartley	Out where? In the canyons?
Tom	On the road.
Hartley	Hell, yes. Gets so dark you can't see nothin'. Why they're widening the darn road and turning over all them bones. Digging up a whole pueblo. Talk about artifacts and shit, I'm telling you. Shards and points, all kinds of stuff coming out of there. Got stuff coming out of these digs, even the Indians won't go near it. *(OUT)*

LIGHTS UP on TOM and MYRA.

Myra	The wolf—he likes to run alone?
Tom	Yeah. Sometimes he can go with a pack. He could even be leader. Like Richard. He was a leader. He was smart and tough. He was canny. He was ruthless. He'd do what he had to. But mainly he goes alone. He likes it alone.
Myra	Can he have a mate?
Tom	He's looking at it. He goes into it with his eyes open. I see his eyes. He's looking at it.
Myra	How did the wolf get wounded?
Tom	The wolf is wounded?
Myra	Well, he wouldn't be so protective if he wasn't hurting.
Tom	He's at the door. The wolf is at the door.
Myra	Is he?

They listen—COYOTES, etc.

Voice Off	You don't know anything but crime, you fuck!
Tom	*(Stands)* Who's out there? *(Looks)* You hear that?
Myra	One of the hands?
Tom	I don't think so.
Myra	It's not just you that's nervous, Tom.
Tom	I'm not nervous.
Myra	Something's been disturbed. They're finding lots of bones. They've dug into a big burial ground on the side of the road. I feel that something has released. And that's why you're feeling—
Voice Off	I feel shut up in a cave.

Tom	Did you hear?
Myra	I'm not sure what that was.
Tom	Did you hear that?
Myra	I'm not sure. *(Pause)* What's the matter?
Tom	Nothing. We told the sonofabitch not to drive. He was too drunk to drive. Richard. Thought we were friends.
Myra	He thought or you thought?
Tom	I thought. He had no friends. Loner. Sidney reminds me of him. Man of the frontier. Rides alone. High stakers.
Myra	My father is a conservative person.
Tom	You got to admire a man like that.
Myra	With many friends.
Tom	Get loaded and fly down the highway. Ninety, a hundred miles an hour. Richard, I mean.
Myra	It was suicide.
Tom	In those days you drank and drove.
Myra	You do, Tom.
Tom	You drove fast.
Myra	You do it, now. Nothing's changed.
Tom	Couldn't tell him shit.
Myra	Can't tell you shit.
Tom	Dog eat dog was the world he lived in.
Myra	It's not the only world.
Tom	It's not?
Myra	No. I feel there's betrayal in there.
Tom	Where?
Myra	I sense betrayal. *(Silence)* I have to go. I'm having lunch with my mother. *(Exits)*
Tom	Okay.

He hears ALBERTO *and* HARTLEY, *off:*

Hartley	ALBERT?
Alberto	YO!
Hartley	DID YA GO DOWN AND SEE?
Alberto	SI!
Hartley	WHA'D YA SEE?
Alberto	NADA!
Hartley	DID YA SEE TRACKS?
Alberto	NO!
Hartley	NADA?
Alberto	NADA!
Hartley	NO NOTHIN'?
Alberto	NADA!
Hartley	HOKAY!

TOM trembles, looks off. (OUT)

LIGHTS UP on TOM *and* FRANK.

Frank	You married?
Tom	I am.
Frank	Don't take her for granted, or one day she won't be there. You'll be alone with your own skin then, amigo, walking the road. Resentful, dazed, and mainly drunk. Maybe get run over like a dog. (Laughs)
Tom	Thank you.
Frank	We need to make *muchos amends, amigo. Reparación.* Not just for our own sins, ongoing, but for the sins of the fathers.
Tom	I accept that.

Frank	Do you? You don't see much. Hard to see. Birth, marriage, old age, death—very strange. If people saw the plain truth, they'd get religion fast, or go mad, or kill themselves. Quick or slow, either way.
Tom	I appreciate it.
Frank	Sure you do.
Tom	I feel like I do.
Frank	What you need, what I've been saying, is reparation—so the line's not lost forever. Let the blind see and the deaf hear.
Tom	I hear you. *(Pause)*
Frank	Do you?
Tom	I think so. *(Looking around)*
Frank	What are you trying to find with that thing?
Tom	My recorder?
Frank	*Sí.*
Tom	Reality.
Frank	*Aí*!
Tom	Catch the sound, you know? I believe in that.
Frank	You hear yourself, ever? Listen to yourself?
Tom	Uh, yeah, sure, sometimes I do. Yes.
Frank	Good. That's good. *Bueno.*
Tom	Can I get a decent meal here?
Frank	Yes, you can.
Tom	Who do I talk to? You?
Frank	You can tell me. Steaks are good here. You eat steak? *(Pause)* Chile sauce, *rojo o verde*? The green is hot, man. *(Pause)* What do you want? *(OUT)*

LIGHTS UP on MYRA and KATHRINE.

Myra	Can't say it was alive, quite.
Kathrine	No, dear.
Myra	Had a heartbeat.
Kathrine	I don't think it was quite alive.
Myra	Then they looked in there, it was still.
Kathrine	These things happen.
Myra	I wonder what it means.
Kathrine	They just happen.
Myra	Don't you think it's, uh, distasteful?
Kathrine	Well, yes. I suppose.
Myra	It's distasteful. Like it was a barnacle, or a slug.
Kathrine	No, no.
Myra	It's more like a current, like an electrical current. Me and Tom, we gave it a start, a jolt, and then its momentum stopped.
Kathrine	It wasn't your fault.
Myra	I know that.
Kathrine	Nor Tom's.

They hear HARTLEY *and* ALBERTO, *off.*

Hartley	*No hay paso.*
Alberto	*¿Dónde?*
Hartley	*Allá!*
Alberto	*¿En la montaña?*
Hartley	*Sí.*
Alberto	*¿Porqué?*
Hartley	*Dice el patrón.*
Alberto	*Hokay.*
Hartley	*No hay paso.*

Alberto	*Hokay.*
Myra	Did you hear someone?
Kathrine	Where?
Myra	Speaking. Outside.
Kathrine	I think it was Hartley and Alberto.
Myra	Oh.
Kathrine	They talk a lot.
Myra	I have to tell you, I have to say it. There are strange things going on, freaky things—chemical things, environmental things, spiritual/criminal things going on.
Kathrine	What kind of things, dear?
Myra	I just told you—criminal things.
Kathrine	Oh. People have always complained, one reason or another.
Myra	We don't see it all. We don't know the half of it. There's an invisible world. *(OUT)*

LIGHTS UP on TOM and DON JOSÉ .

Tom	Don José . *(Pause)*
Don José	Yes? *(Pause)*
Tom	I need, uh, help.
Don José	The idea is to break through. You get your body into the sweat lodge, it's going to suffer. There's your chance. You're making a power, a medicine, spirit world comes into the lodge. But you have to stay in there, with Mother Earth. You pray and you tell the truth. You're not so involved with yourself. Warriors in there, screaming. Outside, shit just goes on, again and again. No will. Warrior has to overcome his weaknesses, his fear, his pain, master his body, touch the power, the thunderbolt.

Voice Off	First you have to die, pal.
Tom	*(Looking off)* What? *(Pause)*
Don José	You have to die. *(OUT)*

LIGHTS UP on TOM and MYRA in their cabin. TOM replays:

(Tape) "There is another reality. It has neither shape nor form, but it can appear to man, or it can come down through the top of his head like a thunderbolt. There is a door there."

Myra	That's good stuff.

TOM turns off recorder. Pause. They hear ALBERTO and HARTLEY, off:

Hartley	*No hay paso.*
Alberto	*¿Dondé?*
Hartley	*Allá!*
Alberto	*¿En la montaña?*
Hartley	*Sí.*
Alberto	*¿Porqué?*
Hartley	*Dice el patrón.*
Alberto	*Hokay.*
Hartley	*No hay paso.*
Alberto	*Hokay.*

TOM shivers.

Myra	You alright?
Tom	It was them again.
Myra	They talk a lot.

Tom	What is it with that fucking Alberto? He whistles and sings to himself like nobody's in earshot. I can't hear myself think. Is he talking to someone? Who could he be talking to?
Myra	That's Hartley.
Tom	The fucker can't speak English.
Myra	Hartley?
Tom	No, Alberto. Hartley keeps saying, "Siesta, siesta," and Alberto says, "No, no." Then he whistles. That's him. Hartley is walking away from him, and Alberto is whistling out of embarrassment.
Myra	He doesn't have a car. He can't go nowhere, and it's Sunday.
Tom	He should ask for a ride. He walks around whistling and singing to himself.
Myra	He watches Mexican television.
Tom	He should go back to Chihuahua.
Myra	He does go. He goes back down there for awhile, not Chihuahua, Durango. He works hard, then he splits for a couple months, then he comes back again.
Tom	Where does he go?
Myra	He goes to Durango. I don't know where that is. He's got two families, one here and one in Durango. Nice arrangement.
Tom	Fuckhead was in my dream.
Myra	Alberto?
Tom	No! Richard!
Myra	How would I know that? *(Aside)* You shit. You piece of shit.
Tom	I don't know what he was doing in my fucking dream, like we were fucking friends or something.

Myra	Everybody's you in your dream, they're all you, all the parts.
Tom	Richard, too?
Myra	Yeah. He stands for something in you.
Tom	What?
Myra	Tell me the dream.
Tom	We were on the run in Michigan. *(Silence)* On the run in Michigan. *(Silence)*
Myra	What happened?
Tom	Windshield cut his head off. Meat in the machinery.
Myra	Oh, my God.
Tom	State police hate that kind of thing. Gots to clean it up, look for the head.
Myra	Tom?
Tom	What?
Myra	Bye! *(Exits)*
Tom	*(Speaking into the tape recorder)* They were heating the rocks. Big bonfire. Red warriors standing around not waiting for anything. They said Richard was in there and I said, "He ain't. He ain't in there." I was glad he died. Lodge power so strong, bullets can't penetrate the skin. Pray for your relatives. Warriors screaming. All my relations. We're in the dark. You can dedicate here, here you can suffer and make amends. I can't tell if I'm screaming. Take the flesh from my bones, please. I am totally ashamed. Put my bones on them rocks and burn them up with the cedar and the sage. I'm sorry for everything I done. Stupid vanity of it all. Sorrow of the undead, in the rocks. Hot. Scalding. I can't breathe. Sweat leader, let me out. Open up. Try and bear it, white-eyes. Open up, please. Don't think about

yourself. I'm going to die, sweat leader. You won't die, white-eyes, not today. I think I'm going to die. I'm afraid I'm going to die. Then the flap blew open and I spun out of the lodge. I broke the circle. All the warriors looking down and away from me as I passed by them, just above their heads in the black heat, their eyes the colors of coral and jade.

Pause. A PETROGLYPH FACE *appears in the window, along with a loud* BANG. TOM *jumps. (*OUT*)*

LIGHTS UP on MYRA *and* AURORA.

Aurora	How is your program?
Myra	My program?
Aurora	Isn't it a radio program?
Myra	A documentary.
Aurora	Right.
Myra	You're in it.
Aurora	Cool. Would you like my report?
Myra	On tape?

AURORA laughs.

	Why do you laugh?
Aurora	It's just a level, you know. There are thought tapes, too. In between, like I explained.
Myra	I don't understand.
Aurora	You can put it on tape.
Myra	You do get the impression, you know, that you're sort of unwinding?

Aurora	Uh-huh.
Myra	Like it's all set up. No, like it has to happen, you know. Like it's already happened, so it has to happen. I'm sorry.
Aurora	No. *Correcto. Eso es.*
Myra	Like a replay?
Aurora	*Aí.* Gots to get even with the movement down.
Myra	What?
Aurora	With the movement up. Anyway, it matters. The Skinwalker's name is Richard.
Myra	Oh!
Aurora	He's a cowboy type.
Myra	Oh, my goodness!
Aurora	He's not cleared.
Myra	What did you do?
Aurora	I tried to burn him.
Myra	Oh!
Aurora	He wouldn't burn.
Myra	Oh!
Aurora	Gots to be a sword. Be the terrible swift sword of the Lord.
Myra	Oh! *(OUT)*

LIGHTS UP on TOM. Replays:

Don José	*(Tape)* "It is not unworthy to sit down and die."

Enter MYRA.

Myra	*(Off)* Hi!
Tom	Hi, Sweetie!
Myra	*(Entering)* Hi!

266

Tom	Was that first "Hi" for me?
Myra	No, for Hartley.
Tom	You went to the rocks?
Myra	Well, yeah.
Tom	How was it?
Myra	How was what? *(Silence)* It was fine. I followed tracks. There were a bunch of cars. Above me I heard voices, like chanting. OMM, or something. I tracked them. It was a group of women. But it was nice. I didn't mind. I went my own way, then I came across them again. One of the women was up on the big rock, spread-eagled, naked, singing. I didn't mind.
Tom	Were they all naked?
Myra	I don't know. It was nice, really, she was just spread out naked on the rock, singing.
Tom	They were stoned?
Myra	No. I don't think so. Just happy to be up there. Like me.
Tom	Who was that woman on the rock?

Enter SIDNEY and KATHRINE.

Sidney	*(Facetious)* Well, now you all get to see this work of art I made.
Tom	Good job, Sidney.
Sidney	He's the Defiant Indian.
Myra	Oh, what's he made of?
Tom	He's beautiful.
Myra	Isn't he, though? I think he's made of brass.
Kathrine	Well, no. His face is copper, and his shield, his shield is of gold.

Sidney	This here is the Defiant Indian.
Hartley	*(Entering)* Excuse me. Oh, that's Kwanah Parker.
Sidney	Oh yeah, that's who it is, all right.
Hartley	He was a great Comanche warrior, and he was half white.
Kathrine	Oh, is that so?
Hartley	Yeah, his mother was a captive who stayed on with the tribe.
Kathrine	Oh, my!
Hartley	Yeah, he was a great war chief. Fierce. Hated the whites, and fought for his people, the Comanche side. But he was a smart one, old Kwanah. I think he was one of the few of 'em who died a natural death.
Kathrine	Is that right, Hartley?
Hartley	Yes, Missus. In some town someplace, in Oklahoma I think it was. Used his mother's last name.
Myra	That's what the road-workers say over at the site, "Well, did you dig up a chief yet?" That's their attitude.
Sidney	What it is, skulls and crossbones, dug out of the refuse.
Hartley	Well, they're finding some crushed-up bones, and skulls with scrapes on them, startles their thinking.
Myra	How's that?
Sidney	*(Signalling to* HARTLEY*)* Sheer amount of garbage. Just threw it out the front door, I suppose.
Tom	But finding a skull's a big thing. A skull is big.
Myra	Why is that?
Tom	I don't remember why.
Hartley	Comanche had regular routes for their raids, and regular times. It was seasonal. Certain time of year, you knew the Comanche were coming through. They went all the way down into Mexico and came back a different route.

	Apache had horses, but the Comanche were the real horse people. Apache could run a hundred miles on foot, though, cavalry couldn't keep up.
Kathrine	Is that right, Hartley?
Hartley	Yes, Missus. They'd kill their horses and run into the Sierra Madre down in Old Mexico. Couldn't be found unless they wanted to show themselves.
Kathrine	Well, dinner's called.
Hartley	Excuse me. *(Exits)*
Tom	This is fantastic wine.
Sidney	We'll take it with us, bring your glass.
Tom	*(Aside, to MYRA)* Who was the woman on the rock?
Myra	Mrs. Saunders. Come on. *(OUT)*

LIGHTS UP on KATHRINE and MYRA.

	There was a woman on the rock. Painted, tattooed. She stood up naked in the rain and sang a song.
Kathrine	Who was she?
Myra	She was...I think she was...actually, I don't know. I'm not sure.
Kathrine	What was she doing there?
Myra	She was chanting. It sounded Indian.
Kathrine	Oh, my.
Myra	I was going to tape her, but it seemed wrong.
Kathrine	We have a friend, she works with wayward girls, teenagers, Navajo mostly. And she says it's the most remarkable thing, the wind comes up a certain way, and these girls, and they're all assimilated as they can be, they get all quiet and frightened and they're eyes get big...

Myra	It's deep. Goes back thousands of years.
Kathrine	I know it. But it's only a minority believes in that stuff. It's the old witchcraft. There's some believe in it entirely. Some don't believe it, but stay cautious. Then there's others, they just scoff at the whole thing. *(Pause)* That woman shouldn't be up there, you know. She's trespassing.
Myra	They come anyway, Mom. They just climb over the fence.
Kathrine	Well, your father's trying to keep 'em out. What if something happened to someone? Or they started a fire? And they leave their trash.
Myra	I know. There's just too much out there for people to look at and dig into. There's places even I haven't seen yet. Hartley, he'll comes across a new site two or three times a year.
Kathrine	Well, your dad is trying to take care of it all.
Myra	Hartley says there's old masks they found at Comanche Gap, even the elders won't touch them.
Kathrine	Why is that, dear?
Myra	They're too sacred. They've got too much power. *(OUT)*

LIGHTS UP on MYRA and AURORA.

Aurora	These people, it's not so cool, they sneak up on me, and they leave money around, see if I'll steal it.
Myra	The Saunders?
Aurora	Yeah, them.
Myra	I don't know them very well.
Aurora	*(Bursts into tears)* Them!
Myra	Oh! Are they treating you badly?
Aurora	*Ai!*
Myra	I'm sorry.

Aurora	Kids gots to suffer, or they won't learn. Real things. Woman's a hopeless neurotic, trapped in her thoughts and feelings. *(Weeps)*
Myra	Aurora?
Aurora	What?
Myra	Mrs. Saunders?
Aurora	Woman's gone spongy, turned herself into a witch.
Myra	I saw her on the rocks, near the petroglyphs.
Aurora	That's her. She goes there.
Myra	Does she...?
Aurora	No, more him. Man's suspicious. Mr. Saunders, he's suspicious.
Myra	Suspicious?
Aurora	They torture me.
Myra	They torture you?
Aurora	You know, they want my light.
Myra	How do they torture you?
Aurora	With mistrust, and with lies. *Celosos.*
Myra	Jealousy?
Aurora	They're jealous because of the kids.
Myra	Oh, I see.
Aurora	They're jealous of my light. Kids know. They feel my light. They look at me, and they lie. I don't like that look.
Myra	The kids?
Aurora	No, them. The parents.
Myra	Doesn't sound good, Aurora.
Aurora	He takes his shoes off and he sneaks around.
Myra	Mr. Saunders?
Aurora	Yes. He'll come in, he'll take off his shoes, and start sneaking around.

Myra	Why?
Aurora	He's trying to catch me. Thinks I'm a witch, a *bruja*. Which I am. I have the light. But don't tell them, don't say anything.
Myra	I won't.
Aurora	Make them paranoid, resentful. I feel sorry for the kids, is all. Day will come, I'll be gone.
Myra	Oh, that would be terrible, Aurora.
Aurora	Just nice to have a friend I can talk to.
Myra	Same here, Aurora.
Aurora	I feel better now.
Myra	Good.
Aurora	I'm tracking the Skinwalker.
Myra	You are?
Aurora	Yes. He's got to make a move. He's in torment, like me. Stress coming down. Causes a turmoil in the spirit world.
Myra	What do you mean? What kind of move?
Aurora	A movement down, like I say. He's got to have a body.
Myra	Oh!
Aurora	Highway accident. Spirit's trying to heal itself.
Myra	You see betrayal there?
Aurora	I'm not clear on it.
Myra	That's okay.
Aurora	There's treachery, though, goes without saying. Treachery abounds. It's unconscious, is what I'm saying. Nobody does it on purpose. That's why you get all this fucked up shit out there. Fucked up, if you'll excuse the language. Just fucked up to the max. *(OUT)*

LIGHTS UP on TOM and SIDNEY.

Tom	These people were here and now they're bones. One day I'll be bones, too. A grimacing skull, half my teeth gone. You think about that, ever?
Sidney	No, I don't think about that much. I think mathematically. I work with numbers. Time defeats all. So I get up and I live my days. I don't think about it. I don't worry about it.
Tom	I hear you there.
Sidney	But it's good policy to preserve your value.
Tom	Mathematically?
Sidney	So much of this, so much of that. It's an exactitude. Numbers don't lie.
Tom	And death?
Sidney	Breathing stops. Brain function ceases. Subside back into the earth. Worms start on you.
Tom	Thank you.
Sidney	What for?
Tom	I don't know, actually.
Sidney	What saves us is the idea, Tom.
Tom	The idea?
Sidney	Of property. Who owns what, when.
Tom	I see.
Sidney	Do you?
Tom	I think I do.
Sidney	It's what makes this country great. (*Out*)

Lights up on Myra and Don José .

Don José	*Es mucho trabajo.* You work out every day, you make a muscle, okay? *Es lo mismo.*

Myra	A muscle?
Don José	*Sí,* a part. It's alive.
Myra	What is it?
Don José	It's something in the brain. It's a part.
Myra	Where is it?
Don José	In the brain. In the head.
Myra	In the head.
Don José	It's like a light. You know, like a switch, or a button.
Myra	Is it an Indian thing?
Don José	It's where we connect.
Myra	You and me?
Don José	Not only you and me. It's the spirit world. Especially. *(Pause)* There's like an inside, and an outside, and that.
Myra	That?
Don José	Where they meet together. It's the spirit world. *(Pause)* It contains them. *Eso es.*
Myra	Do we all have it?
Don José	No. Like I was saying. *(OUT)*

LIGHTS UP on TOM and SIDNEY.

Sidney	A man works hard, makes sacrifices, the land can be his. It's a natural law, you might say. Key idea there is sacrifice. Man's free to risk. 'Course, there are people who think they can do things. People who think wrongs ought to be righted. *(OUT)*

LIGHTS UP on KATHRINE and MYRA.

Kathrine	What do you think of that rock art?

Myra	The petroglyphs are signs from the Old People. Signs on rocks. I think they are tracks. Traces. Like lines of power, or influences.
Kathrine	Do you?
Myra	Yes, Mom. *(OUT)*

LIGHTS UP on TOM and SIDNEY.

Sidney	It's a question of title to the land. An agreement of law. Anyone can do it. But the main thing is the idea of property, and the rule of law. People tend to undervalue the idea. It's like we're on a raft. Nobody knows where the raft is going. But you can get a more comfortable spot on the raft. *(OUT)*

LIGHTS UP on MYRA and KATHRINE.

Kathrine	Look. You can see the trucks going by on the highway from here, but you can't hear them, I'm glad to say. They look like toys. It's an eerie thing, sometimes. *(OUT)*

LIGHTS UP on TOM and SIDNEY.

Tom	Car crash?
Sidney	Yes.
Tom	It's a rainy night in Michigan. Roads are slick. We're drinking in a bar. I see Richard getting into his vehicle. I think to call out: "Hey, Richard, don't drive," but I hesitate. I don't move, I don't say anything, and I have a premonition. I don't know what that is, I don't understand it, like I saw it before it happened, the whole thing, like a

	projection or a wish, like a murderous impulse of mine—
	fulfilled down the road moments later in a vicious crash.
Sidney	Where were you then?
Tom	I was in another car. They didn't have seat belts in those days.
Sidney	No, they didn't.
Tom	He went right through the windshield. He was descended from the mountain people of Virginia, directly into the heartland.
Sidney	Excuse me. (*Exits*)
Tom	Walked around like he had a right to be here. (*OUT*)

LIGHTS UP on HARTLEY and SIDNEY.

Hartley	I was talking to Wayne. Early.
Sidney	Excellent fellow.
Hartley	Marks on the skulls?
Sidney	Yes.
Hartley	Skulls and femurs?
Sidney	Yes.
Hartley	Turns out they were eating each other. The Old People.
Sidney	Well, now.
Hartley	Cannibals, some of 'em.
Sidney	Well, now. I'd not tell Myra just yet.
Hartley	I won't.
Sidney	My, my.

Enter TOM.

Tom	Hi.
Sidney	We were just saying.

Hartley	Scotch-Irish came over in the early eighteenth century, formed the American attitude.
Sidney	They were an abused people over in Europe. Hardened 'em up.
Hartley	Every man for his self and let the devil take the hindmost.
Sidney	Fought and won our independence.
Hartley	Indians woke up one day, there was ten thousand Scotch-Irish forming settlements in the Appalachians.
Sidney	Woke up too late. Could have been a Balkan situation, with French, Spanish, English, Iroquois and Cherokee nations.
Hartley	Stripping the land, corn liquor cutting the fat and gristle in their mouths. Used up the soil and game and moved on.
Sidney	People didn't want certain products, other people wouldn't have made 'em. *(Exits)*
Tom	*(Aside)* No reason to pollute the waters. *(He looks off. Out)*

Lights up on Myra and Kathrine.

Kathrine	Look at those truckers, how they do, driving on into the night. ...*(Out)*

Lights up on Tom, Sidney, and Hartley.

Voice Off	The people have become fat and criminal-minded.

Tom looks over his shoulder.

Sidney	What's that?

Tom	Nothing.
Sidney	I thought you said something.
Tom	No, no. That wasn't me. *(Pause)*
Sidney	Keep in mind, this whole country was once under water. The earth's axis is not the same as it was. We have satellites now, they span the curvature of this planet. Mathematics.
Tom	I was just thinking...
Voice Off	New wounds piling on the old.
Sidney	What's that?
Tom	I don't know what I was thinking.
Sidney	It's like we're ants on a raft. No way of knowing where it's headed. Nothing we can do about that. But we can get a better spot on the raft. *(EXITS)*
Voice Off	MU-TATED.
Tom	Jesus Christ...you hear that?
Hartley	Sidney? He's right, more than likely.
Tom	Sidney?
Hartley	Man knows what he's talking about.
Tom	What did you say?
Hartley	I was saying, Sidney's right, more than likely.
Tom	Oh. I know he is. *(OUT)*

LIGHTS UP on MYRA and KATHRINE.

Myra	You know Aurora?
Kathrine	'Course I do. You've become quite friendly with her.
Myra	I have. I was going to ask you about the Saunders.
Kathrine	Oh, I think they saved that girl. She comes from the criminal class, you know. They took her out of that girls' home over there and gave her a chance. She ought to be grateful.

Myra	I think she's in a situation.
Kathrine	What kind of situation?
Myra	With the Saunders.
Kathrine	Well, she's lucky to have it. That's all I can say.
Myra	Okay. Thanks, Mom. *(OUT)*

LIGHTS UP on HARTLEY and TOM.

Hartley	That dig out by the road, that was me found the skeleton and the skull.
Tom	That was you?
Hartley	That was me, scuffling about. Looked down and there it was. Idea is to save it all from destruction. All it takes is one trespasser to ruin it all.
Tom	*(Distracted)* Uh, I heard you're a fan of Geronimo's.
Hartley	I painted a picture of him once and put it up on a windmill. So you'd see his face as you went by.
Tom	Where was this?
Hartley	In Texas. West Texas. Apache country.
Tom	That's something, Hartley.
Hartley	I admire Geronimo as a religious leader of his people. Taciturn old Geronimo. He had a hard job. He was a war shaman. This was a warrior religion we're talking about. This life here is nothing else but a preparation for the spirit world. A test.
Voice Off	I've been to the other side, fuckhead! And you don't know shit!
Tom	You hear a voice, Hartley?
Hartley	What kind of voice?
Tom	A human voice.
Hartley	No.
Tom	Listen. *(Silence)*

Hartley	I had a dig in my own back yard.
Tom	Where was this again?
Hartley	West Texas. Took a mammoth out of there. Could've started a museum of my own, but I got a paleontologist and an archaeologist in there with me and I kept it as it was.
Tom	Good for you, Hartley.
Hartley	Are you all right? *(OUT)*

LIGHTS UP on MYRA and KATHRINE.

Myra	We've had some losses, made some mistakes.
Kathrine	'Course you have.
Myra	Hard to have a family, keep it going.
Kathrine	You will, dear. Just need to settle down, and stay with it, and work hard.
Myra	Thanks, Mom. *(Breaks into tears)*
Kathrine	Don't cry, dear. *(Pause)* People think they need to pursue their own happiness these days, the children be damned. Think they're entitled, without payment or suffering of any kind. *(OUT)*

LIGHTS UP on TOM and HARTLEY.

Hartley	I had some Hopi working for me in Texas. Crazy mother-fuckers.
Tom	Well, they shouldn't drink.
Hartley	Hated the Rez.
Tom	Sidney?
Hartley	He's a boss. You know, a boss. He's a little remote, you might say. But I like it here. He runs a tight ship. You do your

job. It's quiet. Nobody bothers you most of the time. Place is loaded with old artifacts, shards and arrowheads and fossils and such. I like it just fine. I like ranching. I like the West.

Tom We'll be moving on, Myra and me.

Hartley Hey now, Tom, you see that yonder?

Tom Where?

Hartley Right-chare! My lord!

Upstage, an IMAGE *appears of a deer-dancer, neolithic, huge rack of antlers, upright on two legs, wide, staring eyes, burning eyes. The eyes should be Sidney's eyes. A* FLASH, *a* LOUD DRUM BEAT, *and the* IMAGE *is gone.*

Tom What was that?

Hartley Oh, that was a muledeer, I believe, rose up and looked right at us. Lord have mercy. *(OUT)*

LIGHTS UP on MYRA and KATHRINE.

Myra Skinwalkers. They come through holes. From the other side. They're like...like threads.

Kathrine Oh.

Myra It's not cheesy, you know, Mom. It's neater than that, it's the coolest idea.

Kathrine What is the idea?

Myra There's a wind, like I told you, or a light, a wind of light, you could say. Incorruptible. And they come through.

Myra What do they want?

Kathrine Another chance is what they want, Mom. *(OUT)*

LIGHTS UP on AURORA and MYRA.

Aurora	Skinwalker's about to make his move.
Myra	How do you know?
Aurora	Stands to reason, don't it?
Myra	What reason?
Aurora	I get into this right state, I can hear his thinking.
Myra	His thinking?
Aurora	Yes. He's pissed he's cut off. *Está celoso.*
Myra	Jealousy?
Aurora	Envy and rage.
Myra	What will he do?
Aurora	I don't know. He's got a body. He's found his body.
Myra	That doesn't make any sense at all, Aurora.
Aurora	Okay, fine.
Myra	And you? What will you do?
Aurora	I'm on my way.
Myra	Do the Saunders know?
Aurora	No, and don't tell 'em.
Myra	Of course not.
Aurora	Not your mother, neither.
Myra	I wouldn't, Aurora.
Aurora	*Bueno. Vamos a ver. (OUT)*

LIGHTS UP on FRANK and TOM. TOM is on his hands and knees, beat up, bloody.

Tom	My wife was with her mother. I was alone in the cabin. He just walked in.
Frank	Who?

Tom	A stranger. I tried to close the door on him and he ripped it off its hinges.
Frank	Did he say something?
Tom	Yeah, how he wanted to stick me. He wanted to have the experience of killing someone, especially an Anglo like me, a white man—with his knife. "I'm going to kill you now," he said.
Voice Off	I'm gonna cut your throat, you piece of shit.
Frank	What did you do?
Tom	He charged and I threw the table at him. I kept the table between me and him and I started pleading right away. But he came after me. I ran into the bedroom and tried to close the door on him. We struggled and he tore the door off its hinges. I had this odd thought: "Two doors."
Voice Off	You got no right to live, motherfucker. I'm going to cut your face off.
Frank	And then?
Tom	Then I got right down on my knees and started begging for my life. I tried to look him in the eye, so I'd be real to him. He had this stare. I had to make eye contact. I knew my life depended on it.
Frank	Why didn't you scream?
Tom	It was the wrong move. He'd have killed me. He'd have cut my throat. I had to keep talking, reasoning, begging. Catching his eye. "You don't want to kill me," I said. "I'm nothing to you, I'm nothing. You don't have to kill me, I'm just a nothing." Be he didn't care about that. It didn't matter. He wanted to do me. I kept on talking, and catching his eye, and finally—he saw me. Down on my knees on the floor.

And he took a pause and at last he agreed to some money and I thought I might live. I had about two hundred dollars in my pocket. Funny thing is, I only gave him forty. I worked two twenties off the roll. Trick I learned on the street, as a junkie on the street. He took the forty bucks and the TV and left. I remember thinking, "One second away, a glance away from death." Then I got the ranch hands. The state police came, but I haven't heard another word about it. "He just wanted to kill me," I told them. "He just wanted the experience. The thrill. He was on PCP or something. I had to talk him out of killing me. I made a lot of eye contact. I got down on my knees. He had ripped the fucking doors off their hinges and come at me with a knife. For fun. For the pleasure of it." *(Turns to look)* What? Excuse me?

Frank   You talking to me?

Tom   Uh, no. Sorry.

Frank   What are you doing now?

Tom   I'm looking around.

Frank   Why?

Tom   I wonder if I'll run into that motherfucker again.

Frank   And if you do?

Tom   I'll hurt him.

Frank   No.

Tom   No?

Frank   You don't want to see him again. And if you do, you'll pretend.

Tom   That's right.

Frank   You'll pretend you never saw him.

Tom   Okay.

Frank   You'll look away.

Tom	Right.
Frank	And you'll never be sure. And you'll never want to acknowledge his power. And you'll go on pretending.

Pause. FRANK takes off his glasses. His eyes are huge, bulging. TOM gasps. FRANK starts laughing loudly. (DIM OUT)

LIGHTS UP on TOM and DON JOSÉ .

Don José	People think they are born with power. It's nature's way. It's survival, the effort of survival. But that's not power. It is the chemistry of sex and fear and greed. An illusion. Real power is made of different stuff.
Tom	Okay.
Don José	Real power comes from the struggle of a man with himself. This will force a man to his knees, where he will beg for help, finally.
Tom	From where?
Don José	From above. Or he will twist and contort like a murderer at his electrocution, blind, screaming about injustice, defiant, before he is slammed out of existence by a jolt.
Tom	I see.
Don José	Or he will come unwound in his sleep, like a mechanical doll, and hear the last thump of his heart in a dream.
Tom	I follow you.
Don José	Or he will be crushed like an animal in a toy and be scraped off the road.
Tom	What?
Don José	Or he will be tricked by his daughters and suffocate.
Tom	I beg your pardon?

Don José	Or his organs will rot while he listens to flattery. Lies. His own and others. Lies.
Tom	You mean me?
Don José	Lies. And then he withers and decays and his last words are gibberish. *(Pause)*
Tom	Oh. I hear you now.
Don José	The spirit world is indifferent. It is tuned only to the similar to itself, to that which is like, to a power that is corresponding, arising from the earth with a vibration like itself. *(Pause)* You get that?
Tom	Oh, my God.
Don José	You forgot to turn it on.
Tom	I'm sorry.
Don José	No problem. You missed it, is all.
Tom	Can you say it again?
Don José	No. *(Laughs. OUT)*

LIGHTS UP on TOM and MYRA.

Tom	I think we're done here. I think that's all.
Myra	Aurora says the Skinwalker's gone.
Tom	Aurora.
Myra	I know what you think.
Tom	What? *(Pause, no answer)*
Myra	The skinwalker's you, it's all about you. Your resentments and your pride. *Paria, orgullo.*
Tom	What does that mean?
Myra	Arrogance. I'm quoting Don José .
Tom	I'm done with Don José .
Myra	You scared of him?

Tom	Time to head back to L.A.
Myra	I want to talk to my parents some more. Find out about their lives, their ancestors. They won't be around forever.
Tom	What about the car?
Myra	You can take the car.
Tom	I'll take the car.
Myra	You can drive it to L.A.
Tom	I'll leave it in a lot. I'll mail you the keys.
Myra	You can keep the car.
Tom	What about the tapes?
Myra	I don't believe in it anymore. Days are too short. Life's too short. People wake up around here, they're aware of the dead, go through their days together, they know, every day is closer to their last, the last one. I want to get to know my parents now, before they're gone. *(OUT)*

LIGHTS UP on TOM and HARTLEY.

Hartley	Things work out. They always do. I was fearful of not finding a job. It was very hard to get a job. I'm just the luckiest guy to have this one here, with Sidney. You got to keep on.
Voice Off	Get in the fucking car.
Tom	I better hit the road.
Hartley	What goes around, comes around. You see that with the politicians and such.
Tom	You sure do.
Hartley	I see that all the time. Same with my wife and kids and me. Can't communicate one with the other. Air won't let the words fly between us or something. We're going

	around small for a while, confined. Then the atmosphere
	changes, and we got a big family life again.
Tom	I hear you there.
Hartley	So you keep your head up and watch the road, okay?
Tom	I sure will.
Hartley	And I'll see ya.
Tom	You bet. *(A pause)*
Aurora	*(Entering)* Can I get a ride?
Tom	Where you headed?
Aurora	Hollister.
Tom	Where's Hollister?
Aurora	Hollister, California. It's in the North.
Tom	Yeah, sure.
Aurora	Okay?
Tom	Come on.

They exit. Sound of CAR DOORS SLAMMING. MYRA *enters discreetly.* CAR ENGINE STARTS. MYRA *folds her arms.* SOUND OF CAR MOVING *off down a gravel road. A pause, then a* CAR CRASH, *as in Scene One. A pause.* TOM *re-enters.*

Hartley	So you keep your head up and watch the road, okay?
Tom	I sure will.
Hartley	And I'll see ya.
Tom	You bet. *(A pause)*
Myra	*(Entering)* Can I come with?
Tom	Yes. Of course.
Myra	I've said my goodbyes.
Tom	Well, good then.

Myra	Okay?
Tom	Come on.

They exit. Sound of CAR DOORS SLAMMING. AURORA *enters discreetly.* CAR ENGINE STARTS. AURORA *folds her arms.* SOUND OF CAR MOVING *off down a gravel road. A pause, then a* CAR CRASH, *as in Scene One.* DIM OUT.

The End

Shatter 'n Wade

by Murray Mednick

Shatter 'n Wade *was first performed at the 1990 Padua Hills Playwrights Festival with the following cast:*

Wade: David Officer
Sayer: William Dennis Hunt
Cross: Scott Paulin
Wally: Matthew Goulish
Shatter: Susannah Blinkoff
Bint: Mark Fite
Ann: Allison Studdiford
Martin: Nick Love
Ginnie: Laura Owens
Sally: Elizabeth Iannaci
Bruno: Bob Craft
Bill: Peter Schaaf
The Screamer: Joseph Goodrich

Director: Murray Mednick
Assistant Director: Kim Brown
Music: James Campbell
Lighting Design: Jason Berliner
Stage Manager: Nick Flynn

Shatter 'n Wade was subsequently produced in February, 1991, by Diantha Lebenzon and Wayne Long at the Matrix Theater in Los Angeles and was directed by the author. The cast was the same except as follows:

Wally: James Cox Chambers
The Screamer: Hank Bunker

Set Design: Kenton Jones
Stage Manager: Kathi O'Donohue

Characters

Sayer *Middle-aged; wired; golden hair.*

Martin *Sharp; balding.*

Wally *Early thirties; cowboy outfit.*

Cross *Fifty; white hair.*

Bint *Thirty-one; blue hair.*

Ann *Late thirties; sensitive, emotional; brown hair.*

Ginnie *Late thirties; strong; black hair.*

Shatter *Twenty-two; wired; red hair.*

Wade *Nineteen; bandage on thumb; green hair; carries boom box.*

Sally *Thirties; blonde.*

Bruno *Corpulent.*

The Screamer *Unseen.*

Walk-ons

Scene

In front of the entrance to a meeting hall. Night. SAYER,
MARTIN, WALLY, BINT, and CROSS, hanging out; waiting.
CROSS and MARTIN stand off at opposite sides, the others
stand with SAYER.

Sayer	When I was growin' up there were families! A man had a family! A person belonged to a family and a man had a job and supported the family!
Cross	Did you know that tombs and mausoleums lined the Appian Way from Rome to Brundisium?
Sayer	No. Brundisium? Is that Brindisi?
Martin	So what?
Cross	Different attitude toward the family dead is all. Visibility. That's all I meant.
Sayer	*(To BINT)* Chairs set up?
Bint	Yes, sir. There's people.
Sayer	*(To MARTIN)* Cross here is new.
Martin	I know he's new. We've met, we've talked.

BRUNO enters, approaches behind them.

	(Of CROSS) He says odd things at inappropriate moments.
Sayer	Goin' to the meeting, Bruno? *(BRUNO ignores him, goes inside)* Attaboy!
Martin	You know how people bob their heads?—here, like this— they bob their heads like ducks—guys—guys do it—they get up, they're on their way to the john—they do this— *(Demonstrates as the others laugh)*
Wally	That's it, Martin! *(MARTIN walks off a few steps—he likes privacy)*

Sayer	*(Uneasily)* Hey, anyone see my two mutants? One's got red hair, the other's got green. Ha!
Bint	Uh, uh, no.
Sayer	Kids these days, they do actions. *(To Cross)* You know what an action is?
Cross	Well, yeah.
Sayer	What?

Cross doesn't know.

	Observe.
Wally	Anger is a disease. *(Pause)*
Bint	Anger is not a disease.

The Screamer screams, off.

Sayer	*(To Cross)* You don't know. Watch this.
Wally	*(Formally)* A woman who sleeps around—it's bad news. You have to guard against it, like the Muslims. It's a problem old as the rocks. A good body can get whatever it wants. Whomever, whenever. A wink and a smile, let's fuck around, have a good time. It's elemental. You want to stone such a woman, and destroy her power. Don't you? In a bed, a car, under the stairs, in an alley...
Bint	Say no more!
Cross	Wait a minute. Are those your thoughts? Do you think that?
Wally	Me?
Cross	No, I'm looking at the moon.
Wally	That's not me.
Cross	Because otherwise you have serious problems.

Wally	I didn't think it. I regret it now, okay?
Sayer	Ha!

SALLY arrives for the meeting.

Cross	*(To himself)* Wild.
Sayer	Welcome, Sally!
Sally	Well, I can't believe I'm here, really. I don't know how any-one can arrive at a point of view. One second I'm thinking one thing and the next second I'm thinking the opposite. How can anyone make up their minds about an issue? *(Sigh)* Well, I guess there's feelings.
Sayer	There you go, Sally! *(She goes inside)*
Martin	She's so cute. She's so cute I can't stand it. What is that?
Wally	Marry her, Martin!
Martin	You marry her, Wally! What you need—round off the edges.
Sayer	Ha!
Cross	*(To SAYER)* An action is oratory. It is speaking. *(To MARTIN)* That's what I was talking about. I didn't think it was inappropriate. It is relevant. In the ancient city, in the days of old, that's how it worked. You spoke before the assembly—
Martin	*(Walking away)* Yeah, yeah, rock and roll.
Cross	What's with this guy?
Wally	He never married. Independent fellow, Martin.
Bint	*(Awed)* He's a lawyer.
Wally	Got close to bein' pussy-whipped once and ran like a jackal.
Cross	Who is he to judge?
Bint	He's a judge?

CROSS looks at him.

Sayer	*(To* CROSS*)* Whatsamatter? Everybody has to like you?
	(To BINT*)* What's the worst thing that can happen?
Bint	You can get married?
Sayer	Come on!
Bint	You can die.
Sayer	You do die! Everybody dies! That's not the worst thing! Come on!
Bint	You can be sick.
Sayer	No. You can get better! Come on! *(Pause)* YOU CAN LOSE! LOSERS DON'T WORK! LOSERS DON'T MAKE IT! LOSERS CRAWL LIKE DOGS!
Bint	Okay. *(Walks off)*
Cross	The father was the priest of the household, and he knew the sacred formulas and rites—he knew what to say—in relation to the household gods and to the family dead. You know what I'm saying?
Wally	I don't think so.
Sayer	*(Ruefully)* Where are the families now? Look what happens! Guys make it and live in fortresses behind iron gates. Inside the fortress, nobody's talking. They don't know who each other is. These are the ones on top. In the middle, they are changing partners like rabbits. On the bottom, there are no fathers. The fathers are on the street and there's no money for the women and children! The women are in there exchanging sex for crack! They're doin' it in what they call crack houses! So aids and syphilis are skyrocketing and the kids are gettin' born with it!
Wally	"Skyrocketing." I love it.
Sayer	Wally, the students we got here are beastie boys and bums! They are a tribe of barbarians! They are a primitive-type

	people addicted to noise! It's awful! They are just beating our brains out with the bass and the drums!
Wally	Fantastic!
Sayer	My ex says it's because they got pushed out of the womb, slapped around, and dumped into the school system! Yeah, yeah, rock and roll! Noise and dope! And they start fucking when they're twelve!
Wally	Whoa!
Sayer	I heard Wade today, he's talking about these high school coke dealers, they're teenagers walking around with beepers so they're available day and night, they're driving thirty-thousand-dollar cars and they're afraid of no one! They're too young to do time and they fit snugly into the fuck you, fuck me entrepreneurial tradition! Who can fault them?
Wally	Good, Dr. Sayer!
Sayer	They're loading up, these functional illiterates and know-nothings! They can do business—they are organized and armed. Wade, he's telling me how these kids get initiated into the business—into the gang. You stick a shotgun out the car window and blow somebody away, he says. It doesn't have to be a person you know. It could be anyone—you do a murder and that's how you make your bones.
Wally	It's the fucking cars! You got teenagers shooting around in lethal weapons—they're always on the verge!

Enter ANN.

| Sayer | Ha! |
| Ann | Hi, honey! |

CROSS, startled, goes to ANN as SAYER and WALLY watch.

Cross	*(Trying not to be overheard)* I feel crazed. I feel disassociated. I am not myself. I am appalled.
Ann	Let's take those one at a time.
Cross	What am I? Somebody is acting like he's me, and he's not me and he's outta control.
Ann	What do you mean?
Cross	Crazed. I'm doing things and saying things I don't like but its me and I'm appalled at what I'm doing and saying.

ANN calls to SAYER and WALLY.

Ann	What time is the meeting?
Wally	Uh, it's now!

SAYER opens the door, looks in.

Sayer	Meeting's now!

He goes inside, followed by WALLY.

Cross	There's a guy pretending to be me, and he's outta control.

They watch WADE approach; he stops, stands shyly, walks away.

	I would call it the pain of manifesting, of having to be in this world.
Ann	Then do something about it.

Cross	What?
Ann	Well.
Cross	WELL, WHAT? *(Pause)* I don't want to stand here like I'm dumb and paralyzed.
Ann	I'm sorry.
Cross	I feel like I'm seeing everything very clearly, and guess what, Ann?

WADE re-enters behind them, goes to door, looks in, hesitates.

Ann	No laceration, Cross. At this stage in life, we might not get over it.
Cross	That's what I feel. I definitely feel that. I couldn't agree with you more, Ann. I just don't know where that comment came from.

ANN sighs, looks around to WADE, who is leaving again.

Ann	*(To WADE)* Are there many people in the meeting?

He walks away.

(To CROSS) Odd.

Off, the SCREAMER screams.

God, who is that?

Cross	Do you pray for the dead?
Ann	What are you getting at?
Cross	Do you pray for the dead?
Ann	No, do you?

Cross	No. I don't pray at all. I don't know how.
Ann	Maybe you should learn how.
Cross	A prayer for my ancestors. In the old days, they worshipped the dead. That's how they found meaning.
Ann	Why don't you ever talk to me about what you're doing?
Cross	We were just talking about what I was doing with reference to the meaning of what I was doing, which is research into the ancient world.
Ann	Never mind, we should go in.

BINT reappears, lights up a smoke.

Cross	You go on in.
Ann	What are you doing?
Cross	I am going to continue to stand here.
Ann	Gimme a kiss.

He hesitates, relents.

Come in soon.

Cross	Yeah, sure.

She goes inside. He mutters fiercely to himself.

Goddamn it! I hate that! I hate that shit! What am I! Am I a slug! Am I an actor! Am I a toad! What is that! Damn it! *(Regards BINT smoking)* Looks good and smells good.

Bint	Want one?
Cross	No, thanks. I quit.

Bint	Hey, that's awesome. *(Pause)* That's a wonderful present you've given to yourself. *(Pause)*
Cross	Thank you.
Bint	You should feel good about yourself. *(Pause)* Do you?
Cross	*(Sardonic)* I feel great about myself.
Bint	How long you been not smoking?
Cross	Three months.
Bint	Congratulations. *(Offering his hand)* That's a real statement, a positive affirmation on your part.
Cross	I'd rather smoke.
Bint	How'd you do it?
Cross	I turned fifty.
Bint	Fifty. Whoa.
Cross	Yeah.
Bint	I'm gonna put it out now, go to the meeting.
Cross	Okay.

ANN steps out.

Ann	Cross!
Cross	What?
Ann	Excuse me. Are you coming in?
Cross	No! Not yet!
Ann	All right.

ANN goes back inside. BINT starts to cough.

Cross	What's the matter?
Bint	*(Gulping)* I can't breathe!
Cross	Take it easy.

Bint	It's my heart!
Cross	You wanna glass of water?
Bint	What a shock! I can't believe it! Cindy! Jesus Christ, that was Cindy! Was that Cindy?
Cross	You know each other?
Bint	Hell, yeah—I know her! She still looks good, too! Unfuckinbelievable! *(Gasping)* She looks great.
Cross	Pull yourself together.
Bint	I'm impressed is all, I'm totally impressed. Cindy! She looks fuckin' great.
Cross	Cynthia.
Bint	Cynthia?
Cross	That's her name.
Bint	Oh, wow.
Cross	How do you know...Cindy?
Bint	Hey, are you kidding? This is a charge, man. This is intense. We're talkin' twelve or thirteen years here.
Cross	Really?
Bint	Yeah, I dunno if I can go in there now.
Cross	You can do it. What's your name?
Bint	Bint.
Cross	You can make it, Bint.
Bint	*(Nodding)* Thank you. I appreciate that. I'll wait a minute. Where are you from?
Cross	New York.
Bint	Yeah, I can hear that. You're not from here.

MARTIN re-enters, stops at door.

Martin	Hey, Bint!

Bint	Yes, sir!

BINT doesn't move, so MARTIN goes to them.

Martin	Sayer. He's a fantastic guy. But he's hysterical, ya know? We love him, ya know, but what are we gonna do with him?
Bint	It's not for me to say, Sir.

CROSS shrugs.

Martin	Yeah, yeah, rock and roll. *(Hunches himself, starts for the door, stops)* Bint! Don't let anybody slam the door!
Bint	I'll try, sir!

MARTIN goes inside.

Cross	What happened twelve years ago?
Bint	Cindy?
Cross	Yeah, yeah.
Bint	Nothin' happened. I just knew her. Hey, she was great. Cindy.
Martin	*(Inside)* The world is abusive! Life is abusive! Who is looking to feather someone else's nest? You don't have to go far—if you walk on your ass you'll end up with a sore ass!
Sayer	*(Inside)* Don't interrupt others when they are speaking. Counselor!

Someone closes the door. Off, the SCREAMER screams.

Bint	Weird neighbor.

Cross	*(To* Bint*)* How'd you know her? Cindy?
Bint	Actually, my brother knew her. I met her through my older brother, Brian. *(Pause)* You okay? *(Pause)* Yeah, Brian knew her first.
Cross	And then you knew her.
Bint	What a knockout! Beautiful! Still is. And friendly? Boy! *(Pause)* I mean, she was such a beautiful woman, ya know? *(Starts heaving)*
Cross	Are you having convulsions, or what?
Bint	No, I'm all right. I'm all right. I'm goin' to my brother's house. Tonight. After the meeting. Maybe now, actually. Maybe tomorrow. Clean up. He's a neat guy.
Cross	Sounds like a good idea.
Bint	Yeah, I need a rest. It's harsh out there, harsh. No mercy. You must know, right? New York City.
Cross	New York City. Tell me about Cynthia.
Bint	I was just a kid, an' here's this beautiful woman, gorgeous, and she's just real friendly. It makes an impression. You know what I'm saying?
Cross	I think so.
Bint	Cindy. She was the hottest thing in the valley, man.

Silence.

Cross	Meaning?
Bint	I'm sure she's changed. Ya know, older.
Cross	I'm sure.
Bint	I was still in high school, man. It was like a dream, like a dream come true, like a movie. A kid would go a long way for that ya know, a long way.

Cross	Times have changed.
Bint	I hear ya there. Kids are goin' at it now. No holding back now. Ha! *(Pause)* A beauty, man. A total beauty. And she really got around, I'll tell ya. I guess I was too young to be jealous.

Pause. BILL *walks on.*

Bill	Meeting happening, Bint?
Bint	You bet! It's a happening, Bill!
Bill	Listen to this. There's gonna be a whole new breed of people comin' through: they're called Brazilians. Once they got all the forests down, once they've cut all the trees, then they're comin' over the border! They're gonna invade America! A new species! Brazilians! Okay?
Cross	Thank you.
Bill	Brazil! They got death squads now, knockin' off the street kids! *(Goes inside)*
Bint	*(To* BILL*)* I hear ya!
Cross	Let me ask you something.
Bint	Go for it.
Cross	Why do you talk like that all the time?
Bint	*(Pause)* Is that an insult?
Cross	And why do you love noise so much?
Bint	Who?
Cross	You people. You love noise.
Bint	What people?
Cross	You—the young Californian. The dudes. You like noise. Why is that?
Bint	You mean like loud music?

Cross	Yeah. Loud music. Loud cars. Loud bikes. Loud talk. Empty noise.
Bint	You hostile, man?
Cross	Just answer me the question.
Bint	It's comforting, pal. Comforting.
Cross	Comforting. Thank you.
Bint	You're hostile. I don't need nobody being hostile. It's like the last thing I need, man.
Cross	Take a hike, asshole.

Tense pause.

Bint	I get it. You guys together?
Cross	She's my wife.
Bint	Hey, it's not my fault. How do I know? *(Stepping away)* I'll bet you're a fucking Arab. Arabs can't handle it, man. They like their women closed. *(Makes gesture of turning a key)* Click. *(Laughs)*

Enter SAYER from inside.

	Hello, Dr. Sayer.
Sayer	Hello, Bint. *(Sarcastic)* Comin' to the meeting?
Bint	Yes, sir.
Sayer	You gentlemen know each other?
Bint	No, sir.
Cross	*(To BINT)* Get outta here before I piss on you.
Bint	I don't like that.
Sayer	Go on in, Bint.
Bint	Right, Dr. Sayer! *(Goes inside)*

Martin	*(Inside)* Don't slam the door!

BINT slams door. SAYER laughs.

Sayer	What an assembly, Mr. Cross. *(Takes out a large cigar)*

Enter WALLY from inside, leaving the door slightly open.

Here comes another one. Can't take the heat.

Wally	Hello, Mr. Cross!
Cross	Hello, how are ya?
Wally	*(Half to himself)* Fuckin' Bill's talking.
Bill	*(Inside)*...I think tension grows on the planet, ya know, and it's got to be expressed by, like, war. It's like, ya know, a boil, it's like, lanced by fighting, like on the street, right? You know what I'm saying?
Wally	No, Bill!
Bill	*(Inside)*...The stuff gets kicked off into space, maybe even to the moon. It's not just the asshole in front of you on the freeway fucking up your day, or the crazed sharks biting around in the culture for money and power: It's death squads and invasions and massacres and epidemics! And I'll tell ya something else here: You can't sit on the down-trodden too long—it starts to stink—that's my opinion, that's my point of view on it!

Boos and applause inside.

One more thing: they're trying to buy into Africa now, for a dumping ground, a place to bury the garbage! Africa!

Sayer	Who was that?
Wally	Sounds like Bill.
Sayer	Close the door, will ya?

WALLY closes it.

Cross	*(To SAYER)* Are you gonna light that thing?
Sayer	*(Not lighting up)* They were talking about the dead in there.
Cross	What dead?
Sayer	Children.
Cross	There are no dead, Sayer. People vanish and that's the end of it. No problem about the ancestry, the bloodline, the family name. But in the old days the dead were around, they were in the house or in the tomb or in the field. The dead were near.
Wally	They're in graveyards, Mr. Cross.
Cross	Yeah, but you don't see 'em.
Wally	So what? Who wants to see 'em?
Cross	You don't know anything. And you're a sycophant on top of everything else. *(To SAYER)* The dead are important.
Wally	Why?
Cross	Because once they were alive, sir, like you and me. Like Tacitus, who breathed air and shit and had opinions. Walkin' about with ears and smells and hungers and strategies. *(Pause)* He had a Roman education and he worshipped the dead.

WALLY partly opens the door.

Bill	*(Inside)* YOU WANNA TALK ABOUT CENTRAL AMERICA? YOU WANNA TALK ABOUT THE RIGHT WING? DEATH SQUADS AND TORTURE? YOU WANNA MENTION BRAZIL?

Bruno	*(Inside)* BRAZIL IS NOT IN CENTRAL AMERICA.
Bill	*(Inside)* THEY KILL THEIR WIVES IN BRAZIL! THEY KILL THEIR WIVES WITH IMPUNITY!
Sayer	*(To WALLY)* Shut the door.

WALLY does so.

Wally	Kids don't wanna real education. Don't wanna learn nothin'. This is a good subject for a meeting. Talk about dollars and sense. The economy. Values.

BINT is on his way back out.

Bill	*(Inside)* THEY GOT PACKS OF WILD KIDS ROAMING THE COUNTRY!
Sayer	Don't slam the door.

BINT carefully shuts the door.

Bint	Christ, can't anybody stay in the meeting? *(To CROSS)* I looked at her. I coulda been wrong.
Cross	I'm gonna kick your fuckin' head in.
Sayer	Stand clear, Bint.

BINT steps back. MARTIN comes out the door.

(To CROSS) Reproduction's the most important thing, anyway. That's all that's goin' on. Reproduction. Planet earth don't care 'bout nothin' else. Get 'em all reproducin', vibing into the stratosphere.

Martin	What kind of an idea is that, Sayer?
Sayer	What kind of idea?
Martin	What kind of idea.
Sayer	A big idea. What I've been trying to tell you, Martin. An observable phenomenon, Martin.

MARTIN *goes back in.*

	Why you look at the girls and the girls look back, Martin.
Wally	I love that! *(Pause)* Electricity is what it is. Ever seen it?
Bint	In the air?
Wally	Everywhere. Right, Dr. Sayer?
Sayer	Ha! Right on, Wally!
Wally	Seen the grid from the sky? Satellite point of view? Come on!
Sayer	I got two kids to talk about, myself. That's Shatter and Wade. Shatter's the girl. They're totally dysfunctional.
Wally	For example, forty years ago we beat the Japanese and the Germans and now they're both trying to slap us around. *(To CROSS)* That's an historical truth.

BINT *starts to go back in.*

Sayer	*(Stopping him)* Bint! Ha! Kids don't wanna work, neither one of 'em. Wanna live for free. You take my daughter, Shatter—
Wally	Shatter, I love it!
Sayer	Yeah, that's my wife's idea, "Shatter." Ex. Shatter, she's been living off me. I told her, get out, find a job. You can stay with me a month or two, the minute I find any booze or drugs you gotta leave. I go to empty the trash, there's empty whiskey bottles and beer bottles. I told her, no partying in

	my house. I threw her out. She goes to live with this woman on welfare, the old man is screwing the kids!
Bint	Sonofabitch!
Sayer	Wade, he ploughs right under the axle of a tractor–trailer! Engine's in the back seat, they had to slice him outta there. Kid lives! He's got cuts and bruises and a broken thumb. Third time in a year he's totaled a car. You think he's trying to tell somebody something? Nineteen years old, he's going eighty, ninety miles an hour into a load o' timber, he's leveled by the axle of the truck! Broken thumb and he lives! He's banged up, though. This time it's his mother's car, my ex-wife's. I told him, you're not driving my car! He did his, then he did his girlfriend's, now he's smashed his mother's!
Cross	I have no opinions, Sayer, and no preferences. As far as I'm concerned, you can sell both your kids for meat.
Sayer	Yikes, Cross. *(Lights his cigar)*

MARTIN *comes out, quickly shuts the door.*

Martin	*(Frustrated)* It's a free-for-all in there.
Cross	*(Stepping away)* That's how we get into trouble, Sayer. With our beliefs and requirements.
Sayer	*(To MARTIN)* Trouble, counselor?
Martin	They don't understand the rules of order! They don't understand the goddamn law! The law is clear—you do wrong—wham, bam, into the slammer!
Cross	Our expectations and delusions.
Martin	Oh, that's just your fuckin' attitude of the day, Cross.
Cross	*(Stunned)* What?

Sayer	*(To* Bint*)* You don't work, you don't eat. You can't read, you're illiterate! Hey, Martin! What's a virus?
Martin	Don't do that shit with me, Sayer.
Sayer	A virus is a formula! It is neither dead nor alive! It's in between! It is numbers, Martin, actin' like parasites! And they mutate! *(Goes abruptly inside)*
Cross	*(To no one)* "The first bringer of unwelcome news hath but a losing office."
Martin	What is that referring to?
Cross	I wasn't talking to you.
Martin	That's how people do!—They come around with an attitude— this week they got one attitude, next week they got another one! And don't start talkin' about the fuckin' Romans! They were choppin' people's heads off and throwin' 'em off cliffs and sewin' 'em up into sacks with chickens and dumpin' 'em into the fuckin' river! Fuckin' animals!
Cross	*(Quietly)* It was to deprive them of burial, of the sacred rites.
Martin	*(Going to the door)* Rights!

Bint *opens the door slightly, listens.*

Sayer	*(Inside)* There will always be torture! Because torture is interesting! And I will tell you why! It is a way of playing with the energy of a man! It is a way of saying NO to life! It is rebellion! It is a poking, a tweaking of the invisible, a provocation to God, a denial! It is a stripping away of conscience! It is a form of sexual activity! For some, it is a method of preparing the will for the spirit world! For this life is only pain, pain is its product, its substance, which can be transformed, through endurance, into power!

MARTIN shuts the door.

Martin	*(To no one)* He's a fuckin' maniac. *(To Wally)* You got people in there—they're so fuckin' nervous—they squeak—
Wally	I know it!
Martin	You got people in there—they feel your eyes on 'em—they shrink—their heads turn like fuckin' snails, man!
Wally	I know it!
Martin	You take pills?—I take pills—I take aspirin—I drink coffee— I used to guzzle booze—
Bint	Whoa!

They watch as someone else arrives for the meeting.

Martin	Don't slam the door!

Door slams.

	Christ!
Cross	*(Uncomfortable)* I guess the real meeting's inside. *(Turns to go, hesitates)*
Martin	They don't know! Nobody knows! Electromagnetic fields! Who can talk about that? We've got power stations and cables all over the country fer chrissakes! What are we gonna do, tear 'em down? There's no evidence magnetic fields are causing cancer in kids! You wanna live in society, you got exposure to electric and magnetic fields! You hear what I'm saying? This is a world that uses electricity!
Bint	Whoa! Say no more!

Off, the SCREAMER *screams.*

Cross   Man was meant to walk through earth's direct current, steady-state magnetic field. Man-made alternating currents will cause anything magnetic in their path, including the human brain, to vibrate sixty times a second.

Bint   Whoa!

Cross   *(To* WALLY*)* That's a scientific fact.

Off, the SCREAMER *screams.*

Martin   *(Of the* SCREAMER *)* Someone should shoot that guy. There're all kindsa diseases, fer chrissakes—we just got over polio—remember?

Bint   No.

Martin   That's right—before your time—buy lands—way things are goin'—the Japanese'll beat us to it—be so many fuckin' people there won't be room to piss—buy lands!

Wally   People don't have jobs, you can forget about it. You gotta build.

They watch as SHATTER *goes by.*

Pacific Rim, Martin. Pacific Rim.

Martin   *(Watching her)* Pacific Rim, Wally. *(Of* SHATTER*)* Cute. I can't get over this thing—what drives us?—she's so cute.

Bint   You mean...?

Martin   I mean—she looks at me, I look at her, she looks at me, I look at her—she gets in her fuckin' car! What is that?

Bint	I get it!
Martin	She seems like she's a real honey—I think I'm gonna have a good time—like she's gonna worship my dick and what have you—and what? She starts sayin' things!
Wally	*(Sly)* Scares ya, eh, Martin? Scared they'll leave ya, scareda betrayal.
Martin	Forget about it, Wally.
Wally	You know what it takes? Get on TV? Make a commercial?
Bint	You gotta be gorgeous, right?
Wally	Big lips. That's what it takes, big sexy lips. I know, 'cause I buy ads.
Martin	First they're Daddy's little girl—Daddy's girl. Then calamity falls— *(To* CROSS*)* That's Greek—
Wally	You almost got married, didn't ya, Martin?
Martin	Don't get cute, Wally.
Wally	That's right. Better see what's goin' on. *(Opens door, listens)*
Sally	*(Inside)* I just don't know if you can walk the streets anymore! I can't cross the street near my house! I can't get across because of the cars and the trucks! I just want to say that! Because you can get run over! You can get smashed! They don't stop and they don't slow down! The whole neighborhood is shaking and rocking with the noise! When I was a girl right here a person could cross the street! Hasn't anybody noticed what's going on anymore? I just wanted to say that!
Bill	*(Inside)* Thank you, Sally!
Bruno	*(Inside)* Can I add to that? I'd like to mention the homeless who are on our streets, the vagrants and panhandlers and poor people who are on our streets, who are living in the park and in the alleys and who can be quite aggressive!

318

Ann	*(Inside)* I think that's a good point! But I don't agree with this man's attitude! What kind of a society is this? What kind of a culture is this? What kind of a neighborhood is this?! Where families don't have a decent place to live?! And people have to threaten and beg for their lives?!
Wally	*(Shouting in)* Next time someone asks me for money, I'm gonna crush his face!
Folks Inside	BOO! SHUT THE DOOR!
Martin	Shut the door.

WALLY, laughing, shuts the door.

	I'll tell ya—I'll tell ya what I think—
Cross	What's that?
Martin	I think we should protect the rich—I'll tell ya—I go to the opera—and I see all these white-haired gentlemen in the audience with their ladies—and I'm comforted—I'll tell ya—these guys are holding the whole thing up.
Cross	I see what you're saying.
Martin	If you're gonna take care of people, who should you take care of? The ones who have a stake in everything or the ones who wanna bring it down? Who? Think about it.
Cross	I do.
Martin	It's the upper classes—we wanna make sure they survive— that they take an interest—I'm telling ya the truth, I see all those guys in the audience with their ladies, and I'm reassured—I feel better about the future.
Wally	Yeah, yeah, and they listen to the music.
Martin	Well, not only that—they hold it up—they hold the damn thing up—you gotta be stupid not to see that the ones

with the most investment are the ones most needing the
protection!

SAYER steps out, annoyed.

Sayer	Jesus, can't anyone stay in the meeting? This is serious! Say what you got to say in the meeting!
Wally	*(To himself)* Yeah, yeah, rock and roll.
Martin	Come on!

MARTIN and WALLY start in—a confusion at the door—
SAYER stays out and CROSS starts off.

Sayer	*(To CROSS)* Where you goin'?
Cross	I'm goin' to the bathroom. *(Exits)*

BINT snickers.

Sayer	What?
Bint	I'll bet he's an Arab.
Sayer	He's not. He's a Jew.
Bint	Cross?
Sayer	Russian.

Enter GINNIE.

Ginnie!

BINT sneaks off.

Ginnie	What's up, Sayer?
Sayer	You came to the meeting!
Ginnie	So?
Sayer	You don't come to public meetings.
Ginnie	This isn't going to the meeting, this is standing outside.
Sayer	*(Showing cigar)* This is the real meeting, Ginnie.
Ginnie	Okay.

Pause. WADE's *boom-box music can be heard, off.*

	What's this about power stations and cancer?
Sayer	Transformers and cables, Ginnie, adjacent to the school. Makes waves.

They look around.

Ginnie	God. *(Facetious)* Is there reason for hope, Sayer?
Sayer	Certainly. Anything can happen, Ginnie. Science. We'll unlock the secrets of nature. Who knows what's possible? We can get energy from sand, from sea water. We'll have skylabs. We'll monitor the planet from space. We'll have factories on Mars. We can solve everything. We just don't know now. It's in the future. There is a future, and it is endless, like the sand, the sea.
Ginnie	What do we need?
Sayer	We need more faith, faith in knowledge, in the future. Think of the future. Think of a hundred, a thousand years. Think of it!
Ginnie	That's good, Sayer. You're good. *(Pause)* All these people in the government know how to say is, everything's all

right. Don't predict anything bad happening at all, ever.
Be a reflection on them. Don't predict anything good happening, either. No change at all, Sayer, good or bad.

Sayer   Status quo. You have your reproductive processes and the
eternal menace of the Left. Ha! You got that?

Ginnie   Conglomeration of timid assholes. It's not all right, Sayer.

Sayer   I'm not interested in making this a better world, Ginnie.
Everything is just right and the way it ought to be and
couldn't be otherwise. Let's legalize it and leave it alone.
Come on, I'll escort you in.

Ginnie   Better leave the cigar, Sayer.

*CROSS reappears as GINNIE goes in. SAYER hangs back to
put out his cigar. ANN passes him, looking for CROSS.
SAYER bows and tips his hat.*

Sayer   That was Ginnie. Ol' Ginnie just wants to make sure the
real estate keeps goin' up. Ha!

Ann   *(Distracted)* Oh.

Sayer   *(Pointing)* There he is, Mrs. Cross.

Ann   Thank you.

Sayer   *(Taking her arm)* I just wanted to say, Mrs. Cross, since
you're leaving the meeting—

Ann   I'm not leaving the meeting.

Sayer   It seems to me that certain people are harnessing the
power of the universe in order to transform it into noise!
They are doing it in all ignorance. I saw a program on
television, the talking heads had figured out chaos! They
could see chaos, there on the screen, the very design of
chaos! They didn't know anything. *(Indignant)* They

thought they were important! *(Pause)* And you could see the dying there that were plugged into the machines, into the sockets, into the walls! It had to do with the heartbeat, with heart attacks! The silent, intimidated anguish of chaos! That is, without sense or order or meaning! No meaning to the dying nor to the lives that had gone before! All the moments to this moment plugged into the wall!

Ann   I'm sorry. I'm sorry you saw that.

Sayer   No problem, ma'am. Excuse me.

SAYER goes back inside. ANN approaches CROSS.

Cross   You didn't have anything to do with it.

Ann   I know I didn't.

Cross   So why are you sorry? He's pulling your chain.

BINT re-enters, pretending to be a man of hurried purpose; checks them out; goes to door.

              You know him?

Ann   No. Who is he?

Cross   One of Sayer's boys. A subject! A pal. *(Snickers)*

BINT goes inside, leaving the door ajar.

Ginnie   *(Inside)* So what the hell do you propose, Martin? What's your proposition?

Martin   *(Inside)* MUTUAL PROTECTION! WE LIVE IN A DANGEROUS WORLD! SHUT THE DOOR, BUT DON'T SLAM IT!

BINT slams the door. CROSS snickers.

Ann   *(To CROSS)* Why are you treating me this way?

Cross   Did I ever tell you about the Greeks? Did we ever talk about that?

She turns and walks away from him. Pause.

Shit!

Enter SHATTER, smoking. CROSS watches her, fascinated. ANN goes inside. SHATTER approaches.

Shatter   Do you despise weakness? *(Pause)*

Cross   Yes. *(Pause)* Don't you?

Shatter   Yes, it makes me sick, and I see a lot of it.

Cross   *(Facetious)* Just say, "no."

Shatter   Feels like food poisoning. *(Pause)* Nauseating.

Cross   Do you always talk to strangers?

Shatter   Always. And you?

Cross   Ah. I take your point.

Shatter   This is a good time and place for an action, a discussion.

Cross   An action?

Shatter   It's a protest. We're protesting.

Cross   What?

Shatter   The murder of the universe.

Cross   I see.

Shatter   By man. *(Pause)* By poison and fire. *(Pause)* By noise and anger. *(Pause)* By wind. *(Pause)* What will you do?

Cross   Uh, I'll play a teacher.

Shatter	Okay. *(Pause, formally)* I have to destroy his power. I'll get into a trance and I'll stab him a thousand times.
Cross	Who is he?
Shatter	He has to be cut up, dismembered. I'll destroy his power. If I don't cut him up in a hundred parts, he'll still have his power.
Cross	Did he come to this meeting?
Shatter	Later, maybe I can forgive his spirit. I can evoke his spirit, and offer him forgiveness. Later. Now I must dismember him. First things first.
Cross	Let's talk about it. Let's take it easy.
Shatter	You're full of shit. You're not doing it.
Cross	Are you Shatter?
Shatter	What a bogus disappointing drag you turned out to be. *(Starts to leave)*
Cross	Wait! Listen!

She stops.

	The set for the Greeks, the ancient Greeks, was a giant door. This has to do with the old religion. Wait!
Shatter	*(Stopping again)* Go.
Cross	For the Greeks there was a door, a big upstage door, the door to the household, to the palace. All the action was in front of the door or behind the door, and the chorus moved around like a wave and the messengers and visitors came and went. The action—*(He stops, considers)*—was in motion, in progress, and the murder was behind the door. Wait. Not necessarily the murder. Behind the door was the hearth, and the household gods, and images of the ancestors. Next

to the house or in back of the house was the tomb of the ancestors. The father and his father and his father's father!

Shatter   Was what?

Cross   Was the worship, the religion.

SAYER steps outside, door open.

Ginnie   *(Inside)* Society is not organized for cultural reasons! Society is not organized for justice! Society is organized for survival! Every other consideration is a pain and a joke and a waste of time!

Cross   Survival...

Bill   *(Inside)* May you be loved and liked and may you die immediately!

Ginnie   *(Inside)* That means competition! You stupid clown! That means an economy!

Shatter   I can't stand it.

Folks Inside   Shut the door!

Sayer   Come into the meeting, Cross! Ol' Ginnie is holding forth for the real estate! Ha!

Cross   No!

Sayer   *(Closing the door)* Why not?

Cross   Too much smoke!

Sayer   There's no smoking anymore! *(Seeing SHATTER)* Talking to someone? Trying an action?

Cross   I was saying how the dead were more with us in the old days, Sayer; they had a real place among the living, and watched, and waited, and were fed.

Sayer   As if alive?

Cross   Yes, by virtue of the inheritance, the patrimony. The dead fathers were served by the sons. Burnt offerings, Sayer, sacrificed to the dead.

Sayer   Goddamned kids think everything just appeared, for their use. Forget it all got to be worked for and maintained. Want to live like bloodsucking parasites. *(To SHATTER)* This is Mr. Cross.

Shatter   *(To CROSS)* How are you?

Cross   Devastated.

Sayer   Don't let me interrupt the event, the action, the occasion.

Shatter   We're talkin' power.

Cross   Look up to him and admire him but stay out of his life.

Shatter   Power plays with equal or more power.

Cross   That's the law of power.

Shatter   In obedience to the law of power, women are dishonored. Wives, daughters, secretaries, sisters—dishonored! *(Slaps hands with CROSS)*

Cross   *(To SHATTER)* Very good. *(Pause)*

Sayer   *(To SHATTER)* Where's Wade? Come on!

Shatter   He's around.

Sayer   What's he doing? Come on!

Shatter   He is skulking.

Sayer   How'd he get here? You bring him here? Come on!

Shatter   No.

Sayer   DID HE DRIVE HERE? DID HE DRIVE HERE IN A CAR? COME ON!

Shatter   Yes, Dad.

Sayer   WHERE'D HE GET THE GODDAMN CAR? WHOSE CAR?

Shatter doesn't answer.

FUCKIN' IDIOT!

Cross	*(To* SAYER*)* Who?

SAYER goes back into the meeting.

Shatter	Wade. That's my brother. He stays down in the City of Commerce. He lives in rooms.

ANN re-enters from inside. She and SHATTER *size each other up.* SHATTER *moves off.*

Ann	Who is she?
Cross	That is Shatter. Her brother's name is Wade. They're Sayer's kids.
Ann	I feel sorry for them. The man is out of his mind.
Cross	He's ecstatic.
Ann	Oh, come on.
Cross	Did people call you Cynthia?
Ann	When?
Cross	Whenever.
Ann	Very few. *(Pause)* Why?
Cross	Do you know a guy named Bint and a brother, Brian?
Ann	I know neither a Bint nor a Brian. *(Pause)* What kind of a name is Bint?
Cross	Maybe the family name.
Ann	No.
Cross	As in Cynthia Ann?
Ann	What's the matter with you?
Cross	Sorry. You never bargained for this.
Ann	For what?
Cross	For presiding over this decline of powers, this moral diminution.

Ann	Oh, stop it!
Cross	Please don't talk that way!
Ann	How?
Cross	With the OH prefix.
Ann	*(Choking him)* I'll stop if you stop it!
Cross	Go ahead! Finish it! End the terrible slide!
Ann	My God! I thought I was marrying an intellectual, a historian.
Cross	And instead?
Ann	Instead I got Bozo the Clown. Wait here.
Cross	Where are you going?
Ann	To the ladies' room. Which way?
Cross	The other one.

She goes off. SHATTER reappears.

Shatter	They're lying! They don't know what's real!
Cross	How do you know?

WALLY sneaks out, singing to himself.

Wally	*Why not stay on her good side*
	And be on your own side too
	A man has got a lotta strong
	So what have you got to lose
	A man knows how to play it
	An actor knows how to choose
	Dummies can't find...to say it
	And smart guys get along...
Shatter	*(To WALLY)* Shut up, you fucking male chauvinist putz.

Wally	*(Staring at her)* What?
Shatter	You heard me. You're a male chauvinist putz and a liar. *(To* CROSS*)* Excuse me.
Cross	Sure thing.

Shatter goes.

(To WALLY*)* You two know each other?

WALLY *doesn't answer.*

	How's the meeting…?
Wally	*(Lighting a cigarette)* Wally.
Cross	How's the meeting, Wally?
Wally	Oh, it's just fine. Peoples expressing their views. You ought to participate, it's the American Way.
Cross	I brought my wife.
Wally	There you go.
Cross	Can I stand next to you and breathe your air?
Wally	*(Alarmed)* What's that?
Cross	The smoke.
Wally	Sure thing.
Cross	What are you into, Wally? I mean in life.
Wally	Cattle.
Cross	Oh?
Wally	There are four levels to the cattle business. First you got the ones who make the calves, the cow and calf operation. There's about a million of those in this country. They're marginal. Their place in this business is hard to see. They go to the bank—the bank's got the calves as security—and

get a loan to produce the calves and then they sell the calves to the larger ranches where they pasture. There's maybe a hundred thousand of those. They get the calves up to three hundred pounds and then they're finished off at the feed lots with another coupla hundred pounds. And then they go to the packers. There's only three or four of those. And that's the structure of the cattle business.

Cross	Thank you.
Wally	You're welcome.
Cross	H2-0, Wally.
Wally	What's that?
Cross	That's water, pal.
Wally	I know what water is. Are you saying something?
Cross	Once the earth was a fireball, Wally. *(Pause)* And then it rained. *(Walks away)*
Wally	I hear ya.

Enter WADE.

Wade	I thought I'd come to the meeting.
Wally	So?
Wade	Okay.
Wally	What makes you think I'm interested in that? *(Pause)* You don't know me. We've never been introduced. We've never talked. We have no idea who each other is, do we?
Wade	No. I just thought maybe I'd come to the meeting. I thought it might help me to talk about myself.
Wally	It might.
Wade	I don't know, though.

Wally	*(Referring to the bandage)* What happened to you? Run into a truck?
Wade	Yeah. I don't go out much at all. You can't trust anyone. My sister wants to do an action. I don't know how things work. I can do refrigeration, I guess.
Wally	Do you go out with girls?
Wade	Ha! *(Shyly)* No. Do you think I should?
Wally	Come on! What's your name?
Wade	Wade.
Wally	Come on, Wade! Good for your health!
Wade	Do you do that?
Wally	What?
Wade	You know. I don't think I could do that. You know, like, talk to a girl.
Wally	Pull yourself together! *(Starts away)*
Wade	Do you think all women are the same? I mean, do you think there are any differences at all?
Wally	Yes and no.
Wade	Of course.
Wally	There's no free lunch, I can tell you that. Fuck 'em and watch the spin! Ha!
Wade	Ha!
Wally	Humans!
Wade	Yeah.
Wally	It's like we gotta do it!
Wade	That's what I mean! I mean, the family. Actually, what I mean is, what if this is just a moment? Where it's here and it's gone, you know, where it'll be something else, some other kind of creature? *(Pause)*
Wally	Nah! If I get your meaning, can't be.

Wade	No?
Wally	Why? Because we got all the electronics now. That's why I see it that way. Sure. We've broken through into the electronic world. We've got all kinds of electronics. Never go back, never flash off forever. Sure, that's why I feel that way. Can you feel that?
Wade	Oh yes, I do.
Wally	Okay?
Wade	Thanks a lot. Thanks a lot for talking to me.

WALLY starts off. Enter ANN.

	(To ANN) Are you hungry?
Ann	I beg your pardon?
Wade	I'm sorry. I just think about food all the time. I don't know why.
Ann	You have an eating disorder.
Wade	Are you...?
Ann	Well, yes.
Wade	Is that all right?
Ann	Well, yeah, if you face up to it. *(Pause)* I don't mean that in a violent sense. I just meant, you can see it for what it is and work on it, one day at a time.
Wade	I guess I don't understand.
Ann	That's okay. *(Pause)*
Wade	Are you waiting for someone?
Ann	My husband was here just a moment ago.
Wade	Is he an older person?
Ann	Well...
Wade	People don't intend to look old.

Ann	He's got white hair. But he's not old.
Wade	Okay. *(Silence)* I have poor communication skills. I saw you go into the meeting. I guess you didn't like it.
Ann	I like the meeting.
Wade	You like the meeting?
Ann	Sure.
Wade	You do? My father is in there.
Ann	Which one?
Wade	Dr. Sayer.
Ann	Why don't you come in?
Wade	I can't do that.
Ann	Why not? Don't you have views?
Wade	Views?
Ann	An opinion. You can speak up in the meeting.
Wade	*(Sincere)* Do you think it would do any good? Do you think anybody is doing any good in the world?
Ann	*(Touched)* Yes, I do. Teachers can help. Workers can help. Children can help. It's the children who are dying.
Wade	You don't ever see 'em.
Ann	They're dying of electricity. From the cables, the power stations, near the schools. It is a poison. It can be slow. It's in the air and in the water and in the food.
Wade	I'm hungry all the time.
Ann	Me too.
Wade	Are you?
Ann	Yes, I am.
Wade	For a while, I didn't eat at all. I was starving myself, I guess. Now I eat everything.
Ann	You have to eat—

WALLY comes over; he's very interested in ANN.

Wally	I just wanted to tell this kid—you think the Japanese would be into what they're into if, uhm, you know? Electronics?
Wade	I don't know.
Wally	Electronics! The Japanese! Remember? It's forever!
Wade	Okay!
Ann	*(To WADE)* You have to look at it. When you're hungry, is it a feeling, or do you really need food?
Wally	Oh, you guys talking about eating?
Ann	Well...
Wally	*(Keeping her there)* It's like bugs or something, what people eat. They'll eat anything if it's got like a crust and it's soft and sweet inside. You got chemists, you got biological engineers all over the globe coming up with substances that the human organism will pay money for. Substances, stuff. They'll eat. They wanna eat, they gotta eat. They eat when they're hungry, they eat when they're not. They eat for reasons, any fucking reason. They eat because they're afraid, they eat for sex, they eat for entertainment. They like it, they'll buy more, they don't just eat once. They eat until they're sick, they eat until they die. They don't know what they're eating—it's in a package, it's called food, they'll eat it. So you got these professional junk food manufacturers—I saw a program on this—they make a study of what you like to chomp down on, what kind of texture you like, they plug you right into a computer and they figure out what the human brain will go for in the way of eating shit. Then the chemists go to work and they make it. Say it's like blue cheese, they wanna make a blue cheese deal to go

in the middle of something with just the right texture on the outside, they take a molecule of blue cheese and they break it down and analyze its structure and they build up a molecule which tastes like cheese and smells like cheese but it ain't cheese. It's the ghost of cheese, a facsimile of cheese, a cheese-like substance which is a lot cheaper than cheese, and they put a crust around that, which is equally unreal in that it is not made from anything that has grown in the ground or walked on the earth. Then the marketing geniuses design a bright little plastic package for it and they call it the Blue Cheese Donut Delight! Ha! Okay?

Wade   Are you...?

Wally   I'm in the cattle business. Real food. Meat.

ANN looks for CROSS.

I was telling a white-haired gentleman about it before.

Ann   That's my husband. He must be inside.

Wally   He ain't!

She goes in anyway. He watches her leave, follows to the door, looks in.

Uh-oh.

SAYER starts out. WADE puts distance between them.

Sayer   *(Half in, half out)* THE MOST IMPORTANT DEATH OF ALL IS MINE. IT IS IN FACT THE ONLY DEATH. IT IS MINE IN SOLITUDE, AND THE ONLY ONE.

Martin	*(Inside)* SHUT THE DOOR, Sayer. *(SAYER does so)*
Wally	What I was trying to tell you before, Sayer, about electricity—
Sayer	That wasn't you, that was Bint.
Wally	That was me. Bint doesn't know anything. The power, the electricity, is sucked out of the flow of water, out of the air, out of the little worlds and big worlds, sucked out, drained, and grounded as waste into the earth.
Sayer	Time is running out, running out into the walls, into the machinery!
Wally	That is to say, the flow of electrons, with vibration, movement, currents, waves, is channeled into the machinery and then dumped as waste into the earth.
Sayer	THE MOST IMPORTANT DEATH OF ALL IS MINE. IT IS IN FACT THE ONLY DEATH. IT IS MINE IN SOLITUDE, AND THE ONLY ONE.
Wally	Good, Dr. Sayer!
Sayer	*(Shouting, to WADE)* What is the sun? Come on!
Wade	The sun is a star.
Sayer	No! The sun is a hole! Come on! What is the moon?
Wade	The moon is a planet.
Sayer	No! The moon is a rock! Come on! Where is the earth?
Wade	The earth is between.
Sayer	Right! Between a hole and a hard place! Ha! Come on! Don't you find this entertaining?
Wade	Sure, Dad.
Sayer	Come on! Why are people round?
Wade	Are people round?
Sayer	Well, they have a round shape. And all the microbes are equally round. What do you make of that?
Wade	I don't understand where the competition comes from then.

Wally	Good point, Wade! Ha!

Enter CROSS.

Sayer	Best get back to the meeting, Wally.
Wally	Yeah, yeah, rock and roll...RAP...OP-ER-RA...*(Goes)*
Martin	*(Inside)* DON'T SLAM THE DOOR.
Sayer	Hell of a meeting, Mr. Cross.
Cross	Is my wife in there?
Sayer	For example, cocaine is a product, right? Opium is a product. It's a product. It comes out of the ground, it's a flower. It's a pretty flower, right? So where do we draw the line? What's going on?
Cross	Are they talking drugs now?
Sayer	How can you not talk about drugs? You can't not talk about drugs anymore! You got a group of guys running the coke trade, you got others running the opium, you got the marijuana business. Ain't it the same with tobacco? I mean, where is the difference there? And what about alcohol? It's not good for ya, either. It's an abused substance, fer chrissakes! So you got these fucked up economies, right? You got these populations out of control. You got these huge debts. They owe us money! These people owe us a lot of money! And we got this huge demand here. We got an America with an insatiable appetite for drugs. And these people are supplying the demand. And they owe us money. You see what I'm saying? You look at it clean and there ain't no difference. These agricultural products are meeting a market demand. I mean, what is it we are doing? Let us leave the market be and get our money back, with interest! *(Pause)* Ha!

Cross	Ah.
Sayer	*(To WADE)* How'd you get here? COME ON! DID YOU WALK? DID YOU DRIVE?
Wade	I'm okay, Dad.
Sayer	DID YA RIDE OVER IN A CAR?

WADE doesn't answer. SAYER stares at him.

	(Wheeling, to CROSS) What's a CANCER CLUSTER, CROSS? COME ON!
Cross	No.
Sayer	I still have a bone to pick with you, sir, about speaking and oratory.
Cross	My mother was schizophrenic and abusive; my brother is schizophrenic and retarded; my sister is so shy she's in a convent in Ohio; and I got a great aunt left in the family, but she's had a series of strokes and is losing her mind. Ha.
Sayer	Ha! Back into the fray now, Mr. Cross! *(At door)* Watch out for ol' Ginnie, for she is in a foul mood! *(Goes in)*
Wade	Ginnie's his friend.
Cross	Ah.
Wade	She's conservative.
Cross	Ah.
Wade	I think about suicide a lot.
Cross	*(Dismayed)* Why?
Wade	I don't know. I have thoughts. He's very creative. He's an entrepreneur.
Cross	Who?
Wade	My father.
Cross	True.

Wade	It's hard to live with a man like that.

CROSS sighs.

Wade	She pulled up my big sister by the hair and threw her around the room, against the walls.
Cross	Who did?
Wade	My mother. My sister has problems.
Cross	Everybody, Wade. Everybody in that room's got problems.
Wade	Oh, yeah, sure, I see what you're sayin'. Thank you. I feel better talkin' about it.
Cross	You don't have to thank me.
Wade	Okay.

WALLY comes halfway, hesitates.

Bill	*(Inside)* I don't have a stake in this fucking country and at my age, and you got nothing but contempt for that! I can see it on your face as you go farting through the K-Mart!
Martin	*(Inside)* Fuck you!
Ann	*(Inside)* Did you hear uh, uh…that Doctor…? His talk was of angry children…? That was his theme. That the children are angry, because of all the abortions. When the child is killed in the womb, then the soul of the murdered child is made angry. And they come back, they come back as the newborn, as angry children! *(Cries)*
Ginnie	*(Inside)* It's all right, honey. There, there. Just a theory. Don't take it all to heart.
Martin	*(Inside)* CLOSE THE DAMN DOOR, Wally.

WALLY goes back in, closing the door.

Cross That was Ann.

Wade Oh. Is that your wife?

CROSS nods.

She seems nice.

CROSS nods.

Oh, I forgot to tell you, she was looking for you.

Cross Thank you. *(Of the bandage)* Hurt yourself?

Wade Yeah, I had an accident, I guess.

CROSS stares.

Cross When I was your age I was blasting away at myself, blasting away, like a miner, like a saboteur, like a terrorist. I wasn't investing in my future, I was trying to smash a loop into the sublime.

Wade Oh, that's good!

Cross You're thinking, "That old fart, he's difficult to get along with." Naturally, you don't think it'll ever happen to you. I see what I've become and I can't do anything about it. Time and experience wear you out. I've lived five lifetimes already.

Wade I don't think like that.

Cross You don't?

Wade I'm sorry.

Cross Come on!

Wade	I cruise in the City of Commerce. I live alone in rooms. He drove right into a trailer. He drove right into a truck. He drove right into the bay. He killed himself. He took a hike. That's how I think. The black guys out there take advantage of me. I don't know why.
Cross	You don't?
Wade	Yeah, I do.
Cross	What do you do for fun?

CROSS stares in disbelief as WADE replies.

Wade	I like music, I guess. I drive a lot. I don't like to drive, but I do a lot of it. I don't understand where everybody comes from or where they're going. I just wanna crash it. Everybody's angry. It's not my fault. They all had mothers. They're psychopaths, alcoholics, and addicts. When I'm thinking about it, I'm thinking about smashing her. Do you drive?
Cross	I'm new here.
Wade	Oh, I see. That's it, then. Do you...uh...teach?
Cross	History. Ancient.
Wade	Bitchin'.

CROSS stares.

Cross	It's the most amazing thing: a school in the valley, a house with a porch...
Wade	Yeah...I wanted to love her. I was an innocent child.
Cross	*(Not hearing him)* I should have been a filmmaker.
Wade	Really?

Cross	I keep having this vision. I see this image. It's a film image, a sequence in black and white. A woman, wearing a shawl, a wanderer, is approaching. She is dark, in her forties, greying, still beautiful. Very sad. She is coming for her allotment, her allotment, on a street. The sky is background, a sunset. It is near the sea. The woman approaches, staring at the street. She knows the people in this place, who will provide her allotment, her portion. She is one of those...one of those upon whom vengeance has been taken, and she's saying, "Have you seen my man? Have you seen him? I was just hoping you'd seen my—my husband, he's vanished."
Wade	It's sad. Is that how it ends?
Cross	Yeah...I want a drink. I want a smoke. I want to check out. I'm okay and you're okay. I feel crowded. I'm gone. *(Walks away)*
Wade	Where you goin'?

CROSS doesn't answer, wanders off. SHATTER appears, way off, calls out.

Shatter	Wade! Wade!

WADE steps back.

ARE YOU ANGRY? ARE YOU ANGRY, Wade? COME ON!

WADE takes another step back. SHATTER withdraws. ANN comes out, searches.

Ann	*(Seeing WADE)* Oh!

Wade	Hi.
Ann	I'm looking for my husband. Have you seen my husband?
Wade	*(Shocked)* Well...no.
Ann	*(Distraught)* Oh, where is he? What's wrong?
Wade	He's coming back, I guess.

ANN looks at him.

Ann	What kind of a kid are you?
Wade	I'm a beastie boy and a bum, I guess.
Ann	Oh, God!
Wade	Did I say something wrong?
Ann	Nothing. Never mind.
Wade	What's the matter?
Ann	Oh, I don't know. *(Pause)* I don't know what they think about me. I'm embarrassed how much I care what they think about me.
Wade	They maybe don't think about you at all, I guess.
Ann	Oh, how would you know! You won't even attend the meeting! There's a woman in there who hates my views! Why don't you even go inside!
Wade	Do you think I should?
Ann	*(Distraught)* Oh, God! What's the matter with you? They're trying to help!
Wade	Well...I don't say what I have to say because I don't know. I don't know what I have to say.
Ann	But you can't act as though nothing's happening! It's possible to become monstrous!
Wade	Actually, I have nothing to do with it.
Ann	God. I need a break.

WADE walks away, leaving his boom box. Yelling inside.
ANN wipes the tears from her eyes. GINNIE comes out.

Ginnie	Hi.
Ann	Hi.
Ginnie	I didn't mean to insult you. You weren't the target. *(Pause)* I agree that we should all save money on nuclear arms now. I just hope they don't put it into social programs. Makes for a weak country.
Ann	What about health care?
Ginnie	Nobody has to pay for health here. You just have to know what to do. People come here and live off the fat of the land. Like the Mexicans.

ANN bursts into tears.

All right, all right. Listen to this. I heard a chiropractor the other day, she's talking about the new age: People will live a thousand years, they won't get to puberty till they're a hundred, they'll be as calm as clocks and clear-minded. She's got the idea that billions of years of accident and cosmic debris are in the body. Health is detoxification of enemy vibrations from the past life of the earth. Ha! That and the realignment of entities. As I understand it, an entity is anything that moves. Everything that moves is from the Divine Will toward Being, the explosion of space into space, the first endless moment. All is and isn't, as the Masters say, for in the beginning was Nothing.

GINNIE laughs; off, the SCREAMER screams.

Ann	Who is that person?
Ginnie	You get used to it. You get used to everything.
Ann	*(Cold)* Thank you.
Ginnie	Don't thank me. Self-reliance is what makes a country strong, honey, and violence is a part of that. It's the struggle for life. It's competition. Violence is the key, violence is the mode. What's good for me may not be what's good for you. Should we treat people like children and take care of them? Sex is violent. Eating is violent. Should we stop killing animals for food? At least we don't burn them alive, like in the old days, for the gods and spirits. Politics is violent because that is its nature. Power means violence. It does not mean civility. Civilization means amenities for the powerful, for the ones who can afford it. Culture is an amenity, a way to occupy the mind, to pass the time. Otherwise you work, eat, sleep, fuck, and die. In any event, you die. Working is better than not working. Working is for the morally fit. To lay around, to do nothing, to indulge, to want to be taken care of—this is a life unworthy even of insects.

ANN walks away from her.

	What are we supposed to do, give up our energy? Our light and heat?
Ann	We're gonna bring the whole thing down, them and us! Take the very breath out of the atmosphere!
Ginnie	What difference does it make? Old age and death are curses enough! Earth is nothin' but a pain factory! It will bubble up, when the time comes, with a new set of employees! Insects, probably!

Shatter	Were you talking about incest?
Ginnie	No. Insects.
Shatter	I thought you were talking incest.
Ginnie	Insects.
Shatter	I could say a few things.
Ginnie	Of course, dear.
Shatter	But I won't!
Ann	Excuse me. I...I'm looking for my husband.
	(Walks off)
Shatter	Yeah.
Ginnie	And so's your father, dear.
Shatter	All over the nation men are hurting women, husbands are killing their wives and getting away with it.
Ginnie	So what do you want from me?
Shatter	Ginnie! *(Cries)*
Ginnie	Oh, fer cryin' out loud.
Shatter	Ginnie! I'm livin' in this house. I'm livin' in the back room. Right here in the Valley. The father, he hates his job, he beats his wife and he screws his daughters! Then he wants me to listen to his troubles and feel sorry for him and pay his goddamn rent!

MARTIN steps out, disgusted.

Martin	*(To GINNIE)* I have a choice—I have one choice—I can maintain my fuck-you attitude to the bitter end or I can turn myself around and start a new life.
Ginnie	What do you think it'll be, counselor?

Martin	I don't know—it's late in the day—and I like fighting and I love revenge—so it's a toss-up as far as I'm concerned—I could go either way—there's something very appealing about goin' out with my shit intact to the last—let's go for a ride, Ginnie.
Shatter	Hey! We're talkin' here! My father kicked me out! They put me in a hospital and gave me drugs! If people stopped taking drugs, this whole country would turn to shit! You got that? I'm protesting!
Martin	*(To SHATTER)* Talk! Talk! Rock and roll!
Shatter	I drink and I smoke. I know that. I don't feel good about that. I'd like to talk about it. At least Wade doesn't drink, doesn't smoke. Wade's clean. He is now. He had enough of the City of Commerce and he went home. People pickin' on him in the City of Commerce. Gross shit. Scared li'l white boy. Call him a mushroom. What's he to do now? At least he's a poet.

ANN approaches the door, looks in.

Martin	*(To SHATTER)* Get adjusted! That's the trouble! Nobody makes an adjustment! Move away! Find a home!
Shatter	*(Singing wildly) They'll always negate you* *Prosecute and hate you* *Humiliate and screw you* *Sacrifice and fool you—!*
Ginnie	Stop that!
Shatter	I'M GONNA KILL SOMEONE!
Martin	HEY! CAN YOU DO NO WRONG? ARE YOU A SAINT? WHO ARE YOU TO JUDGE? OBEY THE LAW AND WATCH YOUR ASS! YOU SHOULD GET OUT OF BED IN THE MORNING AND SAY THANK YOU A THOUSAND TIMES YOU WOKE UP IN AMERICA!

ANN *opens the door.*

Sayer   *(Inside)* Something is going to happen—worse than AIDS.
A plague, a virus, it's in the works now. It's being prepared.
Somewhere, in the womb of the earth, in the atmosphere,
is being prepared an antidote to man. The catastrophe is
here, but the correction awaits us. Floods, famine, drought,
the burning of the forests. Massacres. Planes falling out of
the sky. We have despoiled the chain of existence. But these
are ticks, these are spasms, signs and portents. The fulsome
planetary shudder is yet to come. I don't think it will be
nuclear, no—it will be just as total, but more subtle: atomic,
viral. A virulence never seen on earth, because we are so
many. And the poison in the chain—no, the lawful results
of the poisoning of the chain—will destroy all but a few:
the renaissance man, the enlightened, the fit to live. I
won't be here. I am neutral. I am interested in the science
of it, in the laws. I won't be around. I will have met my
Maker, the Initiate of Laws, who regards his Work with
sublime neutrality from a higher world. His Will be done.
Let the survivors remember what happened here—if there
are survivors. I couldn't say. This is only an opinion. It
could be indiscriminate. It's possible. The fit could die with
the unfit.

Ginnie   The sonofabitch is reading! He's making a prepared speech!

ANN *steps back as* BINT *comes out.*

Martin   *(Of* SAYER*)* Who is he?—Who does he think he is?—He
doesn't make a dime!—Nobody pays attention to him!—

Nobody votes for him!—Nobody puts his name in the
fuckin' paper anymore!—Fuck him!

Ginnie   He read from a text!

Shatter   I can't stand it!

Attacks BINT *and beats him.*

Music. SAYER *and the others come rushing out.*

Wally   OH, SHE'S A SPITFIRE, SHE IS!

SAYER *pulls* SHATTER *off of* BINT.

Shatter   *(To* WALLY*)* DROP DEAD, YOU SCUMBAG!

Sayer   *(To* SHATTER*)* HAVE YOU BEEN DRINKING?

BINT *starts crawling off. The* SCREAMER *screams. A huge,
shattering crash, close by.* CROSS *comes running in, finds*
ANN *and takes her in his arms.*

Wade   *(On boom-box tape)* You talk as though you don't know
and maybe you don't, but maybe you better express your
feelings because time is wearing out your sneakers and
fiendish darkness is wearing out your welcome. *(Pause)*
You don't have to smile when I smile and I don't give a
shit if you know or you don't.

Shatter   Wade?

Wade   *(Tape)* The earth will bounce its axis and momentum like the
snap of a ball and shake off the slugs and everything else on
it into oblivion which is a long fall past the moon deader than

absolute nothing and meanwhile I'm hanging here figuring things out responsibly like I know what to do, going from here to there on my rump and saying things with my mouth.

Sayer *(To CROSS)* Where?

CROSS points, SAYER rushes off. MARTIN follows him.

Wade *(Tape)* What I want to do is come alongside with my wheels on straight and eyes level with things as they are and have the knives out for people who bother me—because if you don't win, you lose around here, pal—but my head feels like a tired tree with old leaves in the smog and my chest is like crusty with like thirty-two years of Agent Orange and I wish it would rain.

Ann *(Upset, to CROSS)* What happened?

Cross He crashed, honey. Let's go home. *(Leads her off)*

Wade *(Tape, continuing)* I want to be left alone to die but by the same token I don't. Of all the moments gone and coming how many would be shaken out into the void like dead leaves when the big shake that's on its way is here? Like a ball, like a towel, like a rug—SNAP.

GINNIE turns off boom box.

BLACKOUT.

The End

Dictator

by Murray Mednick

Dictator was first produced in 1997 at Theatre of NOTE in Los Angeles, under the direction of Diane Robinson, with the following cast:

Dictator: Armando Duran
Lawyer: James Lesure
Journalist/Ambassador: Katharine Gibson
Dr. Steward: Christopher Grove
Colonel: Christopher Kelley
Rhea: Christine Avila
President: David Bickford

Characters

The Dictator *Hispanic; 40s.*

The Lawyer *(Jenkins) Elegant black man; 40s.*

The Journalist *(Gina) 31.*

The Doctor *(Dr. Stewart) 40s.*

The Colonel *40s.*

The Mistress *(Rhea) Cuban-born; 30s.*

The Ambassador *(Gina) Now 34.*

The President *The President of the United States.*

The Guard *20s.*

1.

SOUNDS of airplanes going by and occasional car alarms. "Cucaracha" is the ambient music.

Dictator   *(To the walls, mostly in Spanish)* Where are we? Are we near an airport? Which airport? Those planes—what is that? Who is doing this to me? Is it the Colonel? Is it the President? Hey! Say something! You want money? I got more money than everybody! The Colonel, everybody! I got money stuffed in a bank, you and all your babies and babies' babies will never see such money! Hey! Hey!

*

2. Three months later.

New music. Find the DICTATOR greeting the LAWYER (JENKINS).

Dictator   Hello, sir.
Jenkins   Hello, how are ya?
Dictator   I'm not the same. I'm not the man I was. You have news for me?

Jenkins	No.
Dictator	How come I don't see myself on television?
Jenkins	Because you're in jail.
Dictator	You seen my name in the paper? You seen my picture in the paper?
Jenkins	No. There's nothing. Silence. You have disappeared.
Dictator	They locked up my money.
Jenkins	Sorry. I tried.
Dictator	I can't pay you.
Jenkins	That's why I tried very hard.
Dictator	I got a lot to thank you for.
Jenkins	No problema.
Dictator	They were piping "Cucaracha" in here day and night.
Jenkins	That's their idea of a joke.
Dictator	It's not even my country, Mexico. And they finally gave me some videotapes that wasn't soft-core porno.
Jenkins	What'd they give you?
Dictator	They gave me *The Godfather* and *Birth of a Nation*. But I could use a few more books. And something to write on, like a computer.
Jenkins	You can write?
Dictator	I will write a book.
Jenkins	On what?
Dictator	Don't worry. The whole stinking truth.
Jenkins	Forget about it.
Dictator	How the CIA sold coca in L.A. for the Contras. *(Pause)* And kept most of the *dinero* in their own pockets. *(Pause)* Make me a deal. You'll be a rich man.
Jenkins	I wish I could, General.
Dictator	I need an activity, something to do with my time. It could

	be like a hobby. I used to have bad hobbies. This could be a good hobby. What's your hobby?
Jenkins	History of Rome. The Republic, Sulla to Augustus.
Dictator	They were dictators, like me, 80 B.C. to 15 A.D.
Jenkins	I know who they were. But these men were not like you, General. There were not small-time. They were dealing with an empire. Rome. Big.
Dictator	I was big. I was dealing with the U.S. of A.
Jenkins	On the wrong side.
Dictator	Ah, tell 'em to go fuck their grandmothers. *(Looks at walls)*
Jenkins	Stupid. Why play the thug?
Dictator	You think I'm playing?
Jenkins	No, you are a thug.
Dictator	There's a couple more things.
Jenkins	*(Irritated)* What are they?
Dictator	I want to talk to a doctor. I always have a doctor, it's my right.
Jenkins	You have regular checkups.
Dictator	I want a personal doctor. I want to talk to him. I want to have a conversation.
Jenkins	You have medical problems?
Dictator	Me, I don't have no stinking medical problems. *(Smiles)*
Jenkins	Oh, I see.
Dictator	In my country, we got people, they'll dance for days— makes you feel better, and they feel good, too.
Jenkins	A psychiatrist. I'll pass it on.
Dictator	Can you dance?
Jenkins	No.
Dictator	Too bad. Me, I am a very good dancer.
Jenkins	I'm pleased for you.

Dictator	When's my trial gonna be?
Jenkins	You had a trial.
Dictator	I want a real trial. I want to be treated like a living person. I want to testify.
Jenkins	You are not alone in this.
Dictator	I am alone.
Jenkins	A third of the young black men in this country are in prison.
Dictator	You're mad at me for that?
Jenkins	These kids, black kids, they start doing time when they're boys. They don't get an education. They're in the drug economy. They're on the streets or in the can.
Dictator	That's my fault this happens?
Jenkins	Yeah. Greaseballs like you bringing that shit in here from all over.
Dictator	*(To the walls)* I'm sorry for what I did. *(To JENKINS)* I wish to be treated like a serious man. *(Pause)* I had a lot of money once.
Jenkins	Kiss your money goodbye.
Dictator	It's not legal.
Jenkins	Your money was legal?
Dictator	My money was my money.
Jenkins	Your money was shit money.
Dictator	Where is it now?
Jenkins	It belongs to the United States of America. By law.
Dictator	Whose law?
Jenkins	By American law.
Dictator	You know about the Romans?
Jenkins	Sure. They were nothing like you. The Romans had an ideal.
Dictator	What was the ideal?
Jenkins	Rome.

Dictator	I want to learn from them. The game's not over.
Jenkins	It's over. You're not covered. You're not a citizen. You're a nonentity. *(Pause)*
Dictator	International law?
Jenkins	Scumbag like you? *(Pause)*
Dictator	That's not nice. *(Pause)* Will they kill me?
Jenkins	They may not bother.
Jenkins	They got me buried me in here anyway.
Jenkins	Correct.
Dictator	*(To himself)* They go to law school and come out thieves and politicians. Me, I never went to a real school. But I seen the *Godfather* picture nineteen times now. *(To* JENKINS*)* I want to be like you. Handsome and educated. A cool guy, a gentleman, he knows the halls of American power like his own briefcase.
Jenkins	That's me.
Dictator	Are you a happy man? *(Pause)* Black guy like you, you should be more on my side.
Jenkins	Black don't mean I'm stupid. Black don't mean I'm degenerate. I grew up with decent people, decent hard-working people. I'm not on your side. If it was up to me, I'd get all you punks and stop the wealth from pouring out of here like blood from a wound. ¿*Comprende?*
Dictator	What happens to me now?
Jenkins	I don't know what happens to you.
Dictator	You're uncomfortable. Not because you abandon a man in his dungeon, but because the man is intelligent.
Jenkins	Intelligent? They give you a VCR and four walls and suddenly you're intelligent?
Dictator	I'm very intelligent.

Jenkins	You never had to sit still so long before without booze and dope and broads.
Dictator	No, never.
Jenkins	So maybe you're actually learning something now.
Dictator	I think, maybe, there's a chance.
Jenkins	Small chance. They say it's over by the time you're seven years old.
Dictator	I am a war prisoner!
Jenkins	No, you're not. Nobody declared war.
Dictator	An army walks into your territory and shoots your people and blows up buildings and arrests the head of government and this is not war?
Jenkins	No. No war, therefore no war prisoners. When there's a threat to the state, the state can break the rules. It's an old story. The Roman Senate, they had a decree—the *consultum ultimum*. What it did was, it said to the Consul, "Do what you have to—save the state." They went after Gaius Gracchus with it and tried to club him to death. He wanted to break up the big estates, open up the land. You, you played with drug dealers and mercenaries and whores.
Dictator	Gringos included.
Jenkins	Who, for instance?
Dictator	*(Not answering)* What happened to…?
Jenkins	Gracchus? You don't know? They trapped him, and he killed himself.
Dictator	Is that a hint? You're not a bad guy, Jenkins. *(Pause)* You quit the case for good?
Jenkins	Yes. Today.
Dictator	I'm sorry. I was starting to like you. It's okay you don't like me.
Jenkins	It's business.

Dictator	Yeah, yeah. America, business. I want to talk also to the press. It's my right! *(Pause)* I feel bad about what I did. You think I am a dog? I was a king in my country! I was a man to be feared!
Jenkins	I've been giving you a chance to talk. *(Pause)* Last chance.
Dictator	One hand washes the other. Am I right?
Jenkins	Right.
Dictator	Yeah, but I'm not telling you anything.
Jenkins	Fine. Your choice. *(Exits)*
Dictator	*(Continuing)* You're the same as me, a thug. No, I changed my mind. You and me are not the same. You don't like people. Me, I am a social fellow, I like people. You don't like people, you don't like yourself, you're disappointed, your best days are behind you. You, you got your walking papers, you got your own money somewhere in a bank, but you don't believe in it, and you will take a fall. *(Pause)* "Probably. But when I do, it'll be in bed, in my own house. You went right down the toilet."

BLACKOUT.

*

3. Six months later.

Find the JOURNALIST *(GINA) standing at entrance.* DICTATOR *is stunned, as though viewing an apparition. There is a computer, and more books are scattered around the room. Different music.*

Dictator	You're a journalist?
Gina	Yes, I am.
Dictator	You got permission to see me?
Gina	I'm here.
Dictator	Why?
Gina	You asked for the press. They sent me.
Dictator	Why they send you, a beautiful girl like you?
Gina	I applied for the assignment through my agent. I had no idea it was you.
Dictator	Anonymous dictator requests interview.
Gina	Yes. Didn't they tell you?
Dictator	They don't tell me nothin'.
Gina	You got the questions in advance.
Dictator	Oh. I forgot. That was months ago. Sit down, please.

She does so.

	Yeah, so you interview the dictator, it's a big feather in your hair.
Gina	Not really.
Dictator	You like me?
Gina	I don't know you.
Dictator	You'll take my picture?
Gina	Later.
Dictator	When later?
Gina	Later later.
Dictator	Okay. First question.
Gina	You had a chance to go into exile, and avoid prison. Why didn't you take it?
Dictator	I refuse to dishonor myself. I am a war prisoner. I want to

	talk to the International Red Cross. I want to be treated
	according to the Geneva Conventions.
Gina	*(Blurting)* Why'd you do it?
Dictator	Why'd I do what?
Gina	Become a military dictator, a pimp, and a dope-pusher, all at the same time.
Dictator	It seemed like the thing to do. I regret it now.
Gina	Do you?
Dictator	I wanted to have a good time. Who wants to suffer? You'd have to be a stupid idiot. I got a kick out of being the boss. Top dog. Nobody telling me what to do, pushing my face around. Until I got squashed by the Americans. I took a fall and they broke me into pieces. Now I try to put myself back together again.
Gina	How?
Dictator	I do sit-ups. I walk on walls. And...I write.
Gina	You write?
Dictator	Of course. It's the best thing. I'm isolated. I am walled in. My day is settled. I'm not hunted. They feed me. I watch television. I have time. But I feel caged. Yes, I'm edgy. And I'm horny as a monk. You feel safe with me?
Gina	Sure.
Dictator	Sure, the walls have eyes and ears. The walls *are* eyes and ears.
Gina	They say it was the CIA.
Dictator	They say.
Gina	And if it wasn't the CIA, who was it?
Dictator	Who did what?
Gina	Will you tell?
Dictator	No.

Gina	I can help you.
Dictator	How?
Gina	I'll help you on the outside.
Dictator	Nothing outside can help me. Only inside can help me. Big inside. Bigger than this room. Big interior.
Gina	Were the Nicaraguans acting as middlemen for the coke?
Dictator	I don't know no stinking Nicaraguans. *(Smiles)*
Gina	Excuse me. This question was on the list of questions that we agreed upon.
Dictator	I wanted to see somebody for a change. But I don't have any information for you.
Gina	Should I leave?
Dictator	Wait. I do have ideas, and I have time. I want to share. Are you getting this?
Gina	*(Checking her tape recorder)* Yes. Go on.
Dictator	I'm an army man, a military man. But I never read a book on it. Now I'm learning, for example, what it means, a soldier-politician. I went to school, it was kill the lefties and *campesinos* school, sponsored by the U.S. of A. I didn't think about it. Kick the other guy before he kicks you, that was my ideology. You want an army job in my country, you work for the gringos. *(Half to himself)* I myself am a coward by nature. I fear conflict. *(To GINA)* You want to hear how I got into this situation?
Gina	Yes.
Dictator	A difficult childhood. Bad company, misfortune. Lousy circumstances. You know? This is a setup.

He looks at walls—she looks at walls.

Gina	I see.
Dictator	They pay you?
Gina	Absolutely.
Dictator	That's good.
Gina	Should we continue?
Dictator	Continue. *(Pause)* I don't know why. People think, What is success? Must be pleasure.
Gina	I'm not following you.
Dictator	Coke and hundred-dollar bills and dirty movies. *(Pause)* Maybe I don't know anything else.
Gina	Maybe I should go, then.
Dictator	You want to talk about porno?
Gina	Not really.
Dictator	It's not a pretty picture of human life. I will become an author. I will write myself out of this situation. Writing will redeem me. *(Pause)* I wanted to make a lot of money. But poets and monks, they stay poor for life. *Indios*, they don't even have no money. I have ancestors, they were not like me and you. Noblemen.
Gina	Really?
Dictator	I lied. I'm a mongrel dog, I was born in an alley.
Gina	And your parents?
Dictator	Dogs, like me. I'm in a bad mood now. *(Pause)* My ancestry, it's in the language. Latin. *(Pause)* I should learn Latin. I'm a Roman. Never mind. It's all lies. I will write a story, describe my life, maybe lie a lot, get my ass outta here.
Gina	Fine.
Dictator	You don't think I can do it.
Gina	No. Not alone.

Dictator	I had a friend, he was from Texas. A colleague, an apprentice—ha!—I meant to say acquaintance! "Apprentice," what? What do you think?
Gina	Criminal?
Dictator	Yes! Exactly! He had a criminal mind, in that...in that...
Gina	In that?
Dictator	He didn't like himself. Big, Texas ego, but he didn't like himself. You see? I can write, I can express.
Gina	Texas.
Dictator	Well, he gets caught at the border, he's carrying heroin into the U.S.A., big white handsome ol' boy, he's smuggling heroin into the U.S. of A., they lock him in a federal slammer and they throw away the key. In prison, he writes a novel about his childhood, he impresses a few people in New York, and he gets out.
Gina	Who was he?
Dictator	No names. He never wrote another book. I read his book—recently—he used plain words. A book of disappointment and nostalgia, it got him out of jail, the sonofabitch.
Gina	And yours, General?
Dictator	A book of questioning and...rehabilitation. (*Smiles, looks at the walls*) But of course, nothing that shouldn't be known will be revealed. Nothing about the gringos. No gringo connections. (*To the walls*) America, America, they have elections, they get what they deserve. Americans, I know. Tobacco, pills, whiskey, boredom, bad food, they don't admit about life, themselves, nothing. Okay, I shouldn't act big. I'm not sounding good. I never got any learning. But I'm intelligent. I got native intelligence. Someone like

me, he's got one choice, which is the army. I'm still a kid, these two gringo alcoholic whoremongers take me out to a joint—they want me to make a lot of money—I'm an idiot if I don't take the money—only I should spy on the officers and the wiseguys who might have political ideas or personal hatreds—gringo hate. These gringos, they were very hard men. They took me up to the top of a building. Two tall guys, they were much bigger than me. One was from Kansas, and the other from Missouri, but they had the same name cities—same name, two different cities. I came to know them well. They thought I was a piece of shit from beginning to end. And of themselves, they were criminal types, hard men, they're working for the government, things were simple for them. They were serene. They picked me up by the elbows and took me to the edge of the roof. One talked like a cowboy, the other like a banker, without feeling. I was trying to imagine, "Can I survive a fall from here?"

Gina   And?

Dictator   We came downstairs from the building, I was working for the U.S. of A. *(Smiles)*

BLACKOUT.

*

4. Three months later.

Find DR. STEWART sitting with the DICTATOR.

Dictator	I thought you were a psychiatrist.
Doctor	I am.
Dictator	Then let's talk about my problems.
Doctor	We are talking about your problems.
Dictator	I'm not well.
Doctor	More exercise. I know it's hard, but use the machines.
Dictator	I need an anguish pill.
Doctor	I don't have any.
Dictator	Don't forget my stomach and my bowels.
Doctor	Exercise will help there, too.
Dictator	They took away my money.
Doctor	I can't do anything about that.
Dictator	They pay you to come here?
Doctor	Yes.
Dictator	Why do they want me healthy if they're going kill me?
Doctor	I don't know.
Dictator	You could poison me.
Doctor	I could.
Dictator	You think you will?
Doctor	No.
Dictator	You think they'll kill me?
Doctor	I don't know.
Dictator	What then?
Doctor	I don't know.
Dictator	They say, "Go examine the Dictator," and you go?
Doctor	Voluntarily.
Dictator	Why?
Doctor	No special reason.
Dictator	You don't have reasons?
Doctor	It's my life's training.

Dictator	You're in charge of a hospital?
Doctor	I run a V.A. hospital.
Dictator	Where?
Doctor	I can't tell you.
Dictator	So the government knows you and trusts you.
Doctor	Evidently.
Dictator	And you trust them? *(No answer)* Maybe they hope I transmigrofy away.
Doctor	Transmigrate?
Dictator	Yeah, like a worm into a butterfly. Why you laugh?
Doctor	That's something else. You mean metamorphosis.
Dictator	*Eso es.* So, you work with addicts?
Doctor	Addicts and alcoholics.
Dictator	All veterans.
Doctor	All veterans. *(Long pause)*
Dictator	So they picked you for the great scumbag dictator.
Doctor	Are you bragging or complaining?
Dictator	I am an addict, an alcoholic, and a veteran.
Doctor	I won't give you drugs.
Dictator	Why not?
Doctor	You could replace me. The next guy might do it.
Dictator	I need a pill for my brain, for rehabilitation.
Doctor	They might like the idea.
Dictator	Yes?
Doctor	Sure. Tranquilize you, stupefy you.
Dictator	I'm glad to see you. My guards, they're not allowed to talk to me. You have kids and a wife?
Doctor	Yes. We've been married ten years and we have two daughters. And you?
Dictator	Oh, no! Me and women—two weeks, two days, I get bored,

	they want presents, this and that—you watch 'em eat, put on perfume, the romance is over. I tell 'em, "Get outta here, go home." But I feel good for you. Five minutes ago, I thought everybody should be killed.
Doctor	Why?
Dictator	Give the rest of life a chance. Once, I might have had a shot at it.
Doctor	We get men coming in all the time, tired of the pain. Most want to find a way to stay loaded, legally or illegally. Many talk about wanting to die. I tell them, addiction is a relative term. We have a methadone program, group meetings. I tell 'em, at bottom they have a choice. They can go up or they can go down, but they can't stay even. The chemistry won't work that way.
Dictator	I learn. I study. I learn about brain chemistry, what a synapse is. I learned what I knew already from my life, that man is vile, and the history of man, if it is anywhere written for the truth, is a book of terror.
Doctor	I won't debate you, but that means, "I am vile." You see?
Dictator	Yes. I'm writing my own book on it. I just put down what happened. It happened, I put it down. Straight English. But we can never understand each other in any language, because when I say "vile," I have memories, I have experience, they don't belong to you, they don't belong to your class.
Doctor	You read that in a book?
Dictator	No, I never read that.
Doctor	Because it does no good to identify. And vileness has nothing to do with class.
Dictator	Maybe I didn't say it right.

Doctor	Try again.
Dictator	Is this therapy?
Doctor	This is therapy.
Dictator	There are boys down in Mexico, on the border, they choose a nice girl, a middle-class girl, they take her out to the desert and gang-rape her and kill her.
Doctor	Yes?
Dictator	They think nothing about it. They speak another language. It's not even Spanish. It's Spanish thug-talk. It's a language without morals. *(Pause)* All of a sudden I have anguish. *(Pause)* I am turning yellow from the lights in here. I'm staring at the mirror, I see an old man fading, I see his bones. *(Pause)* I can't tell any secrets—
Doctor	—That's all right with me—
Dictator	—Otherwise someone will kill me. One side or the other. I have to be good, right down the middle.
Doctor	I think you're doing very well.
Dictator	But I have thoughts, I have memories, I have knowledge.
Doctor	By the way, are you aware that you squint?
Dictator	I need glasses for reading.
Doctor	Nothing to be ashamed of. I'll examine your eyesight. *(Setting up)* We've observed you squinting. I came prepared. You tell me what you see, I order a lens.
Dictator	I had a vision. I saw my fate. When they caught me, the vicious dictator.
Doctor	Don't be nervous. This won't hurt.
Dictator	While I was being hunted down like an animal.
Doctor	You had time for visions?
Dictator	No, not then. It was being built, it was accumulating. I was going top speed. I had no time for even thoughts. Buildings

blown up, boom! Crash! People exploding, like plastic dummies, bnf! Bnf! The world was turned inside out, and it was flat! Running was like diving, walking was like falling. You have a name, doctor?

Doctor   Stewart.

Dictator   Sitting was like spinning, Dr. Stewart, on a ball.

Doctor   Sit down.

Dictator   I was sitting in the embassy with the Cardinal, when it came to me.

Doctor   *(Turns on machine light)* I see.

Dictator   The Cardinal kept talking about God, and I wondered what he meant. They marched me to the airport. I said goodbye to Flatland, so long Third World.

Doctor   See the lines of letters?

Dictator   Yeah.

Doctor   Which line can't you read? Which one starts to get fuzzy?

Dictator   Uh, the third one down.

Doctor   Try reading the one above it.

Dictator   Sure. X. Z. E. P. ...

Doctor   Okay, now the fuzzy one.

Dictator   Wait a minute.

Doctor   Yes?

Dictator   Wait a minute.

The upstage wall—a panel—is penetrated by the BEAM *OF LIGHT. Visible facing us is a* YOUNG MAN (THE GUARD) *in a white shirt sitting at a console with headphones, a notepad, a computer. A long wait while the* DICTATOR *stares at him, dumbfounded.*

Dictator	You see that, Doctor?
Doctor	What?

The YOUNG MAN looks up, presses a button—the panel goes dark.

Dictator	The light, it went out. You didn't see that? Young man, white shirt, earphones, a computer?
Doctor	No. Now I want you to look through these. We're going to take it one eye at a time…You tell me which image is the sharpest and clearest.
Dictator	There was a dictator in the east, he tried to solve the problem. He killed a lot of people.
Doctor	Pol Pot?
Dictator	Him. He had an ideal. It was not a Christian ideal. He tried to slim it down, make a perfect society.
Doctor	Some people believe in force, they think they can make a new world with it. Personally, I think it's sunspots. Causes mass psychosis on earth.
Dictator	Nobody thinks they're wrong. I never met a person yet, thinks they're wrong about anything.
Doctor	True.
Dictator	They had a thing in Rome, they could do things, called Save the State. That was me, I did things, save the state.
Doctor	Not really. You just did things.
Dictator	Okay. Now I worry about it. This room is wired. They send me visitors so they can hear me say what things. *(Pause, looks at walls)* I'm watched. I take it as a challenge. I go from one wall to the other, maybe to the toilet. Come back, sit down, maybe do it again. I try not to forget what

happened. Wall to wall, to chair, to toilet. Time is killing me. I don't have a friend in the world. I'm feeling sorry for myself. I grew up, my brothers and sisters were begging in the streets and selling their bodies. This I want to write about, it comes out thick, nobody will understand me or agree with me. Now I want to walk through walls. Now I want to turn into another person. I'm insecure. I fuck with whores, I don't think nobody can love me. You grow up like me, you think the world is pissing on you. And they are! One day, we are swimming in the canal near my home, my shack. I knew a gringo soldier, his name was Chuck. Him, I thought he was a benefactor, he gives money, candy, big bully of a fellow, he gives protection, he is watching us swimming, boys and girls, I come out of the water, I sit on edge of canal, all happy, I feel warm water on my back, I'm thinking, "What is this? Warm water? Canal is cold!" Behind me, Chuck is laughing—I jump to my feet! Chuck is pissing on me! In front of my friends, my sisters, this gringo prick is pissing on me! I start to cry, to fight, to kill the bastard! He laughs, he throws me into the canal! I swore, one day I find revenge on this fat American. Still, today, I could rip him apart with an Uzi. *(Long pause, looks at walls)* Who knows where this man is now? In which hell? *(Pause)* When I was running, I ran to the Vatican Embassy. I ran for sanctuary. While I was there, waiting, resting, I saw my—

A KNOCKING, *off.*

Doctor   It's time.

Dictator	—Fate. Since then, I have mainly forgotten. Once in a while, I remember the idea. *(Knocking)*

BLACKOUT.

*

5. Six months later.

Find the COLONEL *facing the* DICTATOR. *More books, no TV. The* DICTATOR *is writing the whole time.*

Dictator	What do you want, Colonel?
Colonel	I wanted you to know, I'm doing great now.
Dictator	What do I care?
Colonel	I went through hell. I suffered.
Dictator	You expect sympathy from me?
Colonel	Not at all.
Dictator	I don't give a fuck about you. We're not pals.
Colonel	I came out the other end, I came out okay. You keep your head on straight, all things are possible.
Dictator	What things?
Colonel	Success, a career.
Dictator	Who sent you to me? Who sent you, that I should hear this bullshit enlightenment?
Colonel	Destiny.
Dictator	Come on, some government hack sent you. Nobody gets in here without permission. It's the President. The President sent you.

Colonel	You can learn from my experience.
Dictator	No, I can't. You got your picture in the paper, you sang on TV—a shitty song, but you sang it—you became a celebrity. Me, I'm a *desaparecido*.
Colonel	Why a shitty song?
Dictator	You got no morals. You got no virtue.
Colonel	I had to tell them shit, but I kept my faith. And where do you get off, talking morals and virtue?
Dictator	Fuck you, I didn't ask for you.
Colonel	You're not behaving intelligently.
Dictator	I know, the walls have eyes and ears. You don't like it, you can go home.
Colonel	Bye, now.
Dictator	Goodbye.

No one moves, DICTATOR *keeps writing.*

Colonel	I know all about being on the spot, I was in everybody's living room.
Dictator	I know. You're a celebrity banana-head.
Colonel	I have my beliefs, I still have them.
Dictator	You got a gun on you?
Colonel	Of course not.
Dictator	You killed a few people.
Colonel	*(Cold)* I did America's business.
Dictator	Let's say you caused a few thousand people to be killed, Colonel. How's that?
Colonel	That's war. *(Pause)* Are your hands clean, you greasy shit?
Dictator	That's not nice. *(Looking at the walls)* No, they're not clean. I been trying to wash 'em.

Colonel	I've come to encourage you.
Dictator	Horseshit. You're a party hack. Talk slow, please. You got a gun, or not?
Colonel	No. Why bother to write that down?
Dictator	Last will and testament. Last words of the dictator and the army hack. I saw you in the hearings, I broke the fucking television. Enough is enough.
Colonel	You want a new one?
Dictator	No, thank you. (*Reads from notes*) They send the consigliere—who is that? The actor? I can't think of his name—never mind, they send him to this old-timer, his days are numbered, because he's been singing, like you. The counselor says, "Remember the days of Rome, the days of our ancestors? In those days a man knew how to save his honor, his dignity." The old-timer gets the message, next time we see him, he's in his bath, he's cut his wrists. You should see the movie. On the other hand, you have nothing to worry about.
Colonel	How's that?
Dictator	You have neither honor nor dignity. (*Long pause*)
Colonel	You piece of greaseball shit.
Dictator	You wanna talk about your testimony? Yeah. It occurs to me—You're surprised? About my English?
Colonel	When I knew you, all you could say was "money" and "more."
Dictator	Right. But of course, I never knew you. Especially according to your own testimony. Speaking of which, the word "testimony," it means "by the balls." The old Romans, they would swear an oath, they swore by their balls, they held their balls and spoke, heh, heh. Of course, that

couldn't be the case with you, you got no balls. I'm watching the hearings, I'm thinking, "This is asshole talk, not balls talk." Fuck it. *(Sadly)* I got an education, I'd be a star now, I'd be in the firmament. So what do you have to say? Talk slow.

Colonel *(Sigh)* I'm doing all right. Legit. I'm in business, a citizen.

Dictator What business?

Colonel We sell bulletproof vests. It's a good product. My name, my image, it's honorable enough, it's respected enough, I'm an asset to the business. We sell to police departments only, strictly on the up-and-up. I had an ordeal, I did my time, but I got through. You're lucky, you don't know what it's like, trials and investigations. Goddamn congressmen grilling you, you think their hands are clean? Anyway, it doesn't matter, I kept to my belief, I kept the country first and foremost.

Dictator This is not my country.

Colonel You getting this? I stayed true, I betrayed no one who wasn't already set up for a fall by their own deeds. We got something to defend here, and it's called freedom. To do business. To live your life, be productive, write books, if that's what you want to do. I have an agent now for speaking engagements. People want to know what I have to say and they'll pay to hear it. There's a lot of patriotism out there, a real feeling for the country. I wouldn't put that down. I'm happy and grateful for the opportunities.

Dictator It's a terrible thing: the memory goes. You have to write everything down. Now I'm reminded, this guy, the canary, he couldn't get off the hook, they'll kill his relatives. I'm sad about that. The walls hear me. The walls watch and listen and judge. They are watching you too, Colonel, as you know. They know what's happening. It's over. Me, I'm behind walls that see me, so I'm paranoid. Maybe you saw the same doctor as me, no? Yes, at Roman trials, for some they said, *Condemno*, others they said *Damno*. I don't know what the difference was supposed to be. That's where it all comes from, Colonel, the condemned and the damned. They call it the Roman Catholic Church, after all. I had a lawyer, he was a Romanist. It's my own religion, I don't put it down, believe me. I'm trying to restore myself also, morally speaking. I had a visit from a doctor, he was a very nice man. *(Looks at walls)*

Colonel   As I was saying—

Dictator   I had a country, they disappeared it.

Colonel   They'll leave you alone here, to make a buck, take of your family.

Dictator   I was born in a garbage can. I have no family.

Colonel   We're not on the same page here.

Dictator   I'm sorry. *(Looks at walls)* I read an article, Joe Stalin's wife, a beautiful woman, she killed herself. I couldn't get it out of my mind. I had to write about it. What was he thinking? He was thinking of the state? What kind of thoughts in his head? What kind of feelings, a beautiful wife who kills herself? How could he live with that? What was he saying to himself?

Silence. COLONEL *looks at walls.*

Colonel   Well, I'm glad to hear you speak this way.

DICTATOR writes.

Dictator	I've been all over, General, and there's no place like America, whatever the problems, the injustices, whatever. I don't think the same anymore. I don't worry about justice. I saw *Birth of a Nation* eleven times. You?
Colonel	Is that a movie?
Dictator	Nevermind.
Colonel	I'd just like to finish up here now, General.
Dictator	Why? You're leaving? Good.
Colonel	Charity and love, General. My final notes for you.
	(COLONEL exits)

BLACKOUT.

*

6. Six months later.

DICTATOR is reading. Sound of woman's voice, RHEA'S, off. DICTATOR jumps to his feet.

Dictator	Who is that? Is that...?

Sound of door opening and closing. Enter RHEA.

	My God, is it you?
Rhea	Don't I get at least a hug?

DICTATOR hugs her stiffly.

	You haven't changed.
Dictator	Wrong. I have changed.
Rhea	Still stiff as a board. You can't hug. You're like a cripple, one arm hangs limp and the other clutches. Your hips are welded to your back, your shoulders are like stones. And your insides are as stuck together as your outsides. What is it? It must be like glue—your heart is glued to your spine, your dick is glued to your liver. That's it.
Dictator	What brings you, Rhea?
Rhea	Relax, darling.
Dictator	Don't call me "darling."
Rhea	You wear glasses now?
Dictator	Only to read.
Rhea	You read now?
Dictator	Why'd they send you, Rhea?
Rhea	I'm on a mission of mercy.
Dictator	You bring a knife? Poison?
Rhea	You like to search me? You can look everywhere.
Dictator	Who sent you?
Rhea	Afraid to touch, darling?
Dictator	Don't call me that.
Rhea	You must be so horny, you have a hard-on now.
Dictator	You came here to check me, see if it works any better?
Rhea	Does it?
Dictator	I don't know.
Rhea	You must really be starving. How about a kiss?
Dictator	I don't feel like it.
Rhea	You've missed me. Say it.

Dictator	Sure. Sure, I did. I've missed you.
Rhea	You don't want to finger me now, see what I've got inside me? I might have a present for you.
Dictator	No. You have to talk like a slut?

RHEA breaks into tears.

I'm sorry. (*Goes to her*) What happened to you?

She sobs convulsively.

What did they do to you?

Rhea	You don't love me.
Dictator	Stop that.
Rhea	You don't. You never did.
Dictator	Please. The walls have eyes and ears.
Rhea	Tell me the truth.
Dictator	I don't know what it is, love. I never learned.
Rhea	You never learned and you never will. It's too late. You can't learn it.
Dictator	Maybe I can.
Rhea	I don't think so. It's not even a joke! (*Laughs hysterically*)
Dictator	Calm down, Rhea.
Rhea	It's true, I don't know you. You're not the same prick.
Dictator	How could I be, Rhea?
Rhea	You're a different prick.
Dictator	Come on, you can talk to me.
Rhea	Let's just fuck, so I can go home.
Dictator	(*Tempted*) Let's talk first.
Rhea	I can't believe this. You've turned into a monk.

Dictator	Where is home, Rhea?
Rhea	How do I look?
Dictator	You look good. You look fine.
Rhea	I'm in shape. I'm refreshed. I eat well, I exercise, I take the sun.
Dictator	You're provided for? Who provides?
Rhea	I'm not a burnt-out whore anymore. I'm in recovery. I'm interested in love now, before it's too late. This is something you could never understand.
Dictator	You're in love?

She breaks into tears.

	Please, Rhea.
Rhea	Why so uptight?
Dictator	I'm embarrassed.
Rhea	Why? It's only us here.
Dictator	Wrong. The walls watch everything.
Rhea	This is awful. What could I have been dreaming?
Dictator	I'm glad to see you.
Rhea	Okay. How are you?
Dictator	I'm having a bad day. It must be grey outside, and cold and wet.
Rhea	It's a nice day. The sun is shining. They don't let you out?
Dictator	Only within the walls.
Rhea	You can't see the sky?
Dictator	From here? I can't see the sky from here!
Rhea	Don't get annoyed. When they walk you, can you see the sky?
Dictator	Yeah! Above the walls is the sky! Twice a week, I go around with guards, I can see the sky!

Rhea	You look pasty.
Dictator	Tell me more, please. How are you kept?
Rhea	I'm kept well. I'm not just a piece of ass.
Dictator	By whom?
Rhea	By short-haired white men. And some homeboys, *tambien*, from California.
Dictator	The F.B.I.!
Rhea	Polite, proper, stupid-looking guys. Well, they're not all so bad. People have to make a living. But they never talk to me.
Dictator	Same here!
Rhea	What is this freedom and democracy? What's it about?
Dictator	You don't know?
Rhea	Why should I know?
Dictator	You're a citizen!
Rhea	I was born in Cuba! I grew up in Miami!
Dictator	That's no answer. You never paid attention, you never learned.
Rhea	And you? You know? You, the Dictator?
Dictator	Yeah, people started voting against me, I beat their brains out. *(Chuckles)*
Rhea	It's true, here you can vote and make money, nobody kicks your head in.
Dictator	*(Looking at the walls)* You still like Fidel?
Rhea	*(Shrugging)* He's a nice man. But in his mind he hasn't been wrong in thirty years. How can you have a relationship with someone like that? And you? How do they keep you?
Dictator	What you see here. *(Pause)* But I have everything I need.
Rhea	Your English, it's wonderful.

Dictator	Thank you. They want to erase me, Rhea, like a bad mark. But I'm intelligent. I'm erasing me myself.
Rhea	Who are you now?
Dictator	I'm a writer.
Rhea	You're not.
Dictator	I am.
Rhea	Read me something.
Dictator	Really?
Rhea	Come on.
Dictator	I don't know.
Rhea	Don't be shy. *(Indicates walls)*
Dictator	Well, maybe a little…
Rhea	Please, darling.

DICTATOR *is irritated.*

Sorry.

Dictator	Okay. *(Finds papers)* Uh, okay. I'll read. Tell you what, I'll just read the opening paragraph, okay, of a story?
Rhea	Yes, please.
Dictator	Okay. *(Trembles, clears his throat, reads)* "As winter approached, people left their homes and began to appear in the streets, out of their minds: ranting bitterly, wandering, shivering, they shook their fists at the cold blasts of wind, and howled. One dark-skinned woman, not yet old, but quite mad, wore a thin red sari and would surely freeze to death before long. There were white circles of cold and terror around her eyes that looked like they were painted on. 'Stay low, Buddy,' she told me, 'stay low.' Then she slunk away like something transforming downward, into an insect,

staying low. I was still a boy then, but I knew that it was useless to try to communicate with crazy persons who have been crushed by absolute certainty, and so I thanked her and watched her go. She was one of the many women who had come out into their neighborhoods insane that year." *(Pause)*

Rhea   Oh.

Dictator What's the matter?

Rhea   Nothing.

Dictator You didn't like it.

Rhea   I did like it.

Dictator Well, I can see plenty of things wrong with it now.

Rhea   It was very good.

Dictator It's just a first draft.

Rhea   I'm amazed.

Dictator It's good to hear it aloud, I could hear things. I'll work on it.

Rhea   I liked it. *(Pause, looks at walls, sighs, etc.)* You have more?

Dictator Oh, yes.

Rhea   Read it.

Dictator No. No, it uh, needs too much work. Really, what did you think so far?

Rhea   I told you.

Dictator No, honestly.

Rhea   Well, there's a thing about women, I guess.

Dictator Yeah.

Rhea   And the kid?

Dictator Yeah, the kid has no legs. He looks down at some point, and he sees that he has no legs. And the next sentence is, the next paragraph, the narrator says, "One of the women, the most grotesque of all, was my mother." And then it

	goes on. *(Pause)* It needs work, I know. *(Reads)* "Emerged from" is better than "came out into," don't you think?
Rhea	I can't remember, actually.
Dictator	Yeah, I think that's better. *(Changes it)* Thank you.
Rhea	I don't know if I can handle this.
Dictator	What?
Rhea	I don't know you. This man is sitting in front of me, we used to be intimate, now he's a stranger.
Dictator	We had some good times, eh?
Rhea	Now he's a writer, in English no less.
Dictator	I always had a little English.
Rhea	Yeah, but not like a professor.
Dictator	What could be a good name for him?
Rhea	You mean, for you?
Dictator	Yeah, a new name. What they call a pseudonym. How about Caesar something? The Great Dictator!
Rhea	What's the last name?
Dictator	That WAS his last name.
Rhea	No, I mean you.
Dictator	Let's see, his mother's name was Aurelia.
Rhea	Nice name.
Dictator	No, we need something gringo. Jones, or Carter. ...What are you thinking?
Rhea	I'm feeling for my sex—I think I like you better now. Caesar. You used to be fun, but we were smashed all the time in those days.
Dictator	You were a party girl, Rhea.

She bursts into tears.

	I'm sorry. Please. I like you, too, Rhea.
Rhea	I'm so ashamed of myself. *(Pause)* You were bad, Caesar, very bad.
Dictator	*(Looks at the walls)* I was a victim of American imperialism! *(Whispers)* Yes, I was bad. I was no better than a dog. Nevermind. They had a job to do. We didn't know any better, truly. That was the life. Now I'm feeling my own sex. *(Looks at the walls)* No.
Rhea	No.
Dictator	No, of course not.
Rhea	Maybe in another life.
Dictator	There will be another life.
Rhea	Are you a Christian now?
Dictator	I mean in this life. *(Looks at walls)*
Rhea	Do you know what you're saying?
Dictator	When?
Rhea	I mean in your writing. I mean about women. That's why you're so stiff and tense, Caesar. The women are crazy and the kid has no legs.
Dictator	*(Distant)* We should stop apologizing, Rhea. We are always apologizing.
Rhea	I don't think I could live with you now, Caesar. You're far away from me now. Before, we had pleasure in common. We had an attitude in common. *(Cries)*
Dictator	Why do you weep so much?
Rhea	I live in Paramus, New Jersey. *(Laughs)* I am watched, and I have nothing for the pain.
Dictator	*(Shouting)* LET THIS WOMAN GO! DO YOU HEAR ME! LET HER GO!
Rhea	Stop. It's alright.

He restrains himself. Long pause. NOISES *off.*

Rhea   They're coming. *(She rises)*

        SOUND *of door opening.*

        Goodbye, Caesar.
Dictator   I'll be seeing you…? *(She shrugs. They embrace)*
Rhea   Good, Caesar. Good *abrazo*.
Dictator   Think of a name, a last name…
Rhea   I'll try.
Dictator   Send me a message…!

        RHEA *exits. Fast* DIM OUT.

                        *

7. Six months later.

Find the AMBASSADOR *(*GINA*) standing with the* DICTATOR.

Dictator   You? An ambassador?
Gina   Well, yes. I'm glad to see you again, as I'd hoped.
Dictator   Why is that?
Gina   You're not glad to see me?
Dictator   I'm shocked. Last time, you were a journalist.
Gina   I'm glad because of the progress that you've made here,
        despite the solitude.
Dictator   Thank you.

Gina	As is the State Department.
Dictator	Save the state, save the state.
Gina	I said I'd try to help, and I have.
Dictator	I believe you. The Colonel was here awhile ago. Charity and love were his last words.
Gina	We approve. We like the direction he's taken, too, of late. Can't have been easy for him.
Dictator	He's still a gringo prick.
Gina	Yes.
Dictator	You agree with me?
Gina	Why not?
Dictator	The man thinks he's a patriot, doing the right thing. *(Pause)* I'm trying to remember last time. What we talked about. I think it was something erotic.
Gina	Not what I recall.
Dictator	Oh, yes. Months, years, I thought about it.
Gina	Really? What?
Dictator	*(Looking at walls)* You. Legs up in the air. Heh, heh. What happens in solitary. Imagine, imagine.
Gina	*(Blushing)* I see.
Dictator	And you?
Gina	What?
Dictator	You think about it?
Gina	No. By the way, I have a message for you. *(Hands him a piece of paper)*
Dictator	*(Reads)* "Truscott." Oh!
Gina	Truscott?
Dictator	You don't know? That's my name! My new last name! From my girlfriend, Rhea, with love. Caesar Truscott! How do you like it?

Gina	Just fine.
Dictator	How is she?
Gina	Just fine.
Dictator	And you?
Gina	Fine.
Dictator	Tell me where she is.
Gina	She's in Paramus.
Dictator	Will I see her again?
Gina	It's possible.
Dictator	Where are we? Are we near an airport? I hear planes going by all the time, it drives me crazy.
Gina	New name, new career. I have helped you, General. I want you to know that.
Dictator	Why did you help me?
Gina	Because I like your writing.
Dictator	Thank you.
Gina	Now we want to help you make a new past also, and talk a bit about the future.
Dictator	What is that sound I hear, waaah, waaah, what is that?
Gina	Those are car alarms, General. So, first of all, regarding the past.
Dictator	You think I'm making up shit just to collaborate with the state, which is a Roman idea, incidentally. Save the state. What is it now? Three years? Four years?
Gina	Three and a half years.
Dictator	Astounding. Three and a half years of airplanes and automobile jungle shrieks.
Gina	You know that Lignam Vitae Press has accepted your book and is interested in your welfare.
Dictator	I got a wire. I was ecstatic.

Gina	That was my doing.
Dictator	Okay, gracias. *Lignam vitae.* Means "live rock." Live Rock Press. This is one of my biggest regrets now, that I never learned Latin. Street kids don't learn Latin. I'd like to read Cicero in Latin. Cicero. He is the father of us all.
Gina	They're very much in your corner, the publishers.
Dictator	What does that mean? I haven't got a dime.
Gina	Morally speaking. Also, my entire staff read your book, and, aside from its literary values, appreciated its attitudes.
Dictator	Attitudes?
Gina	Yes, as towards drug-dealing, prostitution, and the like.
Dictator	No drug-dealing illiterate morons playing footsie with the industrialized democracies.
Gina	Correct.
Dictator	I wouldn't think of it.
Gina	I'm glad.
Dictator	However, the irony is not lost on me.
Gina	Explain.
Dictator	I refer to Laos, Thailand, Pakistan, Mexico, Panama, Colombia, etc., where drug-dealing warlords are playing with taxpayers' money right and left. *(Looks at walls)* But forget I said it.
Gina	I will try.
Dictator	I'm not interested anyway.
Gina	You aren't?
Dictator	Truly, no. I have more serious problems. Loneliness. Regrets.
Gina	I understand.
Dictator	You don't understand.
Gina	Fine. Let's talk about the future.

Dictator	I walk off the path and I'm shot down like a dog. That's the future. Some future. Where's my money at?
Gina	*(Looking at walls)* Your money?
Dictator	I made a lot of money. I did business with certain people at certain times through certain banks; they were *bona fide* U.S. banks, they were supposed to take care of my money.
Gina	You don't have any money, and you're stupid to bring it up.
Dictator	Do you drink?
Gina	None of your business.
Dictator	I'd love to have a drink. Married?

Stiff silence.

	I'm an artist, I think about real things now. I don't drink, I don't get laid, I can't help myself, nothing.
Gina	*(Patiently)* Okay. Caesar Truscott. Good name for an author. An *homo novum*, a new man.
Dictator	I never went to college.
Gina	A new man, worked hard to overcome adversity and achieved a decent life for himself through authorship. Good. But we're not going to sweeten the path, Mr. Truscott. It is an honor and a privilege to be an American citizen. An immigrant must learn to stand on his own two feet.
Dictator	Does this mean I get to be a U.S. citizen?
Gina	No. We're not all the way there yet, Mr. Truscott.
Dictator	But...he is thinking of letting me out of here?
Gina	We're not there yet, Mr. Truscott. We're not quite there. *(Rises)* You have three choices as we see it, Mr. Truscott. We could throw you into a federal pen—no doubt in solitude for the rest of your life—or we could shoot you.

| Dictator | That's two of YOUR choices. |
| Gina | The third—which I support—is letting you out, as Caesar Truscott, author, another person, into the cruel world. But we're not there yet, Mr. Truscott, we're not there yet. *(Exits)* |

DIM OUT.

*

8. Six months later.

DICTATOR in his cell. Enter the GUARD.

Dictator	What is it now, Gerald?
Guard	The President of the United States.
Dictator	The who?
Guard	The President of the United States.

Enter THE PRESIDENT OF THE UNITED STATES.

| President | Good morning, Mr. Truscott. |
| Dictator | Well, I'll be damned. |

Pause. DICTATOR holds a chair for him and the PRESIDENT sits.

President	How are ya, Truscott?
Dictator	Fair to middling, sir.
President	I wanted to have a conversation with you, man to man.
Dictator	*(Looking at the walls)* Are we being taped?

President	No. This is totally off the record. As a matter of fact, this never happened. I don't know you, Mr. Truscott. We've only just met. I used to know—ever so slightly, mind you—a double-dealing punk drug-pusher who made himself into a military dictator for a few months and thumbed his nose at the United States of America.
Dictator	It was a lot of fun. I was on a roll.
President	Not you, Mr. Truscott.
Dictator	Call me Cesar, Mr. President.
President	No.
Dictator	Uh, this dictator you speak of, he used to be acquainted with a certain operative, now the guy is the most powerful man in the world.
President	How things change. You've become a great example of what this country stands for, Truscott.
Dictator	Well, I ought to have more company then. I ought to receive more often.
President	Many are reading your book, Truscott.
Dictator	How many, sir?
President	I don't know, exactly.
Dictator	They ought to send me a royalty report, for chrissakes.
President	What is the book called?
Dictator	*Wild Dog Sorrows*, sir.
President	Oh, yes. *Wild Dog Sorrows*. I'd like to read it sometime.
Dictator	You won't like it, sir, take my word for it.
President	One false move and we'll eliminate you, Truscott, and that'll be that. You and your girlfriend and any trace of you. But I hope for your sake that such a course will be unnecessary.
Dictator	It is my devout wish to become an American citizen, sir.

President	Well, I don't see any reason why not. You won't have a record. Your name is clear. Put in your time, pay your taxes.
Dictator	Is this the final test, then?
President	It is. Of course, you'll then have to make it out there, on your own.
Dictator	Cesar Truscott hits the street.
President	You'll be a shining light, Truscott. And of course, I'll do what I have to do to defend our freedoms and our interests.
Dictator	You know about Roman triumphs, sir?
President	Very little, Truscott.
Dictator	Career and ego, ego and career. Rode through town like gods, sir. I guess they had an ideal behind it all.
President	Which was?
Dictator	Rome, sir. They just called it ROME. It was a patrician idea, very old.
President	Same with us, Truscott.
Dictator	I see that now. I want to open a Latin deli someplace, Paramus maybe, and find a way to live on.
President	Good plan, Truscott. But try not to waste your talent.
Dictator	Thank you, sir.
President	Do you know anything at all about drug cartels in bed with United States government operatives?
Dictator	Nothing, sir.
President	CIA selling crack cocaine in the City of Angels?
Dictator	Not really, sir.
President	Good, Truscott.
Dictator	However, I do know that there are chemicals on this planet which affect the mind, in itself a neurochemical process, and that certain of these chemicals are illegal in the United States; that the demand for these chemicals in the United

States is so fierce that a huge transfer of wealth has occurred and is occurring to the supply-side section of the planet; that a large percentage of the American population, African-American and Hispanic for the most part, survives on black-market distribution of these chemicals; and that a goodly number of these young persons spend a large portion of their formative years in prison.

President   It's an imperfect world, Truscott.

Dictator   That it is, sir.

President   On the other hand, who's to say?

Dictator   Not me, sir.

President   *(Stands)* I'm very glad to have had this opportunity to meet you.

Dictator   Same here, Mr. President.

President   And I do hope you'll have success with your fiction writing, Truscott.

Dictator   Thank you, sir.

PRESIDENT *exits.* BLACKOUT.

*

9. One year later.

The upstage panel is removed, revealing a table, counter, etc.—a deli. A little LIGHT *streams in from a small window above. Same ambient* NOISE *of planes and car alarms. The* DICTATOR *is wearing an apron, sweeping the floor and* *whistling "Cucaracha." D*R. S*TEWART enters and picks up a menu.* D*ICTATOR stares at him a long time, carefully puts aside the broom.*

Dictator   Can I help you?

Doctor   *(Reading menu)* Well, I don't know...

Dictator   You don't recognize me?

Doctor   No...I don't think so...

Dictator   Cesar Truscotta.

Doctor   No...

Dictator   *Wild Dog Sorrows.*

Doctor   Excuse me?

Dictator   A novel. I'm afraid it's out of print.

Doctor   No, I don't think I...

Dictator   *(Takes off glasses)* Formerly obnoxious third world dictator?

Doctor   Oh...

Dictator   You examined his eyes.

Doctor   Yes! *(Standing)* Yes, of course!

They shake hands.

How are you?

Dictator   Please, sit.

D*OCTOR sits,* D*ICTATOR takes off apron.*

Doctor   My goodness! I'm astonished! What happened?

Dictator   They let me out, as a new man. Cesar Truscott, author.

Doctor   A novel!

Dictator	Nevermind, it didn't sell. Now I'm Cesar Truscotta. *(Calling)* Rhea! Rhea!

Enter RHEA.

	Rhea, you remember the doctor I told you about, the psychiatrist who fixed my eyes, Doctor...?
Doctor	Stewart.
Dictator	Dr. Stewart, this is my wife, Rhea.
Doctor	Well, how do you do?
Rhea	I'm very pleased to meet you, Dr. Stewart. Excuse my appearance.
Doctor	Not at all.
Rhea	Please. I'll be right back. *(Hurries off)*
Dictator	As you see, with my esteemed wife, I run a deli. And you? Still with the V.A.?
Doctor	No, I moved on. Private practice.
Dictator	You prescribe drugs?
Doctor	For depression, sometimes, yes. Are you...? Do you...? My office is not far from here.
Dictator	I could always use someone to talk to.
Doctor	Please. Call me. And how's your writing coming along?

Re-enter RHEA, freshened, and dressed up.

Rhea	He gave it up. He doesn't work, he doesn't try.
Dictator	Once I had a vision. Not lately.
Rhea	He hangs around here in the deli. He gossips with the customers.
Dictator	I'm an attraction. Brings 'em in.

Rhea	Would you like a coffee, Doctor? *Café con leche*, Cuban style, eh?
Doctor	Yes, I would. Thank you.
Dictator	You can't force it. If there's nothing there, there's nothing there, forget about it.
Rhea	What a waste! You should write! *(Brings coffee)*
Dictator	Write what, darling?
Rhea	I don't know. Something. Something...uplifting.
Doctor	*(To RHEA)* Thank you.
Rhea	*De nada, Señor.*
Dictator	*(To DR. STEWART)* When I, uh, got out, I tried. I talked to editors, publishers. "I wrote a novel under difficult—yet ideal—conditions, about...well...terror and despair and madness." *(Laughs)* "Well, the market right now, Mr. Truscotta... write something uplifting...and perhaps..." Finally, I said, "Listen, you have something to sell, I'll sell it, you have something to buy, I'll buy it." "We don't understand," they said. "Well," I said, "writing is not a fit profession for a man like me. I think I'll open a delicatessen." *(Laughs, looks at the walls)*

DIM OUT as RHEA joins them at the table.

Rhea	It's a shame, if you ask me.

BLACKOUT.

The End

Switchback or
Lost Child in the Terror Zone

A Jazz Operetta by Murray Mednick

Switchback *was first produced at the 1994 Padua Hills Playwrights Festival/Workshop under the author's direction, with the following cast:*

Rita: Sharron Shayne-Simeone
Brenda: Robin Karfo
C.C.: Mark Fite

The remaining two characters were added in a subsequent draft.

Characters

Tony *A young street prince; 25; dressed in white.*

Rita *His mother; 40s; good-looking, hip, shell-shocked.*

Brenda *Girlfriend of Tony's; 20s; beautiful, high-strung, street-wise; dressed to look like a boy.*

C.C. *Street warrior; late 20s, early 30s; known as the Preacher; dressed in army fatigues.*

Sheila *Girlfriend of Tony's and C.C.'s; late 20s; sleek.*

The interior of a building partially destroyed by artillery fire; this is presently a neutral area in the Terror Zone. Maybe it was once a health club, as there is a swimming pool behind the audience. The stage rear wall has a hole in it, or a large window, revealing a switchback walkway. The switchback could be built onstage, be an image to scale, or a videotape so as to depict C.C.'s entrance and the finale. The baby carriage is of the old-fashioned type. The plane is to scale—a toy model guided from offstage— or video. Down right is a bench; on it, sitting quietly, all in white, is Tony. Gunfire. Rita *rushes in with the baby carriage, as* Brenda *enters from the opposite direction on a bicycle.*

Brenda   He tried to run me over! He doesn't even know me! I am meat! I am garbage!

Gunfire.

I am fun! Fun target! Fun! Fun to shoot!

Gunfire. Shouts off.

You bag! You fart! You maniac! I hope you die!
Rita   Quiet!

Brenda	I coulda been killed! Me!
Rita	Shut up, Brenda!

GUNFIRE stops.

Brenda	This was a safe neighborhood!
Rita	You look like a boy now!
Brenda	Do I resemble Tony?
Rita	You look just like him!
Brenda	There's water in the pool!
Rita	Oh!
Brenda	Is this the place?
Rita	This is the place!
Brenda	There's water in the pool!
Rita	This is it!
Brenda	Who said?
Rita	C.C.!
Brenda	Okay! Where is he?
Rita	He's on his way. *(Looks off)* That must be he!
Brenda	Do I resemble Tony?
Rita	What I say? *(Looks off)* C.C.! He's coming in—here he comes!
Brenda	Who is this guy?
Rita	You know C.C.
Brenda	What's C.C.?
Rita	Curtis Craig, or Craig Curtis.
Brenda	How can he?
Rita	He can cross boundaries, he.
Brenda	Say how?
Rita	He has connections on the other side.

A PLANE appears.

Rita	That be he!
Brenda	Up there?
Rita	That far perspective!
Brenda	You know him?
Rita	Yeah.
Brenda	Way when?
Rita	Before.
Brenda	Say who?

The PLANE circles.

Rita	I said.
Brenda	Say what?
Rita	Tony's friend. A dearest boy. A bosom pal. A companion. You know him well. They call him Preacher.
Brenda	A drug dealer and a pimp. Say?
Rita	I would say.
Brenda	Okay. When do we run?
Rita	7:30.
Brenda	And the baby?
Rita	Baby, too.
Brenda	Baby, too.
Rita	Act right.
Brenda	Say where?
Rita	Right here. Try to relax. And don't start confessing.
Brenda	"Don't start confessing!"
Rita	He's coming in! There he is!

An orange PARACHUTE *appears in the sky. The* PLANE
makes a pass or two and flies off.

Brenda	Let's step on it! Squash him!
Rita	Here he comes!
Brenda	Is that him?
Rita	What I say?

*Enter C.C., folding an orange parachute, wearing army fatigues,
a portable phone, and a .45. He throws the parachute aside.*

C.C.	Greetings on a good day!
Brenda	Good night, sir!
C.C.	Surprised.
Brenda	Pleased, sir.
Rita	Be joined.

C.C. and BRENDA *perform an elaborate handshake.*

	Grateful. Happy.
C.C.	I bring wishes for child.
Rita	Thoughtful.
Brenda	Poignant. And now?

C.C. pops BRENDA *on the nose.*

C.C.	Whim. *(Broad smile)* Fantastic.

BRENDA *falls away to compose herself as C.C. speaks into
his portable phone.*

Poolside. 7:35. Smacked Brenda. Hello?

FLASHBACK. On the bench, find BRENDA joining TONY.

Brenda	You ever use? You used, didn't ya?
Tony	What?
Brenda	You. You used.
Tony	Yeah, I'm clean now.
Brenda	Hey, what do I care? When?
Tony	I'm cleaned up now. I don't do nothin'.
Brenda	When?
Tony	Before.
Brenda	Hey, who hasn't used? Crack?
Tony	I don't do nothin' now, not me.
Brenda	Crack?
Tony	Hey, fuck that shit. I drive a cab. I got the word. Fuck that shit.
Brenda	In school?
Tony	Who went to school? I went to jail. I went to jail school. I got reformed.
Brenda	The word?
Tony	I got the message. I got the news.
Brenda	Say?
Tony	I was fourteen at the time, maybe fifteen. I told nobody.
Brenda	Say?
Tony	Who wants to say something? Who wants to know? People talk too much.
Brenda	You don't wanna kill nobody, either.
Tony	I take precautions. I watch myself.
Brenda	Are you sick?

Tony	I'm only twenty-four, but I feel like I'm aging. I'm not escaping like I thought I would. I drive my cab. I eat good. I watch myself. I could get on TV. Then maybe I could say something.
Brenda	Are you sick?
Tony	I feel great. I feel fine. People in a session, in the joint, everybody is trying to look like they're listening, but all they wanna do is talk their shit, they gotta listen to their own shit. Now I go to groups, I go for counseling, it's the same, I could hear myself.
Brenda	You wanna see me ever?

END FLASHBACK.

C.C.	*(Into phone)* I gave you the goods. You got the goods. The count is right. No. The count is not short. The count is right. Excuse me? *(Clicks off)*
Rita	*(Big breath)* Ah. *(Rocks baby carriage)*
C.C.	*(Of BRENDA)* She can't go.
Rita	No?
C.C.	Just you.
Rita	And the baby?
C.C.	No. Kid stays, Brenda stays, you go.
Rita	Say?
C.C.	Price baby.
Rita	Say?
C.C.	They.
Rita	Who?
C.C.	Other side.
Rita	That's not what you said.

C.C.	What I say?
Rita	Family go!
C.C.	No deal. Only you.
Rita	No!
C.C.	Tony had a lady on the other side. Sheila. You know Sheila?
Rita	I don't know no Sheila.
C.C.	She liked Tony.
Rita	So?
C.C.	She wants his child.
Rita	Why?
C.C.	Love and retribution.
Rita	Love? Retribution?
C.C.	My word is my deed.
Rita	Say?
C.C.	Exactly 8:15. Remember, 8:15. Only you. You alone. 8:15.
Rita	Alone?
Brenda	*(Crossing)* Apologize!
C.C.	*(Laughing)* I'm sorry.
Brenda	*(As TONY, with big strut)* Drop dead you cunt-suckin' fuck!
C.C.	Fine.
Rita	*(Of BRENDA)* That's Tony!
Brenda	*(As TONY)* I hope you eat shit for the rest of your life, you punk!
C.C.	Keep talking dirt. See what good it brings you.
Rita	Shut it, Tony! Brenda!
Brenda	*(As TONY)* I hope you drown!
C.C.	*(To RITA)* Okay, that's enough from him.
Rita	Time out, Bren'.
Brenda	*(To C.C., as TONY)* Hey! How come you got walk-about money and others don't? Are you smarter?

C.C.	I am.
Brenda	*(As TONY, big strut)* They may bleed! *(Of the phone)* And them things is killing machines! Am I right? They eat blood!
C.C.	They are clean machines. And they don't breed.
Brenda	I said bleed!
C.C.	An' they don't eat.
Brenda	*(As TONY)* Them money machines is fed on blood, sir.
C.C.	They are electrical machines, boy. Electro-mathematical.
Brenda	*(As TONY)* No! Why you walk about with money while we get only chits?
Rita	Stop it, Brenda! Tony!
Brenda	*(To RITA)* How can he?
Rita	He gets views. He gets satellite info-mation.
C.C.	One hand washes the other.
Brenda	*(To C.C.)* Explain!
C.C.	I'm a warrior businessman, me. I'm the Captain of Swords, the Commander. One of you I'll spare and save from grief.
Brenda	Explain!
C.C.	People need different things. One needs this, the other that. I give you something, you give something back.
Brenda	Example!
C.C.	Some people have nothing. You're one of them.
Brenda	I have a child! I have a baby!
C.C.	You're mental, Brenda.
Brenda	*(As TONY)* Don't say that, you dumb fuck!
C.C.	I'll have you shot. Are you ready?
Brenda	Shoot!
C.C.	*(Into phone)* You see the little one with the hat? Yeah, that one. *(Pause)* Shoot him.

Brenda	Okay, I'm sorry!
C.C.	*(Into phone)* Hold your fire. But keep an eye on them. Thank you. *(Walks away, singing)*

FLASHBACK. On the bench, find TONY *and* SHEILA.

Sheila	What you got, Guy?
Tony	What you got, Girl?
Sheila	I don't have.
Tony	I got something.
Sheila	It's hard these days, crossing over.
Tony	I got something nice.
Sheila	I can't cross over.
Tony	I got Colombia Red. I got buds and flowers.
Sheila	Oh, how good!
Tony	Came through the line today!
Sheila	Oh, how fine!
Tony	Not much, but some.
Sheila	Wanna trick me for it?
Tony	Say?
Sheila	Are you deaf?
Tony	I'm not deaf.
Sheila	Wanna trick me for it?
Tony	I can't right now.
Sheila	No? *(Laughs)*
Tony	Next time, maybe.
Sheila	You give me the goods?
Tony	I got no problem with that.
Sheila	Then we'll see next time. How I feel.
Tony	You like poetry?

Sheila	You silly boy.

END FLASHBACK.

C.C.	*(Beckons to* BRENDA*)* Come here, girl.
Brenda	*(Aside, to* RITA*)* I'll try. *(Goes to him)*
C.C.	What I do is, I take me an area and I develop a market, a demand. I set up supply and distribution. I study the laws, the procedures. The police. I guard my turf and I watch my back. It's hard work.
Brenda	Are there bodyguards? Are there dogs?
C.C.	Yes. And I have an army, too. Me!
Brenda	Okay, I forgive you. What's your racket?
C.C.	I have soldiers. I have a crew. I have dependents, I have clientele. I love it. I'm the Man, they come to me. Be a business, and I'm the power. Be research and development. Be psychology, be marketing.
Rita	Good mood.
C.C.	Be oratory. Be preachery.
Brenda	You're a fucking gangstah!
C.C.	I've gone to a great deal of trouble on behalf of this lady here.
Brenda	Why?
C.C.	Because of Tony, who was a friend of mine. Now gone.
Brenda	Now gone!
C.C.	*(Charging her)* Blame?
Brenda	*(Quickly)* No blame!
C.C.	Who the fuck do you think you are?
Brenda	Do I remind you of someone?
C.C.	Yeah.
Brenda	Who?

C.C.	Tony.
Brenda	Ha! I am BRENDA!
C.C.	No shit. I knew you once, and you're still a head case. *(Walks away)*
Brenda	Hey, Curtis!
C.C.	Craig.
Brenda	Hey, Craig! *(Pointing)* You live over there now? Other side?
C.C.	Where else could I be the Man? And earn five thousand dollars a day?
Brenda	*(To RITA)* He makes forty million dollars a year!
Rita	We get chits. Chits is all we get.
Brenda	Chits and bullets and a fast death.
Rita	There are too many people and they must eat. An absolute horror. Are we worms? I look at virtual reality, I see worms sliding, giving expressions, thrusting their noses into the camera. Are we worms?
C.C.	Worm-like, I'd say.
Brenda	"There are the working poor and the very poor, which is us. We are the left behind, we. Plus fire, flood, quake, and riot."
C.C.	Such is nature, girl.
Brenda	What I say?
Rita	*(To C.C.)* Do you like parks and pools?
C.C.	What time is it?
Rita	Say?
C.C.	I like parks and pools. *(Tries to grab baby, foiled by RITA)*
Brenda	Kidnapping? Baby stealing?
Rita	Shut up, Tony/Brenda.
Brenda	*(To C.C.)* What's your business there, Curtis?
C.C.	There are extraterrestrial substances, be always in demand. They are the coca, the poppy, and the tobacco. The opium

poppy is a funny-looking blue plant from another planet. Some places here it grows like a weed. Not from earth. Strong. Addictive. Invest. Now for earth substances. They are alcohol, coffee, wheat, hemp, and water. Invest.

Rita Alcohol?

C.C. Invest.

Rita Water?

C.C. Invest.

Rita Extraterrestrial?

Brenda Police?

C.C. We got a system here, they don't want to talk to anyone who knows. You have to start with the leaders. We're strictly into supply and demand. It's like we got one economy on Mars and another in the neighborhood. Nobody wants to talk about real things. They'd have to see themselves in it all.

Brenda Police?

C.C. The police know. But what are the police gonna do? They throw one guy away and ten more are lined up to fill the hole. They're locked into a vicious game, goin' nowhere. No winners, no losers. Police suffer.

Brenda Can I go to the bathroom?

C.C. And they'd have to face my private army. And shit has to move. Police got to eat, too. *(Into phone)* Don't fire. Remember, gentlemen, I have my army. And they are waiting. And they are watching. And they are nasty. *(Clicks off. To BRENDA)* Go take a leak.

Brenda Thank you. (Leaves)

FLASHBACK. *On the bench,* BRENDA *discovers* TONY.

Brenda	Tony!
Tony	Yo!
Brenda	What you doin' here, boy?
Tony	I'm movin' in wit' you.
Brenda	Say?
Tony	You gonna be my girlfriend. I'm tired of hanging here by myself. You're a little strange—but who am I, right? I'm off the streets, and I should have a home. Am I right?
Brenda	Marry me?
Tony	Later we'll get married. Now we'll have an apartment. Me and you. You won't have to worry.
Brenda	Oh!
Tony	I'll take care. You make it nice. I'll drive, I'll bring home the goods. One thing only…you gotta stay on them head pills, B.
Brenda	I know that. Sex?
Tony	I take precautions. I watch myself.
Brenda	Family?
Tony	Don't go so fast.
Brenda	Will you die, Tony?
Tony	Not me.
Brenda	Tony?
Tony	Not me.
Brenda	Oh!
Tony	Don't worry about it, B. I'm feeling fucking great.

END FLASHBACK.

Rita	What was on earth before?
C.C.	I was not here before.
Rita	Where were you, C.C.?

C.C.	I was unborn.
Rita	How old are you? We were *all* unborn! There's fifty-four billion more unborn than born! Are we talking the transmigration of souls here? Where are all the fucking people coming from if they weren't here before, if you're talking transmigration of souls? And if they were here before, where were they?
C.C.	So I don't know.
Rita	How did they get here?
C.C.	What time it is?
Rita	Them drugs!
C.C.	Through the sky. So. You get life and freedom. A home. Safety. They get the kid.
Rita	Not mine.
C.C.	Let go.
Rita	Oh, no.
C.C.	Do it for me, Rita.
Rita	Why? I hardly know you, you!
C.C.	I watched over your son, Tony. We did time. And he was a pal of mine.
Rita	You weren't there!
C.C.	*(Manipulative)* I'm interested in you. I care about you. I feel a deep rapport. I'd like to save you before you come to grief.
Rita	Bullshit. You flew in here to steal the child. For the other side!
C.C.	Not true, darling. *(As* TONY, *with strut)* This is the last time, Mom. I promise. I swear to God, that's it. I'm gonna clean up and go away to another country. Mom? Death goes where I go, Mom. Death is inside of me. It is dormant, it is waiting. I'm trying, Mom. I love you, Mom. I'll make friends with death.

Rita	Tony! And Brenda?
C.C.	*(As* Tony*)* She's trying, Mom. *(Walks away)*

FLASHBACK. *On the bench, find* Tony *and* Sheila.

Sheila	You crossed.
Tony	Here I am.
Sheila	What you bring me, boy?
Tony	I got words. *(Recites)* "I hate and love. And if you should ask how I can do both, I couldn't say; but I feel it, and it shivers me."
Sheila	Hate and love.
Tony	Catullus. He was a Roman.
Sheila	Nasty boy.
Tony	He'd put his mouth on anything.
Sheila	I'll slap you.
Tony	They killed your friend, Terry.
Sheila	C.C.?
Tony	They caught him crossing over to your side. C.C. had to put a bullet in his head.
Sheila	Dirty dog!
Tony	He had a good time.
Sheila	Watch out.
Tony	He likes you.
Sheila	C.C.
Tony	He likes you.
Sheila	He'll never fuck me. *(She shivers)*
Tony	Are you cold?
Sheila	No. Where I come from, it's cold. This is not cold. Where I come from, this time of year, it's cold. You wanna get inside?

Tony	Yeah.
Sheila	Trick me?
Tony	Where?
Sheila	Inside. Over there.
Tony	You don't owe me.
Sheila	Life's too short, and death is sudden.
Tony	You want revenge?
Sheila	Why? You offering?
Tony	I'm asking.
Sheila	Not today.

END FLASHBACK.

C.C.	I cared about the cunning little sonofabitch.
Brenda	*(Re-entering)* Yo, Rita!
C.C.	*(Aside to BRENDA)* I was hoping you fell in.
Brenda	"Darling!" *(Holding out a hand)* Give us money! Shake it out! All we get here is chits!
Rita	And bullets.
C.C.	Money is not free.
Brenda	How much?
C.C.	Twenty-two.
Brenda	That's high.
Rita	That's high.
C.C.	That's tough.
Rita	Okay.
Brenda	Have a heart, you cheap oaf.
Rita	Money for the road! Money for the journey!
C.C.	Leave the child? Leave the baby?
Brenda & Rita	No!

C.C.	Forget about it.
Brenda	Interest rate's too high. Twenty-two is high.
C.C.	Yes, it is.
Rita	Let's try and forget about it.
Brenda	If the rate was frozen, I could go along with it.
C.C.	Market forces decide the rate.
Rita	Then what's to keep the Asians back?
C.C.	The army. What I say. *(Walks)*

FLASHBACK. *On the bench,* TONY *and* SHEILA.

Tony	I heard you did time.
Sheila	C.C. told you?
Tony	Yeah. What?
Sheila	Screaming and crying.
Tony	Trade?
Sheila	Yeah. I saw the money and it was not real. Scared?
Tony	Not me.
Sheila	You wanna do something?
Tony	We can do things.
Sheila	First you have a girl over there? Other side? Brenda?
Tony	We two have an apartment.
Sheila	How nice for you.
Tony	I could be big. Disks and tapes. MTV.
Sheila	Money is shit, Sigmund Freud.
Tony	Who?
Sheila	You don't know?
Tony	I heard of him.
Sheila	You can barely read English.
Tony	I'm a poet. Authentic.

Sheila	Grungy old Jew.
Tony	Anti-Semite?
Sheila	You're not Jewish.
Tony	I'm half-Jewish.
Sheila	I can't read him, Freud. Like Karl Marx, I can't read him, either.

GUNFIRE.

	What is that fucking music?
Tony	Be machine guns. Stay right here. Don't go away. Don't move.

END FLASHBACK.

Brenda	Sun coming down through holes in the sky! The sun be burning down us!
Rita	Be calm, Brenda!
Brenda	Meta-Murder! And Marxism can't save us! *(Laughs)* Religion! Perhaps Mormonism! Or water vapor could fill the holes. Cloud formations. Water and ice.
Rita	*(Baffled)* The oceans?
Brenda	Make new ozone. Go to Mars, grab some ice. Manufacture ozone. Invest in water. Must find the cool, bring the cool to the hot.

Two GUNSHOTS, near misses.

C.C.	*(Into phone)* Not now, gentlemen. Ha, ha. Yeah! It's the military death disco! Be shoot-to-kill-die-young-America! *(Waves)* Take a moment to enjoy yourselves! *(Clicks off)*

Brenda	*(To RITA)* Are you burning? The skin be a soft and delicate substance. Be careful.
Rita	Am I peeling?
Brenda	Uh, no. Question: Does the sun have a skin? Does it have a membrane, like a skin? Answer: Yes. It is the solar system. Sunspots flash and the rabbit population goes up! *(Laughs)*
C.C.	Thing about the genes. What a man wants, pump his genes.
Rita	We know all about it.
C.C.	Bodies. Look out, people staring inconsolably at bodies, at imagery.
Rita	Don't look.
C.C.	I don't do that anymore. I feel remorseful about looking. I keep my head down now. I keep my eyes straight now. *(Walks)*

FLASHBACK. On the bench, find TONY and SHEILA.

Tony	*(Recites or sings CATULLUS #32)*

I beg of you, my sweet, my Ipsitilla,
my darling, my sophisticated beauty,
summon me to a midday assignation;
and, if you're willing, do me one big favor
don't let another client shoot the door bolt,
and don't decide to suddenly go cruising,
but stay home and get yourself all ready
for nine—yes, nine—successive copulations!
Honestly, if you want it, give the order.
I've eaten, and I'm sated, supinated!
My prick is poking through my cloak and tunic.

Sheila	Whoa! I like that one. I liked it. Ummmm. Nine times. Catullus.
Tony	Him again.
Sheila	But that was not Lesbia. That was some filthy hooker.
Tony	The Romans, they had a lot of troubles. They didn't take care of their poor. They were afraid of their poor. Am I right?
Sheila	You read this? You looked it up?
Tony	I learned it. I take classes.
Sheila	So why ask me?
Tony	Because you're smart.
Sheila	No. Because you're bragging on yourself. Next time bring your own. And bring some other shit, too.
Tony	What you got?
Sheila	You can trick me for it. *(Laughs)* But don't tell the Preacher. What you do. Bragging on yourself.
Tony	He wouldn't hurt me. Man's a pal of mine.
Sheila	Yeah, yeah. You should come over to my side.
Tony	No.
Sheila	Why not?
Tony	My mother. My people.
Sheila	Brenda. You're all gonna die over there.
Tony	We're all gonna die anyway.
Sheila	Not me, Tony. Not so fast. Let's go. Let's go into one of these buildings.
Tony	Wait. Snipers.

END FLASHBACK.

Rita	Man says, "I have a feeling of hope." He may mean the opposite: "I have a dread feeling." He don't know. He say.

Then he don't know and I don't know. He thinks you
mean what he means. She say, "That ain't you. That your
mama talkin'." Dreams, they act like memories.
Projections, they seem virtual.

C.C. pulls his gun. BRENDA *ducks.*

C.C.	Tony played games with the other side. Dope games. Mind games. He liked that shit, Tony. I'll take the child.
Rita	Shoot!
C.C.	Would you like a bullet through the head?
Rita	I have seen the dirty face of death.
C.C.	I know you have.
Rita	So fuck off. *(Pause)* There is day and night and there is the sky, and that's all there is.
C.C.	And the child?
Rita	And there is a child.
C.C.	But it doesn't belong to you, Rita.
Rita	Yes, it does. A Jewish child.
C.C.	Brenda's not Jewish.
Rita	Tony's child. *(Pause)*

FLASHBACK. On the bench, BRENDA *joins* TONY.

Brenda	Hey, Tony.
Tony	Yo.
Brenda	What's the matter?
Tony	Mom be always on my bubble.
Brenda	What for?
Tony	Viruses. Whatever.

Brenda	You told her?
Tony	Don't I go for counseling?
Brenda	You told her?
Tony	I could be on TV.
Brenda	No wonder.
Tony	I could tell my story. I could sing it. *(Big strut)*
Brenda	She knows.
Tony	I am no bullshit white boy, me.
Brenda	Where you goin'?
Tony	Cab time.
Brenda	You cross over, Tony?
Tony	Who?
Brenda	You. You cross over? In your cab?
Tony	You're thinking about other people, B. You're not thinking about me.
Brenda	You. Tony.
Tony	Not me.
Brenda	Don't lie, Tony.
Tony	Get it out of your head, B.
Brenda	You going cabbing, or for class?
Tony	I'm working, then I go to class.
Brenda	You got extra money coming in?
Tony	I get tips, don't I? I rap to the fuckers. They love that shit.

END FLASHBACK.

C.C.	*(Of the child, as* BRENDA *rejoins them)* Give it to me and you can go.
Rita	No! Brenda?
Brenda	No!

C.C.	Brenda. More wired than awake, more frenzied than alive. Unfit, wouldn't you say?
Rita	I wouldn't say.
C.C.	Give up the child. Fresh start. Good life.
Rita	And she?
C.C.	Back to the hospital. You go free. I take the child.
Rita	Be a Jewish child.
C.C.	What they want.
Rita	Half-Jewish!
C.C.	What they want.
Rita	For what?
C.C.	Raise it up. Blood offering.
Rita	Slave! Sacrifice!

He is about to fire into Rita's head—when C.C.'s phone rings.

C.C.	*(Into phone)* It's not time yet, people! I am the Preacher. Sheila? Don't ask me stupid questions! And don't call me— I'll call you! *(Hangs up. To RITA)* Dumb fucks. They call me the Preacher.
Brenda	We know!
Rita	Our fathers cut into the equatorial rain forests, and the viruses came out. *(Breaks into uncontrollable tears)*

C.C. looks on helplessly.

Brenda	Tony was a poet! He loved to talk his shit! He walked his talk! *(To C.C.)* Do you?
C.C.	I taught the sucker everything he knew. Am I right?

Brenda	You're not Jewish!
C.C.	So what? *(Laughs)* I could be. I might be. You never know.
Brenda & Rita	You're not Jewish. You can't be Jewish. There's nothing Jewish about you. You have not one Jewish cell in your body. If you were Jewish, you would know it and I would know it. You would be intelligent, for one thing. There would be no question. As it is, you're not, so forget about it.
C.C.	I'm restless and eager to do. I love life and God. I make a lot of money.
Brenda	Ha! You hear that?

Rapid GUNFIRE, off.

C.C.	Stay right here. Don't go away. Don't move. *(Exits to pool)*
Brenda	*(Of the shooters)* Psychopaths, like him.
Rita	They are not sane.
Brenda	They shoot to kill. They shoot for fun.
Rita	It's true.
Brenda	Let's run.
C.C.	*(Off)* Shut the fuck up! Cut!

GUNFIRE stops.

Rita	*(Of C.C.)* A strange creature. Exotic creature, he. An odd duck.
Brenda	Is he judging me?
Rita	Yes.
Brenda	Do you feel he likes me?
Rita	No. I believe he thinks we have a real relationship.
Brenda	You and me?

Rita	No. He and I. What's he doing now?
Brenda	He's taking a dip.
Rita	Maybe he'll forget to breathe and drown himself.
Brenda	Do we snap him?
Rita	Man's a preacher, knows stuff, feels bad.
Brenda	Let's snap him!
Rita	He has employees. They—
Brenda	Let's snap him, grab his phone. Where's his guards? *(Pause, sound of BABY)* Hear the baby?
Rita	Sounds good. *(Rocking)* Excellent baby.
Brenda	Wonderful baby.
Rita	They want the baby.
Brenda	What for?
Rita	Trade. We go, baby stay.
Brenda	Drop dead.
Rita	Wonderful baby.
Brenda	What's he doing, sneaking nips down there?
Rita	Get your juice today? Take your pills today?
Brenda	Yeah, yeah. I've had enough. *(As TONY)* I've had enough. Long line. Biological failures. Hoarse whining. Yellowish complexions. Childish demands. Hassling of nurses. I've had enough.
Rita	Tony!
Brenda	*(Of C.C.)* Did he call you, "darling"?
Rita	He wants the child. He wants the baby.
Brenda	Let's snap the fucker.
Rita	He's kind sometimes.
Brenda	I'm the mother.
Rita	You're not a mother.
Brenda	So let's go.

Rita	No.
Brenda	It's mine. Uh, oh. *(Of C.C.)* He's coming back.

Re-enter C.C., wet.

C.C.	Did you miss me?
Rita	No.
Brenda	Sneakin' nips are ya?
C.C.	*(A bit tipsy)* Ah, refreshed. Public pools: reward. Provide amusement parks and pools, beach-front pleasure, hoops, hip-hop, chits for the indigent, and so on.
Rita	A horror. *(To BRENDA)* Watch out for the mood change.
Brenda	*(To C.C.)* We thought you drowned. Ha, ha, ha.
C.C.	I could drop you down the sewer, Brenda. No trouble at all. Drink your fuckin' junk-juice, Brenda. Fuckin' shit was invented by Hitler. You're not clean. Go back on the rack an' climb the fuckin' walls.
Rita	There it is.
Brenda	Be hard.
C.C.	Ha, ha, fuck you.
Brenda	I got drunk in high school a lot.
C.C.	I'm not drunk.
Brenda	My parents gave me tranquilizers. And then I took to crank. One thing led to another. Then I got on the program.
C.C.	Junk-juice program.
Brenda	Where I met my Tony.
C.C.	You are not Jewish.
Brenda	I know I'm not.
Rita	I AM. Thank God.
C.C.	Not you.

Brenda	I'm Italian.
Rita	My husband was Italian.
C.C.	Jewish parents are not poor. Jewish parents do not give their children drugs.
Rita	Long gone.
C.C.	Were your parents your parents?
Brenda	My parents WERE my parents.
C.C.	Not you.
Rita	My real name is Rita Burns. I got tired of being a waitress. I did know you once.
C.C.	I'll help you find a home, Rita.
Rita	We were poor, and my mother was psychotic. Unbearable stress. There used to be a vacant lot. I played on the fire escape. Strangers came. There was an aunt who smelled like talcum powder and an uncle who smoked. I needed help, but it came too late. I forget to breathe. I'm always holding my breath, me, waiting to get whacked. I was undernourished. Trouble to breathe. My mother, she tried to starve us. In the morning, hard bread and tea. In the afternoon, porridge. Leave me alone, she said, and hoarded dollars in socks. Psychosis lay waiting, like a virus, waiting. She was mean and cold. We are talking child murder here.
C.C.	Be handed down in the family, like with Tony. Am I right?
Brenda	Sir, you are a bag!
C.C.	I could have you hanged on a clothesline, Brenda. Time is running out. You're a junk-juice suckin' junkie and Rita doesn't love you.
Brenda	You don't know! But I know the truth of you! You are no hero, you! You are no savior! You are no preacher! *(Hides under the parachute)*

C.C.	Good. Tony used to be with her. I wasn't in the picture. They set up housekeeping. Brenda, she was clean and sober in every way, and the virus didn't matter, because Tony was asymptomatic. And then one day Brenda stopped taking her pills. She had to be alone. Tony freaked, he'd OD'd on crack, he fell down gasping. Say?
Rita	I won't say.
C.C.	They found him on the floor, coughing. Pneumonia. That's it. They had to plug him into the respirator. And now?
Rita	Now he is ashes.

FLASHBACK. *On the bench, find* TONY *and* SHEILA.

Sheila	You don't see me.
Tony	I don't see you?
Sheila	I'm the class of this city but you stay on your side with crazy Brenda.
Tony	It is not safe over here.
Sheila	Scared?
Tony	Ain't it me who comes over?
Sheila	Scared?
Tony	Not me!
Sheila	Scared?
Tony	No!
Sheila	Scared and run! You're still a baby.
Tony	I seen it all already.
Sheila	Get over it. Enjoy. Take no prisoners. Life's too short and death is sudden.
Tony	Who was serious?
Sheila	Go ahead and die if you want to. With her.

Tony	Not me.
Sheila	What you want.
Tony	I'm feeling fucking great!
Sheila	My people, you see them, it gets like ten below zero, they're freezing to death in cardboard boxes along the railroad tracks. *(Silence)* I want you to bring something over to your side for me. Some money. Some food.
Tony	For you, no problem.
Sheila	My father kicked my mother out of the apartment. She's over there now. Your side. I could see her leaving from my window, down in the parking lot, in the brown slush, crying. She was all by herself. Just one car in the lot, holding my mother. Snipers—from both sides. Everything around grey and black and old snow—winter, bitter, my mother down there hunched over with her face in her hands. My father came running up behind me and grabbed my hair. I could see he was terrified in his fuckin' eyes. He started to run to bring her back, but he couldn't run fast enough. *(Snaps her fingers)* I looked down onto the parking lot and she was gone—just a big dead, dirty corner lot, empty and wet. Bullets slamming into the icy slush.
Tony	I'll talk to the Preacher.
Sheila	You can't trust C.C.! How many times!
Tony	Forget about it.
Sheila	Check her out yourself.
Tony	Okay, I will.
Sheila	Thank you, darling.
Tony	Don't call me darling.
Sheila	I'll give you love. Not like that madwoman, Brenda.

END FLASHBACK.

C.C.   Tell Brenda I can crack her: change her spine forever, me. Result: permanent backache.

Rita   Brenda!

C.C.   Alternative: burn down the neighborhood. A little kerosene and a match: out she comes. Ha, ha, ha.

BRENDA comes out of hiding.

Brenda   Okay!

C.C.   They are waiting for you, Brenda.

Brenda   *(As TONY)* I hope they all die. I hope they are mangled. I hope they burn.

Rita   Why our child? A Jewish child? Tony's child?

C.C.   I told you. Love and retribution.

Brenda   When a child is born, death is defeated!

Rita   Love comes streaming down then. God shows his love then!

C.C.   Over there, no more Jewish people. None left. No survivors. I'll tell you what they did, them. Say?

Rita   No.

Brenda   Say.

C.C.   War. A roundup. Four hundred Jewish people, they ran them through the slaughterhouse.

RITA gags and weeps.

C.C.   Where I come from, nobody loved nobody.

Brenda   It shows!

C.C.	Me and Tony, we came up together. We did time together. We ran the neighborhood, him and me. But Tony was playing with the other side. He insulted the wrong people. Now for the payment.
Rita	No!
C.C.	Is it yours?
Brenda & Rita	Yes.
C.C.	I'll take it.
Brenda & Rita	No!
C.C.	*(Into phone)* Time?
Brenda & Rita	No!
C.C.	*(Into phone)* Time?
Brenda & Rita	No!
C.C.	*(Into phone)* Time?
Brenda & Rita	No!
C.C.	*(Into phone)* Put Sheila on. Hello? I want an extension. Are you deaf? I'm tired. What? *(Clicks off. To RITA and BRENDA)* Be clear to me now, clear as shadows on a bright day.
Brenda	Oh, yeah?
C.C.	Hostile?
Brenda	Give an example.
C.C.	Be with one, fall in love with she. Lose both. Repeat, repeat.
Brenda	I didn't follow that.
C.C.	Emotions and desires: ephemeral. Fade. Can love endure?
Brenda	I have the intelligence to understand that.
C.C.	Okay, listen up. There is a woman with a baby. She loves it to pieces. She's totally attached to it. She'll do anything for it. She's a slave to it and a martyr.
Brenda & Rita	Say?

C.C.	She is jealous of the baby so she won't allow help. Though the baby is difficult and needs a lot of care, she doesn't let anyone else get too close to the baby.
Brenda & Rita	And?
C.C.	Before the authorities, she weeps and laments. Who among us can resist a mother's martyrdom?
Brenda & Rita	Not one of us.
C.C.	And so she continues in thrall to the baby, and the baby in bondage to she. *(Pause)* Be only one problem.
Brenda & Rita	Say?
C.C.	It's not her baby.
Brenda & Rita	Conclude?
C.C.	The baby must be separated from this woman and restored to her rightful blood.
Rita	A parable?
C.C.	No.
Rita	A riddle?
C.C.	Think it over. You have five minutes. *(Exits to pool)*
Brenda	What the fuck?
Rita	That was rude!
Brenda	Sheila? *(Of the carriage)* We have minutes, so let go.
Rita	No.
Brenda	Are we alike at all?
Rita	You're not Jewish.
Brenda	We have nothing in common but Tony.
Rita	We know what's what, the Jews. It's in the Bible.
Brenda	Sheila? *(Off, splashing from the pool. Of C.C.)* I think he likes to wash himself.
Rita	He thinks he's beautiful for a worm-like creature.
Brenda	He's a water freak. We snap him.

Rita	*(Rocking the carriage)* You can do what you want, you.
Brenda	Let's run.
Rita	Not we.
Brenda	Why not?
Rita	Not we.
Brenda	You blame me?
Rita	I'm trying.
Brenda	You blame?
Rita	No.
Brenda	I'm trying.
Rita	I know.
Brenda	Forgive me? *(Pause)* When I met Tony, I had tracks all over, like the pox. I was hookin' for fixes. I got on the program and took my pills. He started cracking, Tony. He knew he was going to die, he. Virus—no forgiveness. Tony. Just a boy. He cracked. I knew he knew he was going to die. He fell down. I? I was panicked. I wanted to go into hospital. I wanted to be alone, me. Nobody dying. Me alone. Tony cracked. He fell down. Me. He made friends with death, Tony. We had a good life. We had a family. We had a future. He had—he made friends with death. Say?
Rita	I forgive you.
Brenda	Say?
Rita	I forgive you.
Brenda	Say?
Rita	I forgive you.

Re-enter C.C., all wet.

Brenda	Here he comes. *(To C.C.)* Who is Sheila?

438

| C.C. | Hey? Man must live and enjoy the flaws. Pussy by the pool, and so on. But I keep my eyes down now. That is, I try. |
| Brenda | Who is Sheila? |

FLASHBACK. *On the bench, find* TONY *and* SHEILA.

Sheila	You don't look good.
Tony	I feel great.
Sheila	Are you using?
Tony	Not me.
Sheila	Okay, Tony.
Tony	You don't know what you're looking at.
Sheila	Do you have any money?
Tony	I don't have any money.
Sheila	What do you do with it all?
Tony	I have responsibilities.
Sheila	Are you sick?
Tony	No.
Sheila	I don't believe you.
Tony	Shoot me.
Sheila	Not so fast. I heard of a story. There's a swordsman, he liked to pick up girls. There's a carnival, where he goes to find one. There's a strange girl, and they see each other. She's dressed funny, you know, like, revealing. She could be the love of his life, his one true love. She warns him: I might be crazy for all you know, maybe you don't want to go dancing with me. Let's go dancing, he says, and see what happens. They have a wild time—until the men from the asylum come. She fights like a tiger but they beat her down. She's killed three men, they tell him, in a breakout to go dancing. Two

men she stabbed, the other she decapitated. Remind you
of someone?

Tony	Brenda!
Sheila	Is she pregnant?
Tony	Who?
Sheila	Brenda. Is she pregnant? *(Pause)* You don't know?
Tony	Yeah.
Sheila	Yeah, you know, or yeah she's pregnant?
Tony	Yeah, she's pregnant.
Sheila	How?
Tony	How?
Sheila	You heard me—yours?
Tony	Mine.
Sheila	I don't think so. I'd like to slap you.
Tony	Go ahead.

She slaps him.

Sheila	I'll kill her. Then I'll rip the child out of her stomach.
Tony	I don't think so.
Sheila	After you die, Tony. Once you're dead, I'll take care of it.
Tony	I won't die.
Sheila	Revenge and retribution.
Tony	No reason, then.
Sheila	What I say.

END FLASHBACK.

Rita	Calm down, Brenda.
Brenda	Fifty times a day I'm wrong! Am I imagining things? *(Sulks)*

440

C.C.	Decision?
Rita	Yes.
C.C.	Will you give me the child?
Rita	No.

C.C. takes BRENDA aside.

C.C.	Fucking ants are taking over the planet. And they bite.
Brenda	Are you nice now?
C.C.	You're cute.
Brenda	How many of you are you?

Off, BABY crying.

C.C.	I'll tell you about Sheila.
Brenda	You're not a bad guy, really. You're nice sometimes.
C.C.	Pay attention. I was dealing hemp, I was just getting started in business. I brought her a nickel bag. I didn't realize she liked me. She wore a see-through gown. She was skinny but cute. She lay down seductively, offering her body in exchange for grass. "Will you trick me for it," said she.
Brenda	Say?
C.C.	I said I couldn't do it at first, loyalty and so on. Shy and confused. I could taste her pussy but I was afraid of dishonor. Once we took a ride on a motor-scooter and necked on Fifty-ninth Street. A man shouted at us to get out of public view. Sex seemed dirty then.
Brenda	I have problems in that area.
C.C.	Sure you do, Brenda. I let it alone and Tony grabbed it.
Brenda	Are you mean now?

C.C.	Then a connection is made. Any good: substances exchanged. Lasts: forever. Mysterious, permanent.
Brenda	Babies are born from it, too.
C.C.	That's right, Brenda. How?
Brenda	I know how.
C.C.	Good for you, Brenda.
Brenda	But not now.

C.C. laughs.

	I have a tendency to want to be alone. But I've enjoyed this part of the conversation.
C.C.	Good.
Brenda	You can be just a regular guy, seems like.
C.C.	You want attention.
Brenda	I suffer that. Along with the feeling of being wrong.
C.C.	Where I grew up, they strung up cats on clotheslines, and tried to fuck the younger ones in the ass. Where did you grow up?
Brenda	Brooklyn, U.S.A. *(To RITA)* This man's cool. Honey, this man's been baptized, or something.
Rita	Light's changing.
Brenda	Man could be a friend of mine.
Rita	This is a special light. I love it. Brenda?

FLASHBACK. *On the bench,* BRENDA *joins* TONY.

Brenda	What you got, boy?
Tony	*(Sings:)*
	If any pleasure can come to a man through recalling

decent behavior in his relations with others,
not breaking his word, and never, in any agreement,
deceiving men by abusing vows sworn to heaven,
then countless joys will await you in old age, Catullus,
as a reward for this unrequited passion!
For all of those things which a man could possibly
say or do have all been said and done by you already,
and none of them counted for anything.

Brenda   What's that?

Tony   Poetry.

Brenda   Are you sick?

Tony   How do I look to you?

Brenda   You need to build up something that could fight it off.

Tony   What for?

Brenda   You could fight it off.

Tony   Okay.

Brenda   You're in very good shape.

Tony   They'll have cars that talk to you and fly. You'll have a home address, it'll be a cubicle with a bed and some shelves, there'll be a number—that'll be your home—be a gigantic barracks!

Brenda   She thinks she's in charge, she thinks she can drive right over me, say? She thinks she can fox me and tell me what to do!

Tony   Who?

Brenda   She!

Tony   Who?

Brenda   Rita! Yeah, well, I'm out here sweetie, I'm gone baby, you no longer run my life, you bitch!

Tony   Wait! The baby!

Brenda	Not yours!
Tony	Say?
Brenda	Mine!
Tony	Where you goin'?
Brenda	Virus, remember! Precaution, remember!
Tony	No! Wait, you!

END FLASHBACK.

Rita	Brenda?
Brenda	Yo, Rita! *(To C.C.)* Ha, ha—fuck you.
C.C.	Fuck you—ha, ha.
Brenda & Rita	You don't know anything. You're a performer, a politician, a hipster philosopher, an artiste. The real horror—you don't know it. The real death—you don't know it. The real abuses—you only dream them, you!
C.C.	Ha, ha, fuck you.
Brenda & Rita	We don't talk the same talk! We don't walk the same walk! We're not on the same ground! We're on different sides of the world! We're on different angles! We on a different edge! The shape is not the same shape! You are in a parallel world, you!
C.C.	Swim-time! *(Exits to pool)*
Rita	He's got us, Brenda. No ID. No money. Insecure and homeless. What he wants, he gets.
Brenda	Can we have an exchange about this?
Rita	Speak.
Brenda	We couldn't handle the responsibility. We can't provide stability. For example, I would have to get off the junk-juice.
Rita	Of course. You wish to stay bloated? You wish to stay

444

medicated? You wish to segue to the junk-juice boat every single sunny day? Is that the proper atmosphere for child-rearing or parenting?

Brenda	It's not done. It's impossible. Be in the bones.
Rita	What I say?
Brenda	I'll cry.
Rita	Okay. I'll make plans.
Brenda	But not today.
Rita	I'm always holding my breath.
Brenda	Say?
Rita	Remember Tony. Last gasp, and death.
Brenda	Take care.
Rita	Say?
Brenda	A person could string out on that.
Rita	You don't know. Blame?
Brenda	No.
Rita	Blame?
Brenda	No.
Rita	I was his mother.
Brenda	No blame.
Rita	Say?
Brenda	I forgive you.

Pause. SPLASHING, off.

	(Of C.C.) Guy's got a real problem with water. Did ya notice? *(As TONY)* Time now to snap the fucker.
Rita	Ah. I'm breathing.
Brenda	(As Tony) Snap his fuckin' neck, snatch his phone, flee to the Yucatán.

Rita	Sarajevo was the place to be. Twenty years from now, people will have said with pride, "I was in Sarajevo in the 90s."
Brenda	They'd like to be sniped and starved?
Rita	They will have suffered and endured.
Brenda	Kids, they learn fast what's what. Survive first, be nice later. Kids are sticking it to each other everywhere. Rio, Brooklyn, L.A.—what time is it?
Rita	Remember Tony. No one remembers very long, do they? Life dropped him like he was a bunch of bananas.

Re-enter C.C., wet.

C.C.	Speaking of me again?
Rita	We don't always talk about you, C.C.
C.C.	Say?
Rita	Tony.
Brenda	I'll tell you what happened. They lock you away and you're alone. You're alone and you got time to think and there's no action. You start to look at yourself. Visiting day, you get to see the ruins—my Tony and me was the same. We did the same and acted the same. Only he was out and I was in, he was loose and I was tied. He got the virus, not me. Only he it was who died the dirty death.
Rita	*(To C.C.)* She's trashing his life. *(Sigh)* That's what he's used to. Tony was a junkie. Once a junkie, always a junkie. Tony?

FLASHBACK. On the bench, TONY—lying down—responds to RITA.

Tony	Mom?
Rita	Tony!
Tony	Get me out of here, Mom.
Rita	I told you a hundred times, Tony. Give it up or it will kill you—and it did.
Tony	No one knew, which spoon, which point—no one even heard of it.
Rita	You stupid kid.
Tony	I was ripping off your goods, Mom. I'm sorry.
Rita	I forgive you.
Tony	I'm sorry, Mom.
Rita	I forgive you.
Tony	Get me out of here.
Rita	I can't, Tony. Pneumonia, Tony.
Tony	Therapy. Group counseling. School and cab, Mom.
Rita	First they have to clear the pneumonia, honey, and then you can go.
Tony	You don't believe me, Mom?
Rita	I believe you.
Tony	Rita.
Rita	I believe you.
Tony	My feet are swollen.
Rita	They are swollen, Tony.
Tony	I fell down on the floor, Mom.
Rita	I know you did. *(Weeps)*
Tony	Don't worry, Rita. I have made friends with death.
Rita	*(Gagging)* Ah!
Tony	Where's Brenda?
Rita	She's in another hospital, Tony.
Tony	Is she coming?

Rita	She's coming soon.
Tony	She's a head case, B. She has demons.
Rita	She loves you. She loves you very much.
Tony	Love, Mom?
Rita	She loves you.
Tony	Time?
Rita	Not time.
Tony	Time!
Rita	Not time yet, Tony.
Tony	Time!
Rita	Say?
Tony	Time!
Rita	Not yet, Tony.
Tony	My shot! Where's my shot? It's time!

END FLASHBACK.

Rita	Brenda?
Brenda	*(As TONY, big strut)* Shut the fuck up! I'm trying to change. I want to change. But you can't force change, you can't will change, and you can't act changed!
Rita	*(To BRENDA)* You're hysterical!
C.C.	And the child?
Rita	You want love and you can't buy it or steal it!
C.C.	"Mom be always on my bubble." *(Laughs)*
Brenda	That's what Tony used to say!
Rita	He was a good kid!
C.C.	Five percent of the time.
Rita	He used to watch for the white-coats. He kept one eye out. Time for his shot. Time for his shot. He'd move you

	out of the way. Time for my shot, Mom. Get out of the way. Time. Then they put him on a morphine drip. *(To C.C.)* Have you no capacity for grief?
C.C.	"I have made friends with death."
Brenda	That's what Tony said!
Rita	Poor Tony. He could not breathe with his own lungs. The respirator breathed him. *(Weeps)*
C.C.	Tony was great. The ace of street kids. The King. I miss him. Even though he ripped me off every chance he got. Manipulative sonofabitch.
Brenda	He always made sure the lights were out and there was food in the refrigerator. He took care. And he was a hustler. I liked that. He would take a job. He drove a taxicab. Something came up through my uncle, a pallbearer, whatever, he was ready. I liked that about Tony. He wasn't one of those young guys: "Excuse me, but don't bother me."
Rita	He was a good kid!
C.C.	He would try to manipulate you in any way he could.
Brenda	We had a good time. He was sweet.

FLASHBACK. *Find* TONY *on the bench, his face contorted.*

Tony	What is that fucking music?
Rita	Respirator, Tony.
Tony	Good times.
Rita	Oh, yeah.
Tony	Good times.
Rita	Oh, yeah.
Tony	C.C.?
Rita	No, Tony.

Tony	C.C.?
Rita	No, Tony.
Tony	Action, Mom.
Rita	He is at war.
Tony	The commander.
Rita	Quiet now, Tony.
Tony	I can't talk.
Rita	You shouldn't talk.
Tony	Get this thing out of my mouth.
Rita	They won't let me, Tony.
Tony	Please get this thing out of my mouth.
Rita	I can't, Tony.
Tony	I'll never make it out of here alive, Mom.

RITA gags.

	Mom?
Rita	Rest now.
Tony	Father?
Rita	You have no father.
Tony	Where?
Rita	Nowhere.
Tony	Prison, Rita.
Rita	I don't know.
Tony	Dad?
Rita	Not here, Tony.
Tony	I forgive you.
Rita	Say?
Tony	I forgive you.
Rita	Brenda!

Brenda	*(Off)* Here I am.

END FLASHBACK.

Rita	We sat with him for months. Respirator music. Incessant. He vanished into it. We fought to have it removed. Then they made us ask him four times: Are you ready to be unplugged, Tony?
Brenda	Are you ready to be unplugged, Tony?
Rita	If yes, blink with one eye, then the other. Four times.
C.C.	And did he?
Rita	I couldn't tell. But the white-coats thought he did. They removed the machine from his throat. We held him in our arms. Twenty minutes later he gasped and died. They turned him over like refuse. They asked us to leave. He was now inanimate matter. Brenda cried with me. When a child appears, he comes from heaven. Even his shit is sweet. Is that so, Preacher?
C.C.	That is so.
Rita	Then I have the following questions: What is the sacred? When does it start?
C.C.	Now we are here, we live. Before: parents.
Rita	That is an answer, but that is not what I asked. That is an answer to a question I did not ask. Is there a sacred? When does it start? When does it end? Was Tony's death a sacred death? The white-coats said, "Ask four times. If yes, then blink an eye. Tell us if you are ready to die or not." Are you ready to die, Tony? I couldn't tell if he blinked. Four times. They unhooked the machine, finally. They turned the switch, they pulled the tube. He struggled to breathe

and then he breathed his last. I wanted to sit quietly, but they rushed in and started cleaning it up. *(Pause)* What an awful disease, a dreadful disease, a disgusting disease. He was a boy of twenty-five. Who did he shoot up with in some filthy hallway? In some tenement dump? In what fucking dope-filled project?

Brenda	What's a virus, Craig?
C.C.	A virus be a moving thing, they aim to replicate. One aim: make copies. Repeat, repeat. But must have living cells. Are parasites. Nature's way: correction. Like war and famine, like quake, riot, fire, and flood.
Rita	Did he notice?
C.C.	Say?
Rita	Tony. The moment of death. Did he notice it?
C.C.	I don't know. I wasn't there. Time, please?
Brenda & Rita	Oh! The time!
C.C.	You have missed your appointment.
Rita	Light changing.
C.C.	Pay attention. I know these people. They won't stay with this much longer. Game: blood and bodies. Exchange of living or dead. They shoot to kill.
Brenda	The time!
Rita	Be dark again. This is what I remember.
Brenda	Say?
Rita	The feeling at twilight.
C.C.	Who is the mother of this child?
Brenda & Rita	I am!
C.C.	When was the kid born?
Brenda & Rita	When Tony died!
C.C.	What did you give for him?

Brenda & Rita Nothing!

C.C.'s PHONE rings.

C.C.   Hello? I told you not to call me. I know what time it is. I'm
             not a kidnapper. I'm not a baby-stealer. I'm trying to do
             the right thing. I've had a harder life than any of you. I've
             earned every penny, every honor. I am the captain, I am
             the commander. I am organized, and I am true. Chance
             has nothing to do with it. You're a bunch of drunken,
             homicidal maniacs who belong in mental institutions
             under heavy guard. *(Pause)* You heard me.

Brenda   Uh, oh.

C.C.   *(Into phone)* You can't give people things or try to help—
             causes hatred and confusion. That you, Sheila? Fuck
             you, ha, ha. Time passes while we have this conversation.
             I hope you can afford it. I see—you may want to be
             killed anyway. No? It's thrilling to murder people? Hold
             your fire. *(Clicks off. To RITA and BRENDA)* Last
             chance for exchange of child. *(Silence)* Done. You're on
             your own.

Brenda   Wait, Preacher.

C.C.   What is it, Brenda?

Brenda   They built a great blaze, and they put Tony into it. There
             was a silent burning, save for the hissing of steam.

C.C.   Say?

Brenda   There was a condensation in the spirit world, a gathering
             of force—like clouds, like rain.

C.C.   Where?

Brenda   In the atmosphere. Cleansing, redemption. Say?

FLASHBACK. Near the bench, C.C. and TONY.

C.C.	Tony!
Tony	Yo, Preacher!

Elaborate handshake.

C.C.	How you doin', man?
Tony	I'm feeling fucking great.
C.C.	That's Tony!
Tony	How's the Preacher Man?
C.C.	Hey, I'm goin' to war, pal. I'm going to straighten out the issue! I will finalize it, me! Are you there?
Tony	I am with you, C.C.!
C.C.	Am I right?
Tony	Right as rain, Preacher!
C.C.	Will they make up poems about the Preacher? Will they make an epic about the Preacher Man?
Tony	I don't think so.
C.C.	I'm sad about the whole thing and I'm sorry. Forgive me?
C.C.	It's the women, Tony. They're on a different path.
Tony	No blame.
C.C.	The child be on its own now.
Tony	I'm the child.
C.C.	Say?
Tony	I'm the child.

END FLASHBACK.

C.C.	*(Into phone)* Get off the line, I'm calling my mother. Hello? Mom? Once I was a handsome young street prince, Mom, I believed in romance, or: Sex was too much for me, and close-ups confused my mind. Is everything on tape? Me, immense ego, low self-esteem. White nigger. Commit: spiritual crime. Did I? I? Falling...closeups. Two-shots. Result: fear. Result: confusion. Just listen. I'm in a hurry. No, be close-up, intimacy: self-love. Be action, fast: revenge, adventure. Heroes, beautiful dames. *(As TONY)* Inside: little boy, little white nigger boy, nobody loved nobody, white nigger Jew boy, slave boy, just a boy, frightened, lonely boy. *(Clicks off)* Dream on. *(Starts off)*
Rita	Wait, you!
C.C.	The core of the earth is molten rock, or liquid metal. It is hotter than the surface of the sun.
Rita	Say?
C.C.	I'll be finishing my thought, which is: The core of the earth is hot, and the crust of the earth is thin, and the sun and the moon.
Rita	Be what?
C.C.	When you look at what a man be.
Brenda	I see what he's saying.
Rita	Say?
C.C.	Be dust. *(Pause)* It's time. This is for the record. *(Into phone)* Whoever makes it up the switchback and lives— she is the mother.
Rita	And you? Where are you going, you?
C.C.	Well, I just have a feeling of fate. I feel like there are waves, and one of them's got my name on it. *(Into phone)* Last word: Ha, ha, fuck you. What else? Nothing else.

Next time I see you, come out firing. We shoot on sight.

(Goes)

Rita   I realize there's an end to my story. There's a be-all and end-all, built in to the story. Be: the end. World collapse.

Brenda   Say?

Rita   What if I didn't believe that? Suppose the world goes on and on? Population: no problem. Viruses: cured. Forests: reborn. America: eternal. What then?

Brenda   The time!

Rita   We're escaping together!

Brenda   I have hypertension. I have angst.

Rita   What time is it?

Brenda   I believed in C.C. for a minute because he had something to say.

Rita   Electro-mathematics, I think it was.

Brenda   The Way of the Psychopath.

Rita   That's it.

GUNFIRE.

Oh! A battle!

Brenda   He is shooting! He is fighting!

Rita   Oh! What now!?

Brenda   He's going into the water.

Rita   Look at him swim!

GUNFIRE stops.

They got him.

Brenda   Is he flapping?

Rita	He is flapping.
Brenda	Is he floating?
Rita	He is floating. *(Pause)* He was a good man, basically. He could see his end coming in a wave.
Brenda	He was loyal, but he had a bad side to him.
Rita	When I die, I hope people say nice things about me.
Brenda	He couldn't tell the difference between what he did and what he saw in his head.
Rita	I see now that I don't have my own fate. My fate is my Mom.
Brenda	Maybe there *are* no reasons. People like to interfere with the pleasures of others, or to inflict torture upon them.
Rita	Let's go.

Pause. BRENDA grabs the baby carriage and races up the switchback. Gunfire. BRENDA makes it to the top, then falls, shot. Pause. RITA trembles with indecision, then rushes up the switchback, retrieves the carriage and runs away.

BLACKOUT.

The End

Murray Mednick is the founder of the Padua Hills Playwrights Festival and Workshop, where he served as artistic director from 1978 through 1995. Born in Brooklyn, New York, he was for many years a playwright-in-residence at New York's Theatre Genesis, which presented all of his early work, including *The Hawk*, *The Deer Kill*, *The Hunter*, *Sand*, and *Are You Lookin'?*. He was artistic co-director of Genesis from 1970 until 1974, when he emigrated to California. Plays produced since then include *Iowa* and *Blessings* (for the PBS series "Visions"), *The Coyote Cycle*, *Taxes*, *Scar*, *Heads*, *Shatter 'n Wade*, *Fedunn*, *Switchback*, *Baby*, *Jesus!*, *Dictator*, and *Freeze*. Mednick's plays *Joe and Betty* and *Mrs. Feuerstein* received dual runs in Los Angeles and New York in 2002; *Joe and Betty* received the American Theatre Critics Association's Best New Play Citation in that year. He is also the recipient of two Rockefeller Foundation grants, a Guggenheim Fellowship, an OBIE, several Bay Area Critics Awards, the 1997 L.A. Weekly Playwriting Award (for *Dictator*) and a 1992 Ovation Lifetime Achievement Award from Theatre LA for outstanding contributions to Los Angeles theatre. In 2002, Mednick was awarded the Margaret Harford Award for Sustained Excellence in Theater by the Los Angeles Drama Critic's Circle.

Padua Playwrights Press books are available from your
local bookseller or visit www.paduaplaywrights.net. They are distributed by Theatre Communications Group, New York.

Other available titles:

Padua: Plays from the Padua Hills Playwrights Festival
Includes plays from the Padua Hills Playwrights Festival by:
Neena Beber, Maria Irene Fornes, Joseph Goodrich,
Murray Mednick, Marlane Meyer, Susan Mosakowski,
John O'Keefe, John Steppling, Kelly Stuart
504 pages, Paperback, ISBN 0-9630126-4-9
$18.95

Three Plays by Murray Mednick
16 Routines, Joe and Betty, and *Mrs. Feuerstein*
Murray Mednick at his darkly comic best.
"A playwright's playwright...Mednick has spent his career
at the forefront of avant-garde theater."—Sandra Ross,
LA Weekly
300 pages, Paperback, ISBN 0-9630126-3-0
$14.95

Best of the West
Includes plays from the Padua Hills Playwrights Festival by:
Susan Champagne, Martin Epstein, Maria Irene Fornes,
Julie Hebert, Leon Martell, Murray Mednick, Susan Mosakowski,
John Steppling, Kelly Stuart
312 pages, Paperback, ISBN 0-9630126-2-2
$14.95

The Coyote Cycle

Seven Plays by Murray Mednick

"...it permanently reshaped my vision of what theatre could achieve—ritual, magic, playfulness, and respect for the playwright-actor bond entered my creative vocabulary and have been my resources ever since...in a day when much of the public has come to doubt the power of theatre, Murray Mednick's Coyote is proof that the best of it can still change lives."—David Henry Hwang

176 pages, Paperback, ISBN 0-9630126-1-4

$15.95